GCSE
Core Science
Higher Workbook

This book is for your higher level **GCSE Core Science** year 10 exams.

It's full of **tricky questions**... each one designed to make you **sweat** — because that's the only way you'll get any **better**.

There are questions to see **what facts** you know. There are questions to see how well you can **apply those facts**. And there are questions to see what you know about **how science works**.

It's also got some daft bits in to try and make the whole experience at least vaguely entertaining for you.

What CGP is all about

Our sole aim here at CGP is to produce the highest quality books — carefully written, immaculately presented and dangerously close to being funny.

Then we work our socks off to get them out to you — at the cheapest possible prices.

BIOLOGY

Contents

CHEMISTRY

Section 6 — Chemicals from Oil

PHYSICS

Section 7 — Heat and Energy

Section 8 — Electricity and Waves

Section 9 — The Universe

Published by CGP

Editors:
Katie Braid, Joe Brazier, Emma Elder, Ben Fletcher, Edmund Robinson, Lyn Setchell, Jane Towle, Dawn Wright.

Contributors:
Mike Bossart, Steve Coggins, Mark A Edwards, Paddy Gannon, Dr Iona MJ Hamilton, Rebecca Harvey, Frederick Langridge, Kate Redmond, Adrian Schmit, Sidney Stringer Community School, Paul Warren, Jim Wilson, Dee Wyatt.

ISBN: 978 1 84146 534 0

With thanks to Katherine Craig and Julie Wakeling for the proofreading.
With thanks to Jan Greenway, Laura Jakubowski and Laura Stoney for the copyright research.

Graph of global temperature variation on page 97 reproduced with permission of the Climatic Research Unit, School of Environmental Sciences, University of East Anglia: www.cru.uea.ac.uk

Pages 82, 125 and 171 contain public sector information published by the Health and Safety Executive and licensed under the Open Government Licence v1.0.

Every effort has been made to locate copyright holders and obtain permission to reproduce sources. For those sources where it has been difficult to trace the originator of the work, we would be grateful for information. If any copyright holder would like us to make an amendment to the acknowledgements, please notify us and we will gladly update the book at the next reprint. Thank you.

Groovy website: www.cgpbooks.co.uk

Printed by Elanders Ltd, Newcastle upon Tyne.
Jolly bits of clipart from CorelDRAW®
Based on the classic CGP style created by Richard Parsons.

The Nervous System

Q1 Suggest why it is important for animals to be able to **detect changes** in their surroundings.

....

Q2 **Tick** the box next to the correct statement below.

- [ ] Light receptor cells contain a nucleus, cytoplasm and a cell wall.
- [ ] Light receptor cells have the same structures as plant cells.
- [ ] Light receptor cells contain a nucleus, cytoplasm and a cell membrane.

Q3 Which of the following is **not** an example of a **stimulus**? Underline your answer.

pressure **hearing** **chemical** **change in body position** **change in temperature**

Q4 In each sentence below, underline the **sense organ** involved and write down the **type of receptor** that is detecting the stimulus.

a) Tariq puts a piece of lemon on his tongue. The lemon tastes sour.

....

b) Siobhan wrinkles her nose as she smells something unpleasant in her baby brother's nappy.

....

c) Xabi's ears were filled with the sound of the crowd cheering his outstanding goal.

....

d) Lindsey feels a wasp sting the skin on the back of her neck. She screams very loudly.

....

Q5 Some parts of the body are known as the **CNS**.

a) What do the letters CNS stand for? ....

b) Name the two main parts of the CNS.

1. .... 2. ....

c) What type of cell carries information to and from the CNS? ....

The Nervous System

Q6 Explain why a man with a **damaged spinal cord** may not be able to feel someone touching his toe.

....

....

....

Q7 John and Marc investigated how **sensitive** different parts of the body are to **pressure**.

They stuck two pins in a cork 0.5 cm apart. The pins were placed on different parts of the body. Ten pupils took part — they were blindfolded and reported "yes" or "no" to feeling both points.

The results of the experiment are shown in the table.

Area of the body tested	Number of pupils reporting 'yes'
Sole of foot	2
Knee	3
Fingertip	10
Back of hand	5
Lip	9

a) Which part of the body do the results suggest is:

i) most sensitive? .... **ii)** least sensitive? ....

b) From the results above, which part of the body do you think contains the **most pressure receptors**? Explain your answer.

....

....

c) John and Marc took it in turns to test the pupils. Their teacher suggested that if only one of the boys had done all the testing, the experiment would have been fairer. Explain why.

....

....

d) Each pupil was tested once. Suggest how you might make the test more accurate.

....

....

Synapses and Reflexes

Q1 **Circle** the correct answer to complete each of the following sentences.

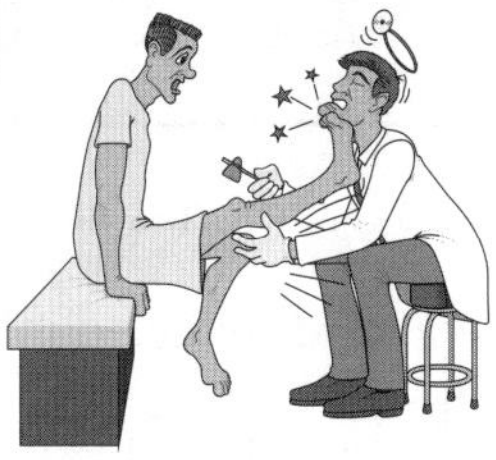

a) The main purpose of a reflex is to **protect** / **display** the body.

b) Reflexes happen **with** / **without** you thinking about them.

Q2 Why is a **reflex** reaction faster than a **voluntary** reaction?

....

....

Q3 When you touch something hot with a finger you **automatically** pull the finger away. The diagram shows some parts of the nervous system involved in this **reflex action**.

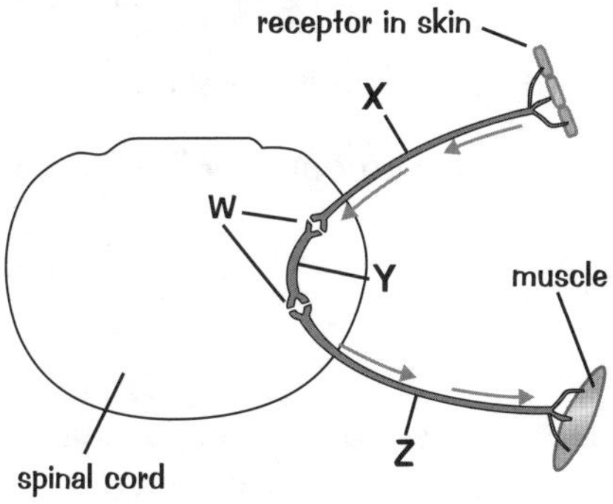

a) What type of neurone is:

i) neurone **X**? ....

ii) neurone **Y**? ....

iii) neurone **Z**? ....

b) In what form is the information carried:

i) along neurone **X**? ....

ii) from neurone **X** to neurone **Y**? ....

c) i) Complete the sentence.

In this reflex action the muscle acts as the ....

ii) Briefly describe how the muscle responds in this example.

....

d) i) What are the gaps marked **W** on the diagram called?

....

ii) Explain how the impulses get across these gaps.

....

....

Top Tips: Whatever weird and wonderful reflexes you're thinking about, just remember that they always involve the same reflex arc — stimulus, receptor, sensory neurone, relay neurone, motor neurone, effector, response. So once you've learnt it, you can apply your knowledge to anything.

Hormones

Q1 Complete the passage below about **hormones**.

Hormones are .... messengers. They are produced in .... and released into the .... They are carried all around the body, but only affect certain .... cells.

Q2 Fit the answers to the clues into the **grid**.

a) Transports hormones around the body.

b) A hormone produced by the ovaries.

c) A hormone produced by the pituitary.

d) Hormones are secreted by ___________.

e) A hormone involved in the menstrual cycle.

Q3 Describe the major differences between responses brought about by **hormones** and those due to the **nervous system**.

....

....

....

....

Q4 Tick the boxes to show whether the following responses are mainly controlled by the **nervous** or **hormonal** systems.

	Nervous system	Hormonal system
a) Hearing the alarm clock and turning it off.	☐	☐
b) Your heart beating faster when you remember you have an exam that day.	☐	☐
c) Smelling toast burning.	☐	☐
d) Your hairs standing on end when you're cold.	☐	☐
e) The 'fight-or-flight' response.	☐	☐

The Menstrual Cycle

Q1 There are three main **hormones** involved in the menstrual cycle.

Complete the table to show **where** in the body each hormone is produced.

HORMONE	WHERE IT IS PRODUCED
FSH	
oestrogen	
LH	

Q2 **FSH**, **LH** and **oestrogen** have specific functions in the menstrual cycle.

a) Describe **two** functions of FSH.

1. ....

2. ....

b) What effect does oestrogen have on the production of FSH?

....

c) Describe the function of LH.

....

Q3 The diagram below shows how the **uterus lining** changes during the **menstrual cycle**.

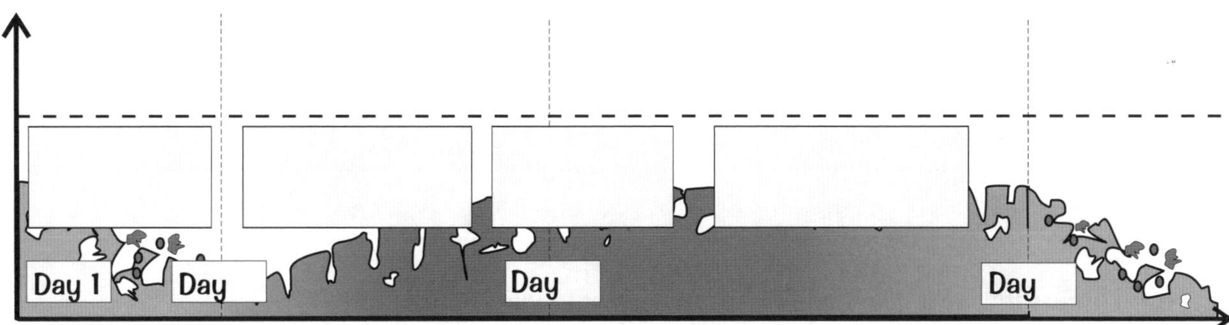

a) Fill in the day numbers in the boxes where they are missing.

b) Fill in the remaining boxes using the labels below:

Uterus lining builds up

Egg released

Uterus lining maintained

Uterus lining breaks down

Controlling Fertility

Q1 Hormones can be used to **increase fertility**.

a) Underline **two** hormones from the list below that can be taken by a woman to increase her fertility.

FSH oestrogen insulin LH progesterone

b) Briefly explain how these hormones increase fertility.

....

Q2 The **combined pill** contains oestrogen and progesterone.

a) State **two** benefits of taking the combined pill.

....

....

b) Explain how oestrogen in the pill reduces fertility.

....

....

....

c) Suggest why a woman might take a progesterone-only pill, rather than the combined pill.

....

Q3 **In vitro fertilisation** can help couples to have children.

a) Explain how **in vitro fertilisation** works.

....

....

....

....

b) Discuss the advantages and disadvantages of in vitro fertilisation.

....

....

....

....

Plant Hormones

Q1 Cedrick placed some **seedlings** on the surface of **damp soil** and left them for **five days**. The appearance of a seedling is shown in the diagram.

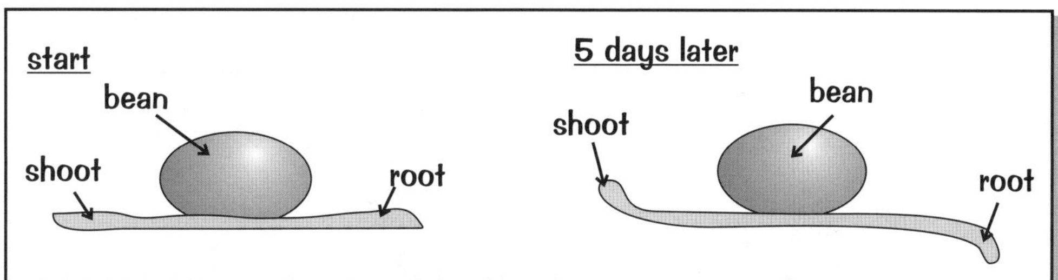

a) What **hormones** are responsible for these changes? ....

b) Where are these hormones produced? ....

c) Explain the responses of the shoot and the root to **gravity**.
For each one, say whether the response was **positively** or **negatively geotropic**.

i) the shoot ....

....

ii) the root ....

....

Q2 Vicky used three seedlings to investigate plant growth. Each seedling was prepared differently (see table). All three were placed in the same conditions, exposed to light from **one** direction and left for five hours. She recorded her results in the table below.

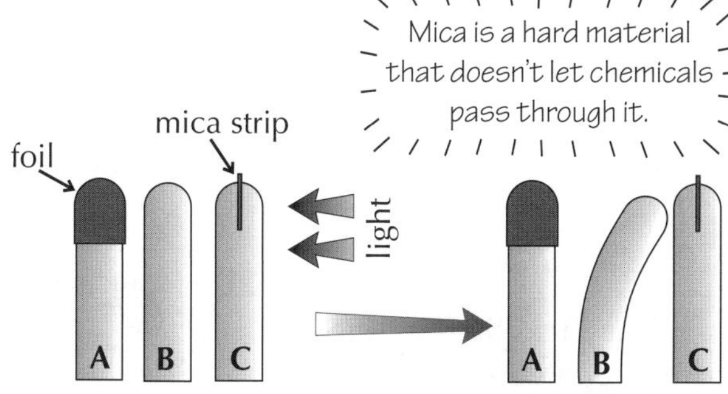

Seedling	Preparation	Observation after 5 hours
A	foil covering tip	no change
B	left alone	tip bent towards the light
C	mica strip through centre of tip	no change

Suggest why seedling A and seedling C failed to respond to the light.

Seedling A ....

....

Seedling C ....

....

Commercial Use of Plant Hormones

Q1 Describe four ways in which **plant hormones** can be used **commercially**.

1. ....

2. ....

3. ....

4. ....

Q2 Roger owns a fruit farm which grows satsumas. The fruit is picked before it is ripe and transported to market.

fruit picked → fruit packaged → fruit transported to market → fruit displayed

a) Suggest why the satsumas are picked before they are ripe.

....

....

b) **i)** How could the unripened satsumas be ripened in time to reach the market?

....

ii) At what stage in the diagram above should the satsumas be ripened?

....

Q3 Charlie sprayed a batch of **dormant** barley seeds with a dilute solution of a plant hormone. This caused all the seeds to germinate.

a) Define the term **dormancy**.

....

b) Suggest **two** reasons why it is useful to be able to control when seeds germinate.

....

....

Homeostasis

Q1 Homeostasis is an important process in the human body.

a) Define **homeostasis**.

....

....

b) Why is homeostasis important for **cells** in the human body?

....

c) Hormonal communication systems are involved in homeostasis.
Name the **other** type of communication system involved.

....

Q2 Write a definition of the term '**negative feedback**'.

....

....

Q3 The graph below shows how **negative feedback** systems operate in the body.

a) Circle the correct word in each pair to complete the sentence below.

In a negative feedback system the response produced has the **opposite / same** effect to the change detected — it **increases / reverses** the change.

b) Fill in the missing words in the labels on the graph.

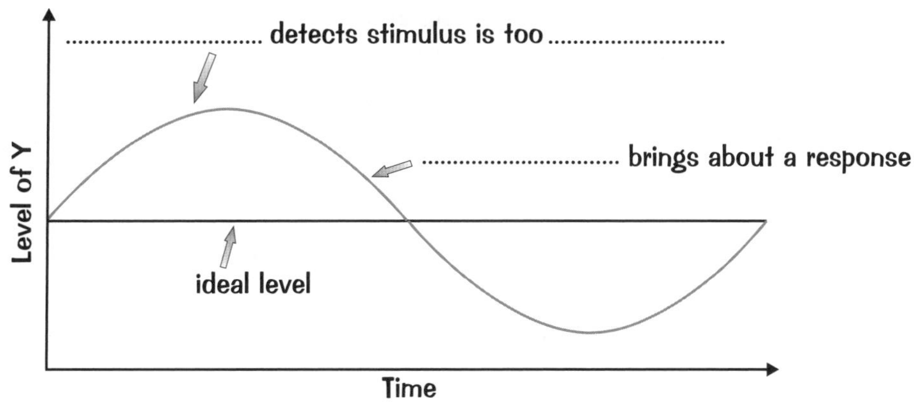

c) What name is given to the part of a negative feedback system that receives information and coordinates a response?

....

Controlling Ions, Temperature and Blood Sugar

Q1 The human body is usually maintained at a **temperature** of about **37 °C**.

a) Which part of your body monitors your body temperature to ensure that it is kept constant?

....

b) Why do humans suffer ill effects if their body temperature varies too much from 37 °C?

....

....

Q2 Your body has various techniques for adjusting body temperature to keep it constant.

a) Explain how **sweating** helps to lower your body temperature.

....

....

b) **i)** Explain what **vasodilation** and **vasoconstriction** are.

....

....

ii) How do vasodilation and vasoconstriction help to keep your body temperature constant?

....

....

Q3 The graph shows the **blood sugar level** of a healthy person over a period of 5 hours.

a) What might have caused the drop in blood sugar level at point A?

....

....

....

b) The blood sugar level rose quickly at point B. What could have caused this increase in sugar level?

....

c) Why does the body's blood sugar level need to be constantly maintained?

....

Controlling Water Content

Q1 Choose the **correct words** to complete the paragraph below.

> On a **cold** / **hot** day or when you're exercising, you **sweat a lot** / **don't sweat much**, so you will produce **more** / **less** urine. The urine will be a **pale** / **dark** colour as it contains **less** / **more** water than usual. We say that the urine is more **concentrated** / **dilute** than usual.

Q2 Would a man on a treadmill lose **more** or **less** water from his lungs than he would if he sat still? Explain your answer.

....

....

Q3 The concentration of water in the blood is adjusted by the **kidneys**. They ensure that the water content never gets **too high** or **too low**.

a) **ADH** is a chemical needed to control the body's water content. What type of chemical is ADH?

....

b) Complete the diagram below by circling the correct word in each pair.

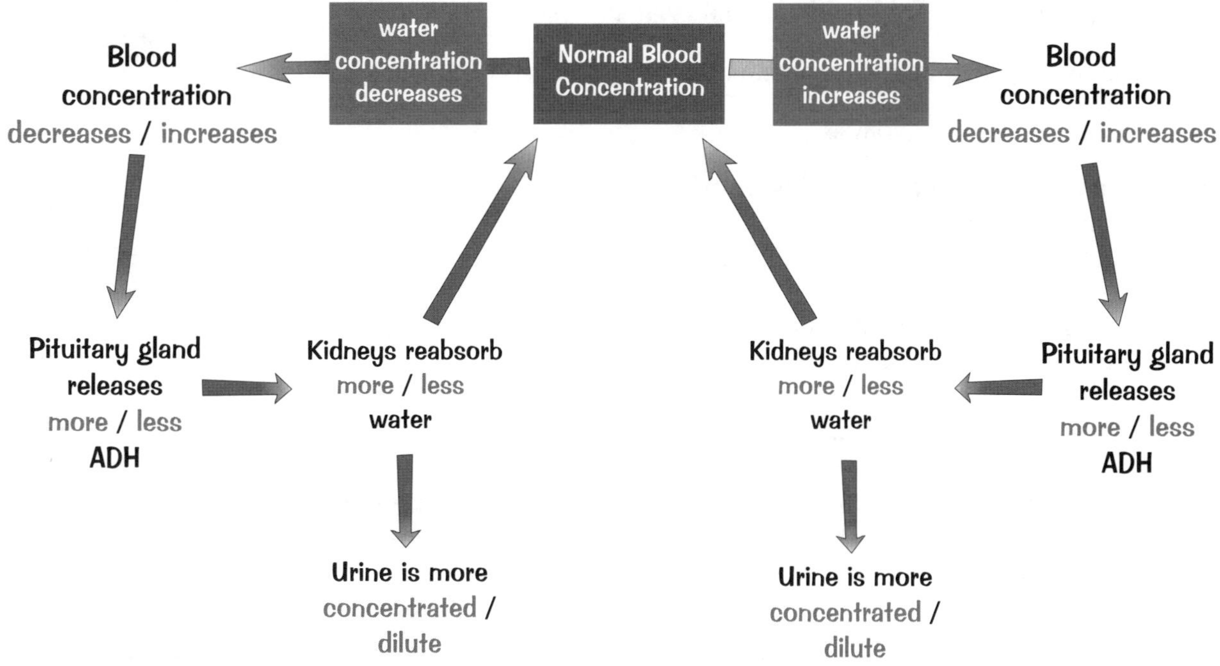

Mixed Questions — Section 1

Q1 The diagram shows a runner waiting to start a race in the Olympic Games.

a) Give one sense organ that the athlete is relying on at the start of the race, and state the type of receptors it uses.

....

b) When the athlete starts the race, information will travel around his body via neurones. What is the difference between motor neurones and sensory neurones?

....

....

....

c) The day of the race is extremely hot, so the runner's coach tells him to drink lots of water.

i) Give three ways that water could be lost from the runner's body.

....

ii) Explain why the amount of urine that people produce can depend on the air temperature.

....

....

Q2 The diagram represents the **menstrual cycle** in a particular woman.

a) What is the length of the complete menstrual cycle shown?

.... days.

b) What happens on day 16 of this woman's cycle?

....

c) Oestrogen is one of the main hormones that control the menstrual cycle. Name another hormone involved.

....

d) Explain how the oestrogen in the contraceptive pill prevents pregnancy.

....

....

Mixed Questions — Section 1

Q3 Ronald eats a meal that is very high in **salt**. Which of the answers below explain correctly how Ronald's body gets rid of this excess salt? Tick one or more boxes.

- Ronald's liver removes salt from his blood. ☐
- Ronald loses salt in his sweat. ☐
- Ronald's kidneys remove salt from his blood. ☐
- Ronald's saliva becomes more salty, and the salt is lost when he breathes. ☐
- Ronald gets rid of salt in his urine. ☐

Q4 **Hormones** are chemical substances.

a) How do hormones travel around the body?

....

b) Tick all the factors below that describe how hormones work.

- ☐ slow response
- ☐ response lasts for a short time
- ☐ response lasts for a long time
- ☐ acts on a very precise area in the body

c) Plants contain hormones too.

i) Where in a plant is the hormone **auxin** produced? Circle the correct answers.

at the tips of shoots   in leaves   at the base of the stem   in flowers   at the tips of roots

ii) Describe the **difference** between how auxin affects cells in the shoots and in the roots of plants.

....

....

iii) Name **one** use of auxin in agriculture.

....

Diet and Metabolic Rate

Q1 Tick the box next to the correct definition of a **healthy diet**.

- [ ] A diet containing protein, carbohydrates, fibre, vitamins and minerals but no sugar or fat.
- [ ] A diet containing the right balance of different foods and the right amount of energy.
- [ ] A diet containing equal amounts of protein, carbohydrates, fats, fibre, vitamins and minerals.

Q2 Complete the following sentences to show the functions in the body of different food groups.

a) Protein is needed for .... and ....

b) Carbohydrates provide much of your ....

c) Fats are needed to .... and for ....

d) Vitamins and minerals are needed in .... amounts to stay healthy.

Q3 Answer the following questions about **metabolism**.

a) Explain what is meant by the term 'metabolic rate'.

....

....

b) Circle **three** factors from the list below that will affect a person's metabolic rate.

proportion of muscle to fat in the body

proportion of hair to bone in the body

inherited factors

amount of exercise

number of brothers and sisters

Q4 Wendy and June both work as IT technicians. Wendy is training to run a marathon and goes to the gym every evening. June doesn't enjoy sport and prefers playing chess in her spare time. Who needs more **protein** and **carbohydrate** in their diet — June or Wendy? Explain your answer.

....

....

....

Top Tips: Mmm, what I couldn't do with 6000 Calories per day... Anyway, remember that everyone needs a balanced diet, but not everyone needs to eat exactly the same stuff.

Diet and Metabolic Rate

Q5 Different people need to eat **different amounts** of food because they have different energy requirements.

Calories are a measure of the amount of energy in food.

a) It is recommended that the average woman eats about 2000 Calories per day, while the average man should eat about 2500 Calories. Explain why there is a difference.

....

....

b) Cyclists riding in the Tour de France bike race need to eat about 6000 Calories per day during the race. This is more than twice what the average man requires. Explain why.

....

....

Q6 The bar chart shows the proportions of each **food group** that make up three different foods.

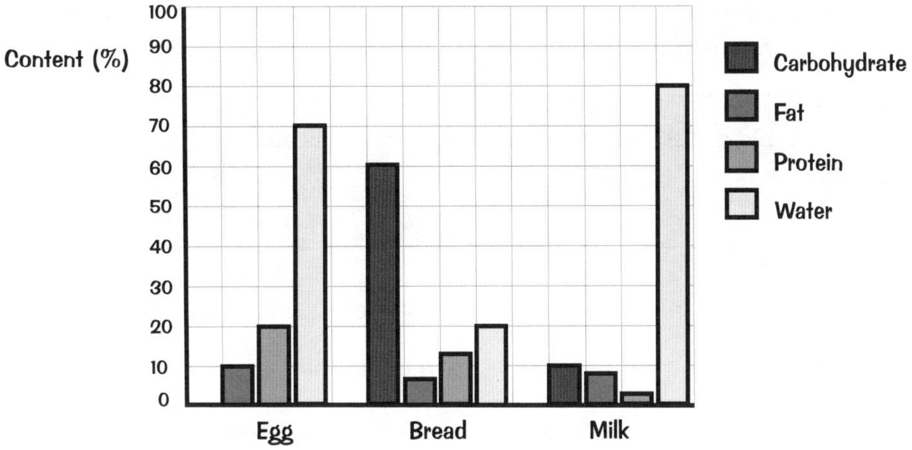

Content (%)

100
90
80
70
60
50
40
30
20
10
0

Egg Bread Milk

Carbohydrate
Fat
Protein
Water

a) Which food contains the highest proportion of fat? ....

b) What is the difference between the amount of carbohydrate in 50 g of bread and the amount of carbohydrate in 50 g of milk? Give your answer in grams and show your working out.

....

....

The % in the bar chart is like the no. of grams you'd have in 100 g of the food.

c) For my lunch I have scrambled eggs on toast and a glass of milk. Suggest another food I could have to make this a more balanced meal. Explain your answer.

....

....

Factors Affecting Health

Q1 A person may have poor health due to being **malnourished**.

a) What do we mean when we say a person is 'malnourished'?

....

b) Deficiency diseases are often associated with malnutrition. What is a deficiency disease?

....

Q2 How can a person be both '**fit**' and **malnourished**?

....

....

Q3 Fifty men and fifty women were asked whether they thought they were **obese**.
Each was then given a medical examination to **check** whether they were actually obese.

	Thought they were obese	Actually obese
No. of women	9	16
No. of men	5	11

a) What percentage of women in this survey were obese? ....

b) What are the most common causes of obesity in developed countries?

....

c) Underline any health problems in the list below that have been linked to obesity.

heart disease **hepatitis** **influenza** **cancers** **scurvy** **type 2 diabetes**

Q4 Answer the following questions about **health**.

a) Why are people who exercise regularly usually healthier than people who don't?

....

....

b) Give **two** ways in which inherited factors can affect a person's health.

....

Evaluating Food, Lifestyle and Diet

Q1 Circle the correct words to complete this passage on **weight loss**.

To lose body mass, a person needs to take in **more** / **less** energy than they **use** / **store**.

Eating **more** / **less** fat and carbohydrate means the body takes in less energy.

Exercise **increases** / **decreases** the amount of energy used by the body.

Q2 Two reports on **low-fat foods** were published on one day. **Report A** appeared in a tabloid paper. It said that the manufacturers of 'Crunchie Bites' have shown that the latest girl band, Kandyfloss, lost weight using their product. **Report B** appeared in a *Journal of Medicine* and reported how 6000 volunteers lost weight during a trial of an experimental medicine.

Which of these reports is likely to be the most reliable and why?

....

....

Q3 The **nutritional labels** of two different burgers are shown below. Both burgers have the **same weight**.

A:

NUTRITIONAL INFORMATION	
	per burger
Energy	2538 kJ
Protein	33 g
Carbohydrate	51 g
of which sugars	12 g
Fat	30 g
of which saturates	7 g
Fibre	2 g
Sodium	0.9 g

B:

NUTRITIONAL INFORMATION	
	per burger
Energy	2718 kJ
Protein	19 g
Carbohydrate	56 g
of which sugars	16 g
Fat	39 g
of which saturates	12 g
Fibre	1 g
Sodium	1.9 g

a) Which is the most **unhealthy** burger? Explain your answer.

....

....

b) Sharon eats burger B three times a week. She reads and goes to the theatre regularly, but doesn't do any kind of exercise. Explain how Sharon's choice of lifestyle could affect her health.

....

....

The Circulatory System

Q1 Complete the passage using the words provided below.

carbon dioxide	vessels	nitrogen	oxygen	nutrients
particles	veins	arteries	capillaries	tubes

Blood is vital to the working of the body. It is carried around the body in blood .... The blood is carried away from the heart in .... and brought back in .... It supplies the tissues with .... and .... for energy, and carries .... to the lungs, where it is removed.

Q2 The **heart** keeps blood pumping around the body.

a) The heart is a **double pump**. Explain what this means.

....

b) **i)** What type of cell makes up the walls of the heart?

....

ii) Why is a blood supply to the cells in the walls of the heart essential?

....

Q3 The pictures below show cross sections of three **blood vessels** — an artery, a capillary and a vein.

A B C

a) Write the name of each blood vessel by the correct letter.

A = ... **B** = ... **C** = ...

b) Explain how the following structures are related to the **function** of the blood vessel.

i) Strong and elastic walls of arteries ....

....

ii) Walls one cell thick in capillaries ....

....

iii) Valves in veins ....

....

Heart Rate and Blood Pressure

Q1 Fill in the blanks in the paragraph, choosing the correct words from the list below.

lower higher stops seventy relaxes artery two vein

Blood pressure measurements record the pressure of the blood on the walls of an .... When a doctor measures your blood pressure, ... readings are taken. The .... pressure is the pressure when your heart contracts. The other reading is the pressure when your heart ....

Q2 You can measure your **heart rate** by recording your **pulse rate**.
Explain why pulse rate can be used to measure heart rate.

....

....

Q3 The table below shows the blood pressure measurements of five adult men.
Normal blood pressure is in the range of **90/60** to **120/80**.

	Blood Pressure
Chris	110/80
Dan	85/50
Steve	120/80
Ahmed	120/80
Nigel	150/95

a) How many men have blood pressure in the normal range? ....

b) Explain why normal measurements are usually given as a range of values.

....

c) Which of the men has high blood pressure? ....

d) High blood pressure can damage arteries and cause the build up of fatty deposits.
Explain how **fatty deposits** in blood vessels could cause a **heart attack**.

....

....

....

Factors Affecting Heart Disease

Q1 Each of the factors below **increase** the **risk** of heart disease. Tick the correct boxes to show whether the each of the factors are **lifestyle** factors or **non-lifestyle** factors.

	Lifestyle	Non-lifestyle
a) Poor diet	☐	☐
b) Excessive alcohol intake	☐	☐
c) Family history of heart disease	☐	☐
d) Smoking	☐	☐
e) Stress	☐	☐

Q2 Circle the correct word to complete the following sentence.

Infrequent / **Regular** moderate exercise reduces the risk of heart disease.

Q3 Heart disease is more common in **industrialised** countries than in **non-industrialised** countries. Tick the box next to the explanation(s) below that you think are valid, reasonable explanations for this.

Industrialised countries are the wealthy, developed countries, e.g. Britain and the US.

☐ People in non-industrialised countries eat less junk food and so have a lower fat diet.

☐ Poorer people in non-industrialised countries will have to walk more because they cannot afford cars and so they get more exercise.

☐ Poorer people in non-industrialised countries cannot afford the treatment for heart disease and so are more likely to die of it.

Q4 a) What are **epidemiological studies**?

....

b) Suggest how epidemiological studies could be used to identify the lifestyle factors that increase the risk of heart disease.

....

....

....

Drugs

Q1 a) What does the term 'drug' mean?

....

b) i) What does it mean if you are **addicted** to a drug?

....

....

ii) Give **one** example of a drug that is very addictive. ....

c) **Statins** are a prescribed drug. What are statins used for?

....

Q2 **Stimulants** are used by some athletes.

a) Why might an athlete use stimulants?

....

b) Give **two** ethical arguments against an athlete using stimulants.

....

....

Q3 Scientists are still **not sure** whether there is a link between using cannabis and developing mental health problems, despite the fact that lots of studies have been carried out. Explain why this is.

....

....

Q4 A drug trial involved 6000 patients with **high cholesterol levels**. 3000 patients were given **statins**, and 3000 were not. Both groups made lifestyle changes to try to lower their cholesterol, based on advice given. The decrease in the patients' cholesterol levels is shown on the graph.

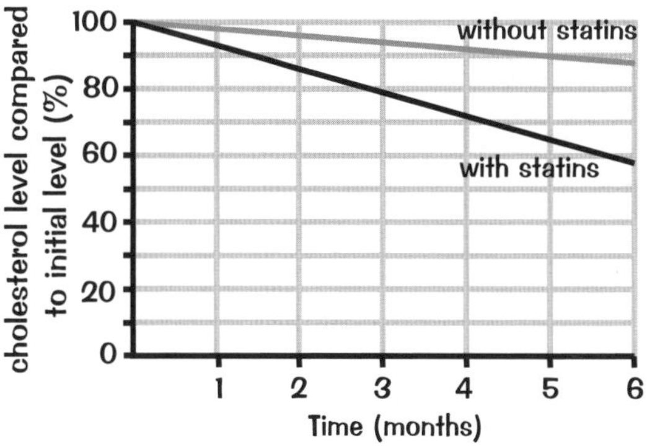

a) Why was the group without statins included?

....

b) Suggest a conclusion that can be drawn from these results. ....

....

Testing Medicinal Drugs

Q1 Write numbers in the boxes below to show the **correct order** in which drugs are tested.

☐ Drug is tested on live animals.

☐ Human volunteers are used to test the drug.

☐ Drug is tested on human cells and tissues.

Q2 Before drugs are made freely available, **clinical trials** must be performed.

a) Give **two** reasons why clinical trials have to be done before drugs are made freely available.

....

....

b) Briefly explain why a drug is tested on **healthy** volunteers first.

....

....

Q3 **Thalidomide** is a drug that was developed in the 1950s.

a) What was this drug originally developed for? ....

b) Thalidomide was not fully tested. What effect did it have when given to pregnant women?

....

....

c) Name **one** disease that thalidomide is now used in the treatment of. ....

Q4 A pharmaceutical company is trialling a new drug. They are using a **placebo** in the trial and are conducting the trials 'double-blind'.

a) What is a placebo?

....

b) Why are the scientists using a placebo?

....

....

c) What is a double-blind trial?

....

....

Recreational Drugs

Q1 Look at the following examples of **health problems** and underline any that are related to **drinking alcohol**.

mumps

liver disease

addiction

lung disease

unconsciousness

Q2 Recreational drugs include **cannabis**, **ecstasy** and **heroin**.

a) Give **two reasons** why someone might use recreational drugs.

1. ....

2. ....

b) Give **one** negative effect that cannabis, ecstasy and heroin can have on the body.

....

Q3 There are three main opinions about the **link** between cannabis and hard drugs. Explain the idea behind each of the following:

a) Stepping stone:

....

b) Gateway drug:

....

c) Genetics:

....

Q4 The use of **legal drugs** causes lots of problems in this country.

a) Why do alcohol and smoking have a **bigger impact** than illegal drugs in the UK?

....

b) Give two ways in which misuse of alcohol and smoking **negatively** affect the **economy** in the UK.

....

....

Top Tips: You'd think it'd be the hard, illegal drugs that cause the most damage to society. But actually the legal drugs are the ones that cause the most problems. This is why it's so important to know all about them. Just because they're legal, it doesn't mean they don't have risks.

Fighting Disease

Q1 What is a **pathogen**?

....

....

Q2 Underline the correct description of an **antigen**.

A 'foreign' cell.

A chemical that causes disease.

A molecule that destroys bacteria.

A molecule that causes an immune response.

Q3 Decide whether the following statements are **true** or **false**.

		True	False
a)	Some pathogens can make you feel very ill.	☐	☐
b)	Infectious diseases can be passed on genetically.	☐	☐
c)	All pathogens are bacteria.	☐	☐
d)	Infectious diseases are not caused by living organisms.	☐	☐
e)	Some pathogens can be spread between organisms very easily.	☐	☐

Q4 Fill in the gaps in the passage below using the words in the box.

Each word can be used only once.

small **replicate** **cells** **damaging** **toxins** **damage** **poisons**

Bacteria are .... organisms which can multiply rapidly inside the body. Some can make you ill by .... your body cells or producing .... (..). Viruses are not .... Viruses .... inside your cells and .... them — this is what makes you feel ill.

Fighting Disease

Q5 The body has several methods of **defending itself** against the entry of **pathogens**. Below are examples of how some bacterial pathogens can enter the body. In each case, describe how your body prevents against illness.

a) *Staphylococcus aureus* can cause blood poisoning by getting into the blood through cuts.

....

....

b) *Streptococcus pneumoniae* can enter the body from the air as a person breathes.

....

....

Q6 **White blood cells** protect the body from infection.

a) Some white blood cells can produce antibodies to deal with invading microorganisms. Can an antibody recognise a wide range of microorganisms? Explain your answer.

....

....

....

b) Give **two** other ways that white blood cells protect the body from infection.

....

....

Q7 If you have already had chickenpox you will usually be **immune** to the disease and will not suffer any symptoms if you are exposed to the infection again. Explain why this is.

....

....

....

Top Tips: Pathogens are all nasty little blighters that can make you ill if they manage to get inside you. Luckily, your body has a few handy ways of defending itself. Just make sure you don't get your words muddled — antigens, antibodies and antitoxins are easy to get mixed up.

Fighting Disease — Vaccination

Q1 Circle the correct words to complete the passage below.

> Illness can be due to microorganisms **dying** / **causing damage** before the immune system can destroy them. If you become infected with a microorganism you have been vaccinated against, you **will** / **won't** have specific antibodies in your blood before the infection.

Q2 **Vaccination** involves injecting dead or inactive microorganisms into the body.

a) Tick the correct boxes to say whether the statements about vaccinations are **true** or **false**.

	True	False
i) The injected microorganisms have the same antigens as the live pathogen.	☐	☐
ii) White blood cells produce antibodies against the antigens on the injected microorganisms.	☐	☐
iii) After a vaccination, the white blood cells can produce antibodies to fight all kinds of diseases.	☐	☐
iv) Vaccinations can wear off over time.	☐	☐

b) Why are dead or inactive microorganisms used in vaccinations?

....

Q3 Describe **two problems** that occasionally occur with **vaccines**.

....

....

....

Q4 John gets injected with the **tuberculosis (TB) vaccine** but James doesn't. Soon afterwards both boys are exposed to the TB bacteria. Explain why James gets ill but John **doesn't**.

....

....

....

....

Fighting Disease — Drugs

Q1 A new medicine called 'Killcold' contains **painkillers** and **decongestants**.

a) Explain why its name isn't strictly accurate.

....

....

b) Why don't doctors give antibiotics for colds?

....

c) Why is it more difficult to develop drugs to destroy viruses than it is to develop drugs to kill bacteria?

....

....

d) Why is it important for a doctor to prescribe the right type of antibiotic for an infection?

....

Q2 a) Write numbers in the boxes below to show the **order** the statements should be in to explain how bacteria become resistant to antibiotics. The first one has been done for you.

- [1] Bacteria mutate and sometimes the mutations cause them to be resistant to an antibiotic.
- [ ] The population of the resistant strain of bacteria will increase.
- [ ] When you treat the infection, only the non-resistant strains of bacteria will be killed.
- [ ] The individual resistant bacteria will survive and reproduce.
- [ ] So if you have an infection, some of the bacteria might be resistant to antibiotics.

b) Name **one** type of bacterium that has developed resistance to antibiotics.

....

Q3 **Microorganisms** can be **grown** in the laboratory on a Petri dish to investigate the effect of antibiotics and disinfectants. Explain why:

a) A lid should be kept on the Petri dish before and after the microorganisms are added.

....

b) The microorganisms should be transferred using an inoculating loop which has been passed through a flame.

....

Fighting Disease — Past and Future

Q1 Ignaz Semmelweis worked in a hospital in Vienna in the 1840s. The graph shows the percentage of women dying after childbirth, before and after a **change** that he made.

a) What was the change and why did it help?

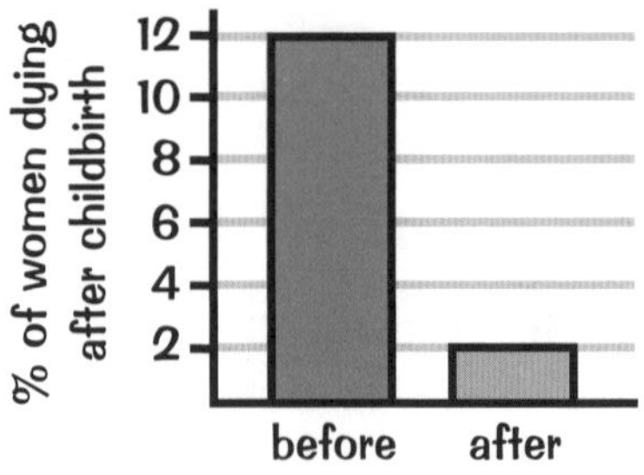

....

....

....

% of women dying after childbirth
12
10
8
6
4
2
before
after

b) After Semmelweis left, the doctors went back to their old ways. Why do you think this was?

....

....

Q2 **Antibiotics** were discovered in the 1940s.

a) Describe what has happened to the number of deaths from infectious bacterial diseases since the introduction of antibiotics.

....

b) Antibiotic-resistant strains of bacteria are becoming more common.

i) Give **one** example of how humans have increased the rate of development of resistant strains.

....

ii) Give **one** way that drug companies are trying to tackle the problem of resistant strains of bacteria.

....

Q3 Some bacteria and viruses **evolve quickly**.

a) Give **two** reasons why a new strain of bacteria could spread very rapidly in a population of people.

....

....

b) A new strain of bacteria could cause an epidemic. What is an epidemic?

....

c) It can be difficult to find an effective **vaccine** against diseases caused by pathogens that evolve rapidly. Explain why.

....

....

Mixed Questions — Section 2

Q1 Draw lines to match each of the **structures** below with its correct **function**.

Structure	Function
valves in veins	withstand the high pressure of blood leaving the heart
permeable walls of capillaries	allow substances to diffuse in and out of the blood
thick, elastic walls of arteries	keep blood flowing in the right direction

HMS DRACULA

Q2 An athlete has been found taking **anabolic steroids**.

a) Why might an athlete use anabolic steroids?

....

b) Give **one** negative health effect of using steroids.

....

Q3 Gavin and Joan carried out an experiment at school to investigate the effectiveness of six different **antibiotics** (1-6). They grew some bacteria on a sterile agar plate. They then placed discs of filter paper, impregnated with the six different antibiotics, onto the bacterial culture.

The clear zone is where there's no bacterial growth.

a) What has happened in the **clear zone** labelled on the diagram?

....

....

....

agar plate
bacterial growth
clear zone
discs of paper impregnated with antibiotics
1 2 3 4 5 6

b) i) Which of the antibiotics (1-6) was the **most effective** against these bacteria?

....

ii) Would this antibiotic also work against the flu, or a common cold? Explain your answer.

....

....

Mixed Questions — Section 2

Q4 Circle the best word or phrase from each pair to complete the sentences below.

a) **Carbohydrates** / **Vitamins** are needed in tiny amounts to keep you healthy.

b) **Overeating** / **Undereating** can cause obesity.

c) An overweight person usually has a **higher** / **lower** metabolic rate than an average person.

d) A farmer is likely to need a lot **more** / **less** energy than someone working in a call centre.

e) Carbohydrates are broken down into sugars to provide **energy** / **materials to build new cells**.

Q5 The **MMR vaccine** has a small risk of serious **side effects**, including meningitis or convulsions. However, the Government recommends that **all** children are given the MMR vaccine.

a) Which diseases does the MMR vaccine protect against?

....

b) Give **one** reason why the Government still recommends that all children are given the MMR vaccine.

....

....

Q6 Tick the boxes below that are next to **true** statements.

Heroin is an example of an addictive, illegal drug. ☐

Alcohol doesn't tend to cause serious problems because it is legal. ☐

You can't get addicted to alcohol. ☐

Some studies have found a link between cannabis use and mental health problems. ☐

It has been proven that the desire to take cannabis and other drugs is genetic. ☐

Q7 Paul catches a **cold**.

a) How do his white blood cells recognise the pathogen?

....

....

b) Shortly after recovering, John is infected with a cold-causing pathogen that he hasn't had before. Will he get ill? Explain your answer.

....

....

Genes, Chromosomes and DNA

Q1 Put the following in **order of size**, starting with the biggest.

cell organism gene

nucleus chromosome

....

Q2 Tick the boxes to show whether the following statements are **true** or **false**.

		True	False
a)	The nucleus of a cell contains instructions for how an organism develops.	☐	☐
b)	Genes are short lengths of chromosomes.	☐	☐
c)	DNA is made up of chromosomes.	☐	☐
d)	There are 23 pairs of genes.	☐	☐
e)	Genes are instructions for a cell that describe how to make proteins.	☐	☐

Q3 **Proteins** are either **structural** or **functional**.

a) Give **one** example of a structural protein.

....

b) Give **one** example of a functional protein.

....

Q4 Describe the difference between an organism's **genotype** and its **phenotype**.

....

....

....

Top Tips: If your plans involve becoming an evil genetic mastermind, you've come to the right place for practising the basics. No matter how hard it seems, keep at it — and one day you could be the ruler of your own army of mutant killer bunnies. Carrots would never be safe again...

Reproduction

Q1 Circle the correct words in each statement below to complete the sentences.

a) Sexual reproduction involves **one** / **two** individual(s).

b) The cells that are involved in sexual reproduction are called **parent cells** / **gametes**.

c) Asexual reproduction produces offspring with **identical** / **different** genes to the parent.

d) In sexual reproduction the sperm cell contains **the same number of** / **half as many** chromosomes as the **fertilised** egg.

e) **Asexual** / **Sexual** reproduction creates offspring with different characteristics to the parent(s).

Q2 Complete the following sentences.

a) Offspring that are identical to their parent are called ....

b) The human male gamete is a ..sperm.....................

c) The process that occurs when two gametes fuse is ....

Q3 Lucy cut her hand, but a week later she noticed that the cut had almost disappeared. The skin covering it looked just the same as the skin on the rest of her hand. This happened by the same process as **asexual reproduction**.

a) Where did the new skin cells on Lucy's hand come from?

....

....

b) Suggest why the skin on Lucy's hand looked the same as it had before she had cut herself.

....

....

c) Suggest why it took a week for the cut to heal.

....

....

Q4 Explain how a human baby receives genes from both its father and its mother, but still only has 46 chromosomes in its cells.

....

....

....

Genetic Diagrams

Q1 An allele for the colour grey (**G**) in mice is dominant over the allele for the colour white (**g**). A heterozygous grey mouse (**Gg**) was bred with a homozygous white mouse (**gg**).

a) Complete the genetic diagram on the right to show the potential combinations of alleles in the offspring of the two mice.

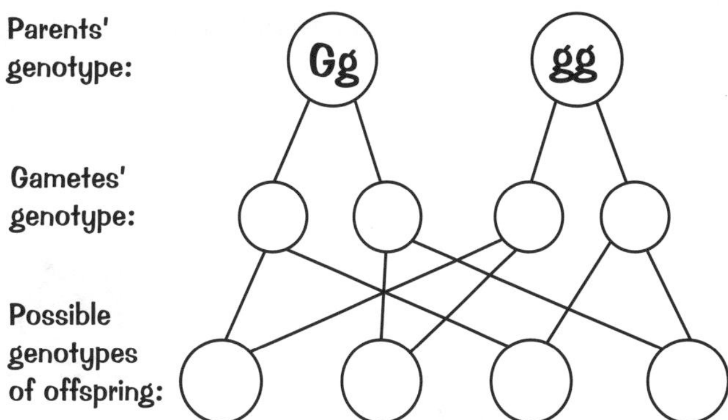

b) What is the likely ratio of colours in any offspring (grey : white)?

....

c) If the mice had 12 babies, how many would there most **likely** be of each colour?

....

Q2 The **family tree** below shows a family with a gene for x-ray vision. The **normal** vision allele (**N**) is **dominant** over the allele for **x-ray** vision (**n**).

a) Based on the expression of this gene, write the combination of **alleles** each grandchild has.

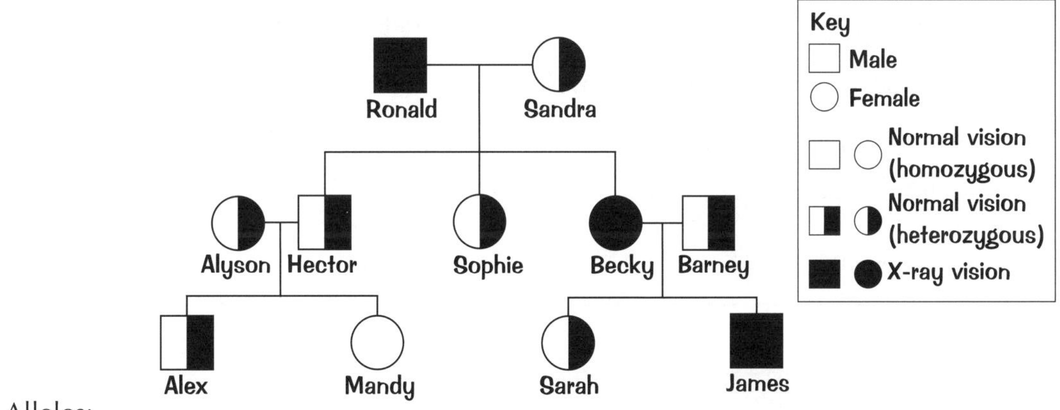

Alleles: ....

b) **Hector** and **Alyson** are expecting another baby. What is the chance that the new baby will have **x-ray** vision? Give your answer as a **percentage**.

....

c) Hector thinks that the baby will **definitely** have **x-ray** vision because Alex and Mandy don't. Is Hector right? Explain your answer.

....

....

Genetic Diagrams and Sex Chromosomes

Q1 In humans, the allele for cheeks with **dimples** (**D**) is **dominant** over the allele for cheeks with **no dimples** (**d**). Adam's mum has no dimples and his dad is **heterozygous** for the trait.

a) Complete the Punnett square below to show the genetic cross between Adam's parents.

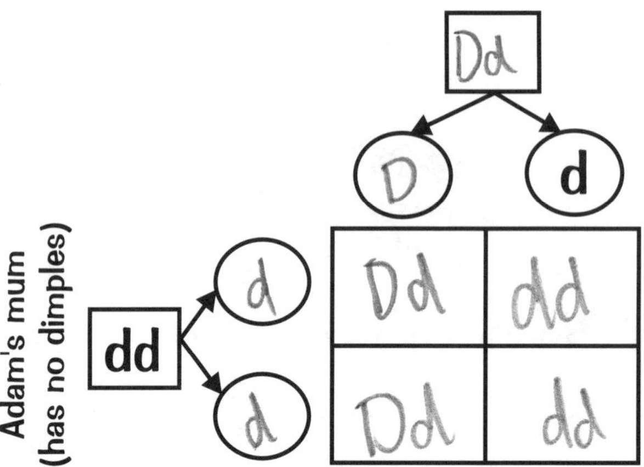

b) If Adam's parents had another child, what is the **percentage chance** of it having dimples?

50%

Q2 Fill in the gaps in the passage below about how a person's **sex** is determined.

Everybody has one pair of chromosomes that determine whether they are male or female. These chromosomes are called the .... chromosomes. There are two types, the .... chromosome, which can be found in males and females, and the .... chromosome, which is found in .... only.

Q3 The sex of a developing human embryo is controlled by a **gene** that causes the production of a specific **protein**.

a) Explain how the protein controls the sex of a developing embryo.

....

....

....

b) Which chromosome do you think the gene that codes for the protein is found on?

....

Genetic Disorders

Q1 **Huntington's disease** is caused by a **faulty** allele of a single gene.

a) Is Huntington's disease caused by a dominant or recessive allele? ....

b) It is possible for a person to pass the disorder on to their children unknowingly. Why is this?

....

....

c) Give three symptoms that someone suffering from Huntington's disease might display.

1. .... 2. .... 3. ....

Q2 Libby and Anne are pregnant. They both have a history of **cystic fibrosis** in their families, but they don't know if their babies will have the disorder.

	Drew	Libby	Billy	Anne
Parent's phenotype:	Carrier	Carrier	Carrier	Normal
Parent's genotype:	Ff	Ff	Ff	FF
Baby's genotype:	?		?	

Remember — alleles with capital letters are dominant. Alleles with a small letter are recessive.

a) It is possible to have the allele for cystic fibrosis, yet not know it because you show no symptoms. How is this possible?

....

....

b) Give three symptoms that someone suffering from cystic fibrosis might display.

1. ....

2. ....

3. ....

c) Complete the table to show the **percentage chances** of Libby's and Anne's babies being carriers or sufferers of cystic fibrosis.

	Carrier	Sufferer
Libby		
Anne		

Sketch a genetic diagram if it helps.

Cloning

Q1 Plants can be cloned from **cuttings**, as shown in the diagram below.

Draw a line from each description below to its correct place on the diagram.

The cuttings are kept in moist conditions until they are ready to plant.

Cloned plant

Cuttings are taken, each with a new bud on

Parent plant

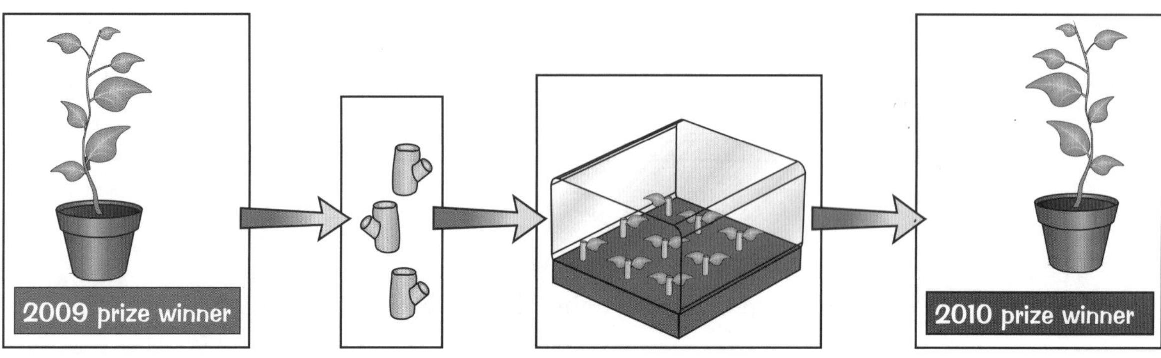

Q2 **Dolly** the sheep was cloned from an adult cell.

Write the correct letter (A, B, C or D) next to each label below to show where it belongs on the diagram.

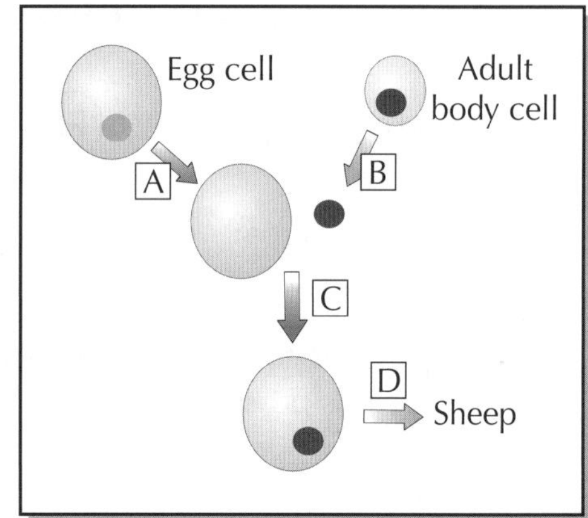

removing and discarding a nucleus ....

implantation in a surrogate mother ....

useful nucleus extracted ....

formation of a diploid cell ....

Q3 Summarise the **issues** involved in cloning.

....

....

....

....

....

....

Top Tips: For some strange reason the scientists who made the first clone decided that what the world really needed was another sheep. So they created Dolly. It's baaa-rking mad if you ask me.

Genetic Engineering

Q1 **Genetic engineering** has produced a range of useful products.

a) Put the following stages of genetic engineering in order by numbering them 1– 4.

☐ Enzymes are used to cut another organism's chromosome.

☐ The gene is cut from one organism's chromosome using enzymes.

☐ The gene is inserted into the organism's chromosome.

☐ The gene for the characteristic is selected.

b) Describe one example of genetic engineering involving bacteria.

....

Q2 **Genetic engineering** has been used to create crops that are resistant to herbicides.

a) Circle the correct word in each pair to complete the following sentence.

Useful genes are inserted into the plants' DNA very **early / late** in their development — shortly after **fertilisation / harvesting**.

b) Many people are concerned about the use of **genetically modified crops**.

i) Suggest **two advantages** of using genetically modified crops.

....

....

....

ii) Suggest **two disadvantages** of using genetically modified crops.

....

....

....

c) Describe **one** other example of the use of genetic engineering in plants or animals.

....

....

Top Tips: Lots of people fret about whether it's ethical to use genetic engineering. It's a really complicated debate and there's no right answer. All you can do is make sure you know both sides of the argument. That way you'll develop an informed opinion — and pick up some marks in the exam.

Adaptations

Q1 Pictures of a **polar bear** and a small rodent called a **kangaroo rat** are shown below.

Diagrams are not to scale.

a) Which of these animals do you think has the smallest body surface area? ....

b) Which animal has the smallest body surface area **compared to its volume**? ....

This is a tricky one. Remember, long, thin shapes have a big surface area <u>compared to their volume</u>.

c) Explain how this animal's **shape** helps to reduce its body surface area compared to its volume.

....

d) Does having a **smaller** body surface area compared to volume mean that more or less **heat** can be lost from an animal's body?

....

e) The kangaroo rat lives in hot desert regions. Explain how its body surface area compared to its volume helps it to survive in these conditions.

....

....

....

Q2 The picture shows a **cactus** plant.

a) Where are cactus plants usually found? Underline the correct answer below.

In Arctic regions **In the desert** **In the mountains** **Near the sea**

b) Explain how each of the following parts of the cactus help it to survive in its normal habitat.

i) Spines ....

....

ii) Stem ....

....

iii) Roots ....

....

Adaptations

Q3 Complete the passage using some of the words from the list below.

temperature	salinity	extremophobes	pressure	light levels	extremophiles

Microorganisms that have adapted to live in extreme conditions are known as .... For example, bacteria living on deep-sea volcanic vents can cope with very high .... and ....

Q4 Some plants and animals are adapted to **avoid being eaten**.

a) i) The fox on the right lives in the Arctic. State **one** feature of the fox that helps it to avoid predators.

....

ii) Explain how the feature described in **i)** helps the fox to avoid predators.

....

b) Wasps are brightly coloured. Explain how this helps protect them against predators.

....

c) State a feature of another organism that helps it to avoid being eaten.

....

Q5 Hayley measured some cubes to find out their surface area to volume ratio. Her results are shown in the table.

Length of cube side (cm)	Surface area of cube (cm^2)	Volume of cube (cm^3)	Surface area: volume ratio
2	24	8	3:1
4	96	64	
6	216	216	
8	384	512	
10	600	1000	

a) Calculate the **surface area : volume ratio** for each cube and write your answers in the table.

Just divide the surface area by the volume.

b) As the cube size becomes larger, what happens to the value of the **surface area : volume ratio**?

....

c) Would you expect the smallest cube (length 2 cm) or the largest cube (length 10 cm) to lose heat more quickly? Explain your answer.

....

d) Use your answers above to explain why a mouse has a thick covering of fur.

....

....

Variation

Q1 Complete this passage by circling the **best** word or phrase from each highlighted pair.

> Usually, organisms of the same species **have differences / are identical**.
> This is partly because different organisms have different **genes / cells**, which are passed on in **gametes / body cells** from which the offspring develop. **Siblings / Identical twins** are exceptions to this. But even these usually have some different features, such as **hair style / eye colour**, and that is due to their **diet / environment**. The differences between individual organisms are known as **variation / inheritance**.

Q2 Helen and Stephanie are identical twins. Helen has dark hair and Stephanie is blonde.

a) Do you think that these are Helen and Stephanie's natural hair colours? Explain your answer.

....

....

b) Helen weighs 7 kg more than Stephanie. Say whether this is due to genes, environment or both, and explain your answer.

....

....

c) Stephanie has a birthmark on her shoulder shaped like a monkey. Helen doesn't.
Do you think birthmarks are caused by your genes? Explain why.

....

....

Q3 Mr O'Riley breeds racehorses. He breeds his best black racing stallion, Snowball, with his best black racing mare, Goldie.

a) Why is there no guarantee that any foal born will be a champion racer?

....

....

b) Will the colour of the newborn foal be due to genes or to environment?

....

Top Tips: Features controlled by genes (e.g. hair colour) can be passed on to an organism's offspring — but features controlled by the environment (e.g. hair style) normally can't be passed on.

Evolution

Q1 Put crosses in the right columns to say which characteristics refer to which **group of organisms**.

	Plant	Animal
Travels to new places		
Makes its own food		
Is fixed to the ground		
May be single celled		

Q2 The diagram below shows the **evolutionary relationships** of four different species.

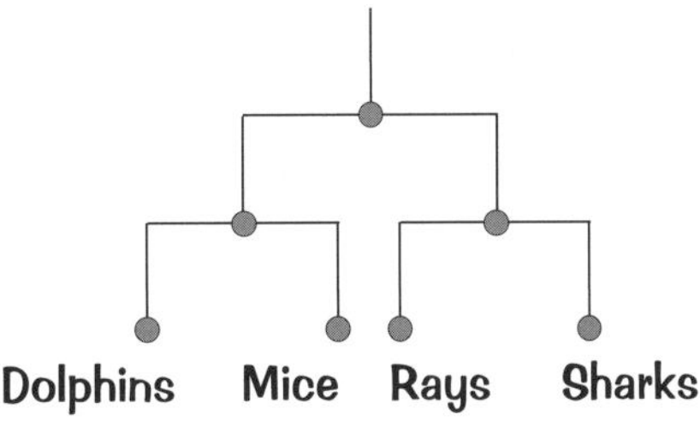

a) Tick the box next to the pair of species below that has the most recent common ancestor.

☐ Mice and Rays.

☐ Rays and Sharks.

☐ Mice and Sharks.

b) Sharks and dolphins share similar characteristics even though they are not closely related. Suggest **one** thing this could tell us about their ecological relationship.

....

Q3 The theory of evolution by **natural selection** was developed by Charles Darwin. Tick the sentences below that describe aspects of natural selection correctly.

☐ There is variation within species caused by differences in their genes.

☐ Genes don't vary enough within species to make members of the same species look different.

☐ The best adapted animals and plants are most likely to survive.

☐ Some characteristics are passed on through reproduction from parent to offspring.

☐ Animals that have successfully adapted do not need to produce offspring.

Evolution

Q4 The buff tip moth's appearance **mimics a broken stick**, making it well-camouflaged. The statements below describe how this feature might have evolved. Write numbers in the boxes to show the order the statements should be in.

☐ Ancestors to the buff tip moth showed variation in their appearance. Some had genes that made them look a bit like a stick.

☐ So the stick-like moths were more likely to survive and reproduce.

☐ Genes that made the moths look like sticks were more likely to be passed on to the next generation.

☐ Short-sighted birds in poor light didn't spot the stick-like moths.

Q5 A and B are fossilised bones from the legs of **ancestors** of the **modern horse**. Some scientists believe that animals with legs like fossil A gradually developed into animals with legs like fossil B.

A

B

a) Suggest **two** reasons why this change may have happened.

....

....

....

....

b) Read the passage below.

> It is thought that there was a stage in the development of the horse between A and B, during which the leg bone would have looked like C.
> Animals with legs like fossil D are closely related to animals with legs like fossil B.
> However, those animals with legs like fossil D aren't direct ancestors of the modern horse.

C D

Use all the information in this question to label the evolutionary tree below with the letters A-D.

....

....

....

Modern horse

Q6 A student incubated a sample of bacteria on an agar plate. The bacteria multiplied to form a plaque. He then added an **antibiotic** to the bacteria. Most of the bacteria died. He incubated the plate again and the remaining bacteria reproduced to form a new plaque. He added the **same** antibiotic to the bacterial plaque and **none of the bacteria died**. Explain these results.

....

....

....

More About Evolution

Q1 Which of the statements below give a reason why some scientists did **not** at first agree with Darwin's idea of **natural selection**? Circle the letters next to the correct statements.

A He could not explain how characteristics could be inherited.

B Characteristics that are caused by the environment can be inherited.

C They thought he was making up the evidence.

D They felt that Darwin was influenced by religious rather than scientific ideas.

E There wasn't enough evidence to convince many scientists.

F They didn't trust men with beards.

Q2 Complete this passage by circling the **best** word or phrase from each highlighted pair.

Bismarck / Lamarck argued that if a characteristic was used a lot by an organism then it would become **more developed / stunted** during its lifetime. For example if an anteater used its tongue a lot to reach ants in anthills, its tongue would get **longer / shorter**. He believed this acquired characteristic would be passed on to **the next generation / animals living nearby**.

Q3 More than one hypothesis has been suggested to explain how evolution occurs.

Tick the boxes by the pieces of evidence below that **do not support** Lamarck's hypothesis:

☐ Kestrels have good eyesight to help them to spot mice from far away.

☐ People with dyed blue hair do not have children with blue hair.

☐ Hummingbirds have long tongues that enable them to feed on nectar from long flowers.

☐ Sheep whose tails are cut short give birth to lambs with full-length tails.

Q4 Lamarck and Darwin came up with **different ideas** to explain how evolution works.

Give **two** reasons why scientists may come up with different ideas to explain similar observations.

....

....

Top Tips: Scientists often come up with different hypotheses to explain their observations. The only way to find out which is right is to find evidence to support or disprove each one.

Competition and Environmental Change

Q1 The resources below are **essential** for life.

Light

Plants

Water

Minerals from the soil

Animals

Food

Space

Mates

a) Draw lines to connect the boxes to show which resources are essential for plants, essential for animals and essential for both.

b) What would happen if two species in a habitat need the same resource?

....

c) Give one way that organisms are dependent on other species for their survival.

....

Q2 **Algae** are tiny organisms that are eaten by **fish**. The graph shows how the size of a population of algae in a pond varied throughout one year.

Algae population size

Jan Feb Mar Apr May Jun Jul Aug Sep Oct Nov Dec

Time (months)

a) Suggest **two non-living factors** that may have changed in the pond to give more algae in April than in January.

....

....

b) The number of **fish** in the pond increased rapidly during one month of the year. Suggest which month this was. Explain your answer.

....

....

....

c) Suggest **two other living factors** that may have changed in the pond over the year.

....

Top Tips: If there's a change in the size or distribution of a population, use information you're given plus your own knowledge to work out the living or non-living factors that might have caused it.

Measuring Environmental Change

Q1 Mayfly larvae and sludgeworms can be studied to see how much **sewage** is in water.

a) What is the name for an organism used in this way? ....

Juanita recorded the number of each species in water samples taken at three different distances away from a sewage outlet. Her results are shown on the right.

Distance (km)	No. of mayfly larvae	No. of sludgeworms
1	3	20
2	11	14
3	23	7

b) Give one thing that she would have to do to make this experiment a fair test.

....

c) What can you conclude about the two organisms from these results?

....

....

d) Suggest why sewage may decrease the number of mayfly larvae.

....

....

e) Suggest a method of measuring the water pollution without using a living indicator.

....

Q2 Dave is investigating the local air quality. He collects data on the **sulfur dioxide concentration** in the air at different sites in his town. His data is shown in the table below.

a) At which site is the sulfur dioxide concentration the **highest**?

....

Site	sulfur dioxide concentration (micrograms/m^3)
1	9.8
2	9.4
3	7.1

b) Dave measured the sulfur dioxide concentration directly, using specialist equipment. Give one advantage and one disadvantage of using **non-living methods** to measure pollution.

Advantage: ....

Disadvantage: ....

c) i) Give an example of an **indicator species** that could be used to monitor **air quality**.

....

ii) Suggest **one** reason why Dave did not use indicator species in his study.

....

....

Pyramids of Biomass and Number

Q1 The **pyramid of biomass** below describes a seashore food chain.

crab

winkle

algae

a) Which organism is the producer?

....

b) Which organism is the primary consumer?

....

c) Which trophic level has the greatest biomass?

....

Q2 A single **robin** has a mass of 15 g and eats caterpillars. Each robin eats 25 **caterpillars** that each have a mass of 2 g. The caterpillars feed on 10 **stinging nettles** that together have a mass of 500 g. Study the pyramid diagrams shown then answer the questions that follow.

A B C D

a) Which is most likely to represent a pyramid of **biomass** for these organisms? ....

b) Explain how you decided on your answer to part **a)** above.

....

c) The stinging nettles are the first trophic level. Where does their energy initially come from?

....

Q3 In the 1950s a chemical called **DDT** was used to control animal pests. DDT was later discovered to be toxic and was detected at very high levels in organisms across food chains, as shown below.

a) Describe what happens to the level of DDT found in organisms as you go up the trophic levels.

....

....

Osprey (13.8 ppm DDT)
Pike (2.8 ppm DDT)
Silverside fish (0.23 ppm DDT)
Algae (0.04 ppm DDT)

'ppm' = 'parts per million'

b) Work out by how many times (e.g. 2 times or 70 times) the level of DDT has risen in the following:

i) in the top consumer compared with the producer ....

ii) in the secondary consumer compared with the producer ....

c) Suggest why a pyramid of biomass is a suitable diagram for displaying the problem with DDT.

....

Top Tips: Pyramids of biomass should be drawn to scale, and will almost always end up pyramid-shaped with the producers having the greatest biomass.

Pyramids of Biomass and Number

Q4 The following diagram shows a garden food chain. The **number** and **biomass** of the organisms at each stage in the food chain is shown below.

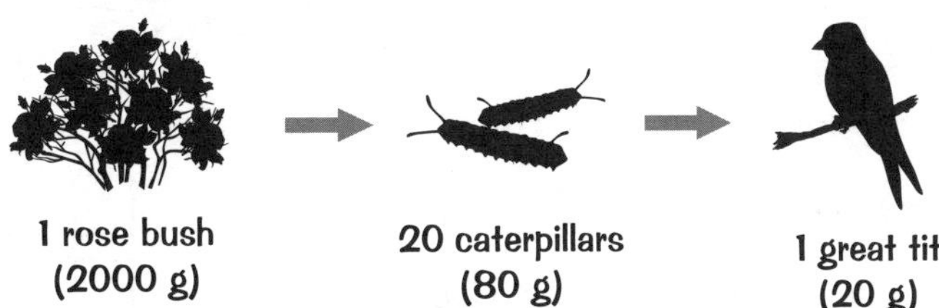

a) Draw and label a **pyramid of biomass** for the food chain in the grid below. Each **large** square of the grid should represent **200 grams**.

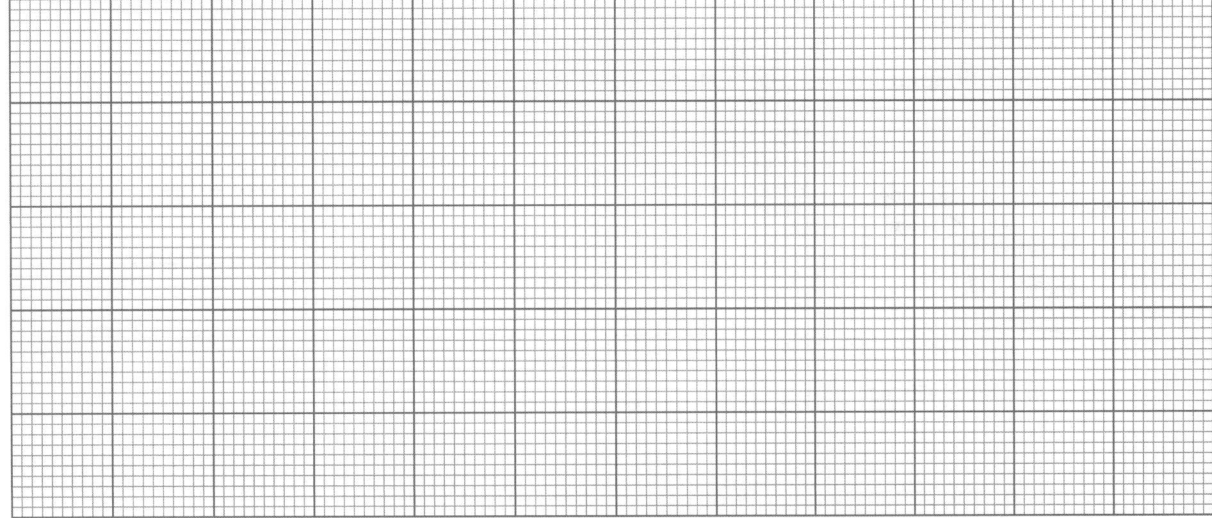

b) Draw and label a **pyramid of numbers** for the food chain in the grid below.

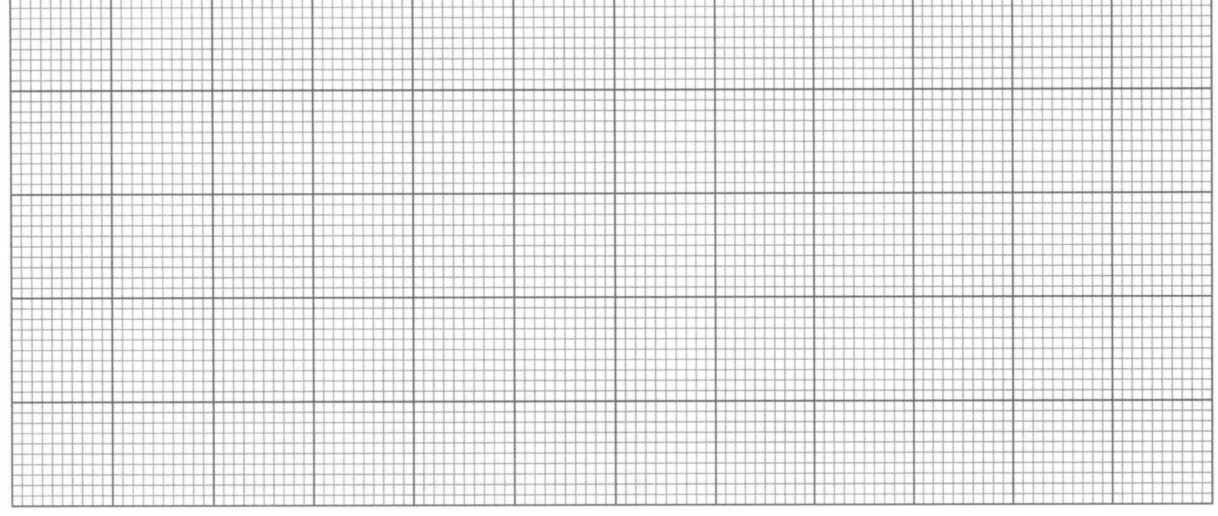

c) Explain the difference between the two pyramids.

....

....

Energy Transfer and Decay

Q1 Indicate whether these statements are **true** or **false**.

		True	False
a)	Without sunlight, nearly all life on Earth would die.	☐	☐
b)	Food chains generally have no more than five steps.	☐	☐
c)	Materials are not lost from food chains — they are recycled.	☐	☐
d)	Elements like carbon are passed along food chains.	☐	☐
e)	Energy only is passed between the steps of food chains.	☐	☐
f)	Food chains that include animals with constant body temperatures are less likely to lose energy as heat.	☐	☐

Q2 Look at the picture of the **compost bin** below. Then choose **three** of the features shown and explain how each feature aids the process of decomposition.

Feature	How it aids decomposition

Q3 Complete the sentences below by circling the correct words.

a) Nearly all life on Earth depends on **food** / **energy** from the Sun.

b) **Plants** / **Animals** can make their own food by a process called **photosynthesis** / **respiration**.

c) To obtain energy animals must **decay** / **eat** plant material or other animals.

d) Animals and plants release energy through the process of **photosynthesis** / **respiration**.

e) Some of the energy obtained by animals is **gained** / **lost** through **growth** / **movement** before it reaches organisms at later steps of the food chain.

f) Some energy is lost between steps of a food chain because it's used to make **edible** / **inedible** materials such as **hair** / **flesh**.

Q4 The sentences below describe how **elements** are **recycled** in a food chain. Sort them into the correct order by numbering them 1 to 6. The first one has been done for you.

☐ **Energy released in respiration is lost by decay, heat and movement and the production of waste.**

☐ **Materials are recycled and returned to the soil by decay.**

1 **Plants take up minerals from the soil.**

☐ **Plants use minerals and the products of photosynthesis to make complex nutrients.**

☐ **Nutrients in plants are passed to animals through feeding and used in respiration to provide energy.**

☐ **Waste and dead tissues are decayed by microorganisms.**

Energy Transfer and Decay

Q5 Living things are made from materials that they take from the world around them.

a) **i)** Name four **elements** that living organisms contain

....

ii) Where do organisms get these elements?

....

b) Explain how the elements inside organisms are returned to the environment.

....

....

Q6 In a **stable community**, the materials that are taken out of the soil and used are balanced by those that are put back in. Decide whether each of the following examples describes a stable community or not — write **stable** or **not stable** in the spaces provided.

a) A farmer plants a field of wheat. In Autumn he harvests the crop. ....

b) In Autumn leaves fall from trees to the grass below where they decay. ....

c) James rakes up the leaves on the ground of his orchard. ....

d) When Julie mows the lawn she leaves the cuttings on the lawn's surface. ....

Q7 Study the diagram of **energy transfer** shown.

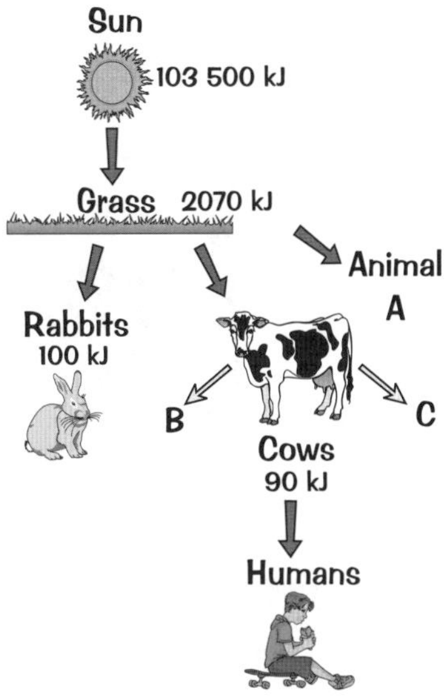

a) Using the figures shown on the diagram, work out the percentage of the Sun's energy that is available in the grass.

....

b) The efficiency of energy transfer from the grass to the next trophic level is 10%. Work out how much energy is available in animal A.

Remember, animal A isn't the only animal at the next level.

....

c) **B** and **C** are processes that represent energy loss. Suggest what these processes might be.

....

d) Why do food chains rarely have more than five trophic levels?

....

....

The Carbon Cycle

Q1 Complete the passage by inserting the most appropriate words from the list below.

respiration carbohydrates microorganisms carbon dioxide detritus photosynthesis eating waste

Green plants and algae remove .... from the air and use it in .... At night plants return this gas to the air through ...., a process that occurs at all times in living organisms including animals and .... Animals obtain a supply of carbon by .... plants. Through digestion, carbon is made available from fats, proteins and .... that are stored in plant tissues. Carbon is released from dead tissues and animal .... by .... feeders.

Q2 Draw lines to match the statements below with their correct endings.

Plants use...	carbon by photosynthesis.
Microorganisms release...	carbon dioxide by decaying waste and dead tissue.
Animals and plants release...	carbon through feeding.
Animals take in...	carbon dioxide to build complex molecules.
Plants take in...	carbon dioxide through respiration.

Q3 The diagram below shows a version of the **carbon cycle**.

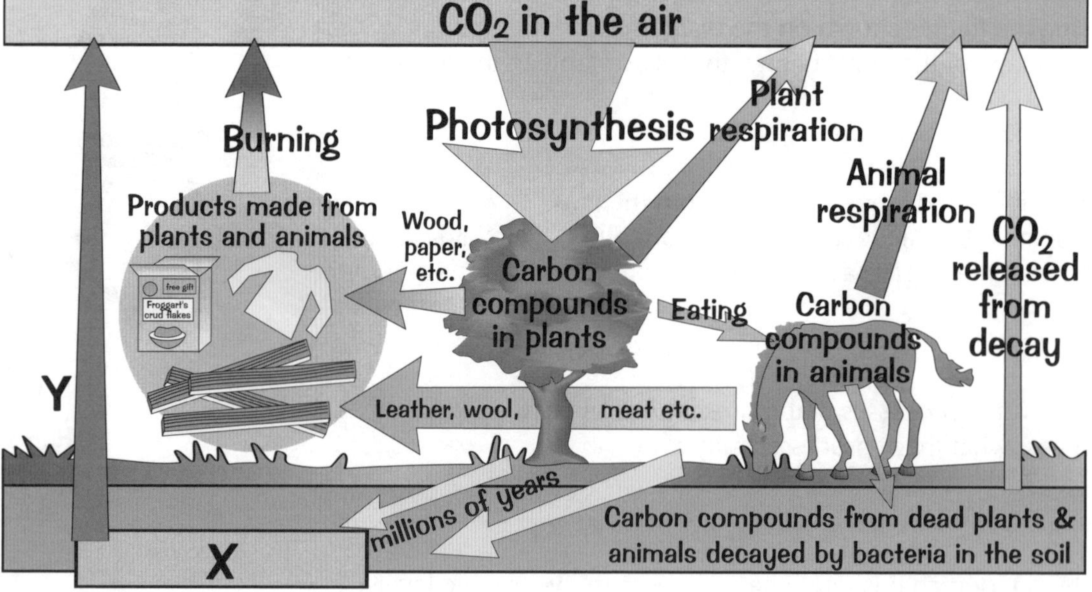

a) Name substance **X** shown on the diagram above. ....

b) Name the process labelled **Y** on the diagram above. ....

The Nitrogen Cycle

Q1 Match up each type of **organism** below with the way it obtains **nitrogen**.

Plants	By breaking down dead organisms and animal waste
Animals	By absorbing nitrates from the soil
Decomposers	By eating other organisms

Q2 The nitrogen cycle is dependent on a number of different types of **bacteria**. Explain the role of each of the following types of bacteria in the nitrogen cycle.

Type of bacteria	Role in the nitrogen cycle
a) Decomposers	....
b) Nitrifying bacteria	....
c) Denitrifying bacteria	....
d) Nitrogen-fixing bacteria	....

Q3 Below is a diagram of the **nitrogen cycle**. Explain what is shown in the stages labelled:

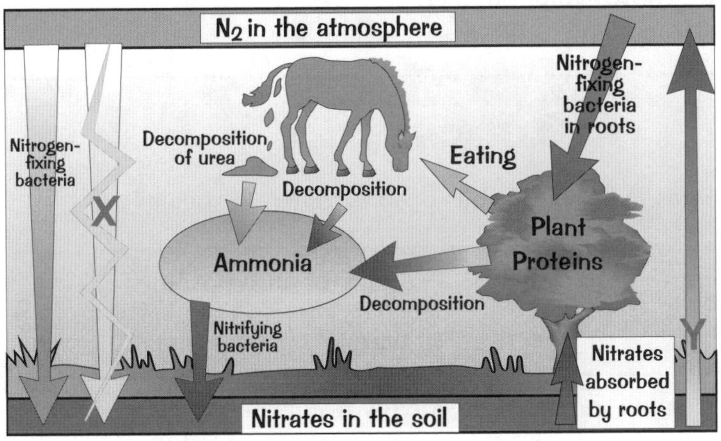

a) X ....

....

....

b) Y ....

....

....

Q4 A farmer was told that if he planted **legume plants** his soil would become more **fertile**.

a) Explain how the legume plants would increase the fertility of his soil.

....

....

b) Explain how this would improve plant growth.

....

....

Mixed Questions — Section 3

Q1 The graph shows how the **body temperatures** of a camel and a goat change throughout the day in a hot desert.

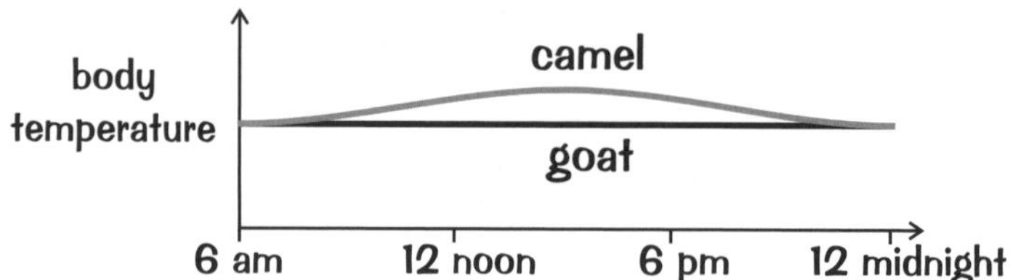

a) Between 6 am and 12 noon, what happened to the body temperature:

i) of the camel? ....

ii) of the goat? ....

b) Which one of the animals keeps cool by sweating? ....

c) Explain why animals that use sweating to keep cool can't survive well in deserts.

....

d) Camels have evolved to tolerate changes in body temperature. State the name of Darwin's theory of how evolution occurs.

....

Q2 The normal numbers of **chromosomes** in the body cells of some different species are:

donkeys — 31 pairs of chromosomes	**horses — 32 pairs of chromosomes**
lions — 19 pairs of chromosomes	**tigers — 19 pairs of chromosomes**

Mating between different, closely-related species occasionally results in offspring. However, the offspring are usually **sterile**. For example, a **mule** is a cross between a donkey and a horse, and a **liger** is a cross between a lion and a tiger.

a) Use the information above to work out the number of chromosomes in the body cells of a mule.

Hint: Think about the number of chromosomes in the gametes of donkeys and horses.

....

....

b) Mules are almost always sterile, but ligers can occasionally produce offspring of their own. Explain this by considering the number of chromosomes of ligers and mules.

....

....

Mixed Questions — Section 3

Q3 An experiment was done with two **fertilised natterjack toad eggs**. The eggs came from completely different parents. The nucleus of **egg A** was put into **egg B**, and the nucleus of egg B was **removed** (see the diagram below).

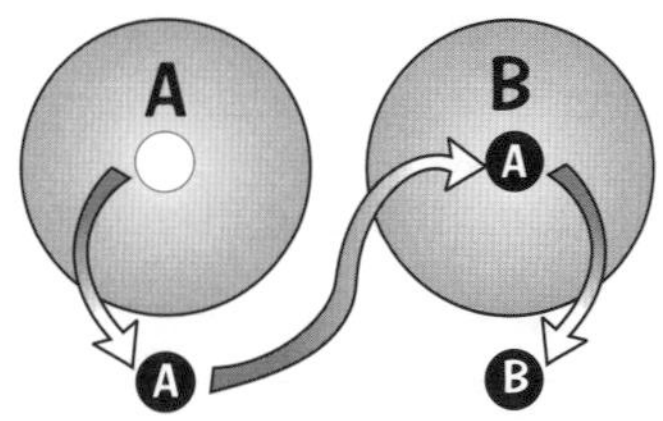

a) Egg **B** grew into a toad. Would you expect it to look more like the parents of egg **A** or the parents of egg **B**? Explain your answer.

....

b) The technique used to create Dolly the sheep also involved removing genetic material from an egg cell. However, Dolly was a **clone**, whereas the toad produced in this experiment was not. Explain why this is.

....

....

c) Because of their permeable skin, amphibians are '**indicator species**'.

Explain what this term means.

....

....

Q4 In **guinea pigs**, the allele for short hair **(H)** is dominant over the allele for long hair **(h)**.

a) Is it possible for two short haired guinea pigs to produce long haired offspring? Explain your answer.

....

....

b) Is it possible for two long haired guinea pigs to produce short haired offspring? Explain your answer.

....

....

Atoms and Elements

Q1 Complete the following sentences.

a) Atoms always have a charge of ....

b) An atom which has lost or gained electrons is called an ....

c) A neutral atom has the same number of .... and ....

d) If an electron is added to a neutral atom, the atom becomes .... charged.

Q2 Complete this table.

Particle	Charge
Proton	
	0
Electron	

Q3 What am I?

Choose from: **nucleus** **proton** **electron** **neutron**

a) I am in the centre of the atom. I contain protons and neutrons. ....

b) I move around the nucleus in a shell. ....

c) I am positively charged. ....

d) I have no charge. ....

e) In a neutral atom there are as many of me as there are electrons. ....

Q4 Draw a diagram of a **helium** atom.

Label each type of **particle** on your diagram.

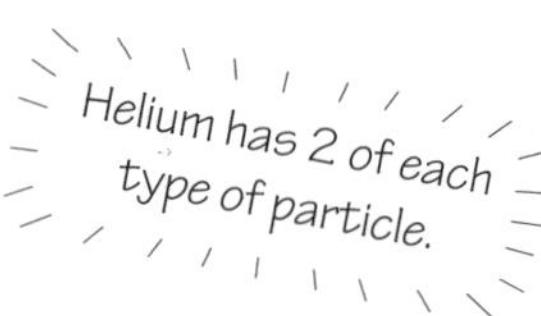

Q5 Look at these diagrams of substances. Circle the ones that contain only **one element**.

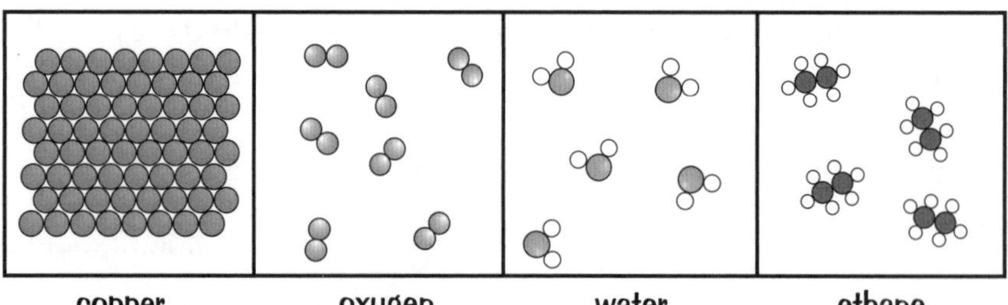

The Periodic Table

Q1 Choose from these words to fill in the blanks.

left-hand **C** **right-hand** **horizontal** **similar** **elements** **K**
Cl **different** **vertical** **metals** **P** **non-metals** **compounds**

a) A group in the periodic table is a .... line of elements.

b) Most of the elements in the periodic table are ....

c) There are about 100 different .... in the periodic table.

d) Non-metals are on the .... side of the periodic table.

e) Elements in the same group have .... properties.

f) The symbol for chlorine is .... and the symbol for potassium is ....

Q2 **Sodium** appears in the periodic table as shown below.

23 Na 11

a) Circle the atomic number on the diagram to the left.

b) How many protons does Na have? ....

c) How many electrons does Na have? ....

d) How many neutrons does Na have? ....

Q3 Elements in the same group undergo **similar reactions**.

a) Tick the pairs of elements that would undergo similar reactions.

A potassium and rubidium ☐ **C** calcium and oxygen ☐

B helium and fluorine ☐ **D** calcium and magnesium ☐

b) Explain why sodium and potassium undergo similar reactions with water.

....

....

Q4 **True** or **false**?

	True	False
a) Group 7 elements are known as the noble gases.	☐	☐
b) All of the noble gases have the same number of electrons in their outer shell.	☐	☐
c) Helium is a noble gas.	☐	☐
d) Noble gases have the maximum number of electrons in their outer energy level.	☐	☐
e) All noble gases are unreactive.	☐	☐

Electron Shells

Q1 a) Tick the boxes to show whether each statement is **true** or **false**.

	True	False
i) Electrons occupy shells in atoms.	☐	☐
ii) The highest energy levels are always filled first.	☐	☐
iii) Atoms are most stable when they have partially filled shells.	☐	☐
iv) Reactive elements have full outer shells.	☐	☐

b) Write out corrected versions of the **false** statements.

....

....

....

Q2 Describe **two** things that are wrong with this diagram.

1. ....

....

2. ....

....

Q3 Write out the **electronic structure** for the following elements.

a) Beryllium ....

b) Oxygen ....

c) Silicon ....

d) Calcium ....

e) Aluminium ....

f) Argon ....

Q4 Do the following groups of elements contain **reactive** or **unreactive** elements? Explain your answers in terms of **electron shells**.

a) Noble gases ....

....

b) Group I metals ....

....

Electron Shells

Q5 **Chlorine** has an atomic number of 17.

a) What is its electronic structure? ....

b) Draw the electrons on the shells in the diagram. 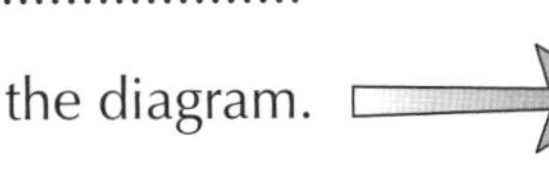

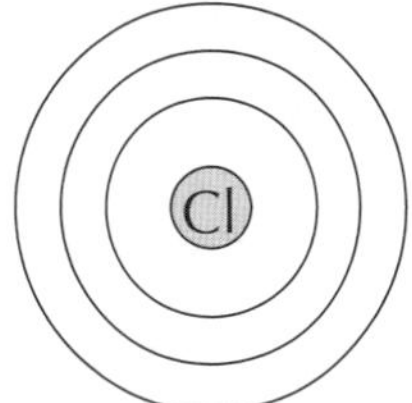

c) Why does chlorine react readily?

....

Q6 Draw the **full electronic structures** for these elements. (The first three have been done for you.)

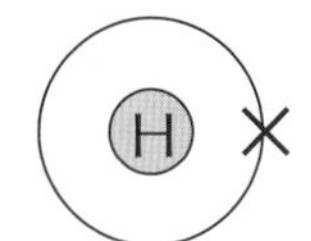

Hydrogen

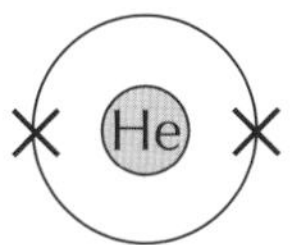

Helium

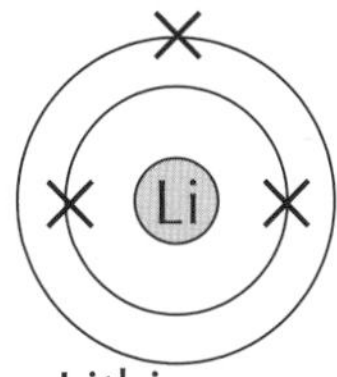

Lithium

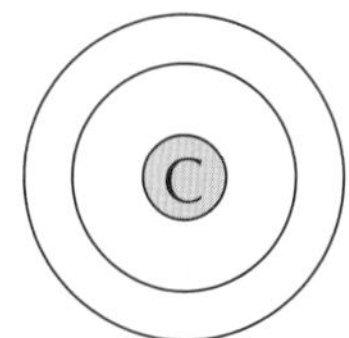

a) Carbon

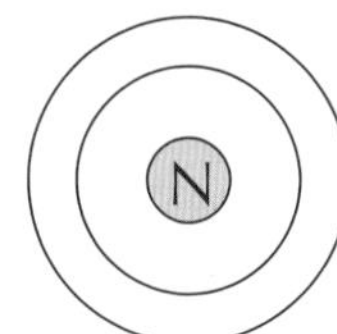

b) Nitrogen

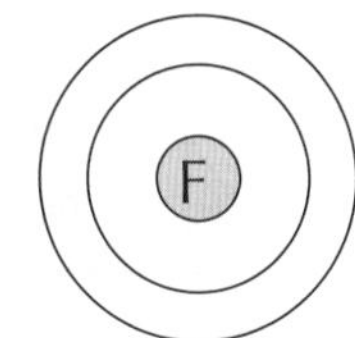

c) Fluorine

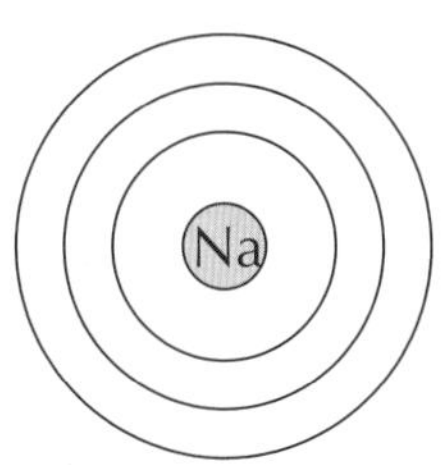

d) Sodium

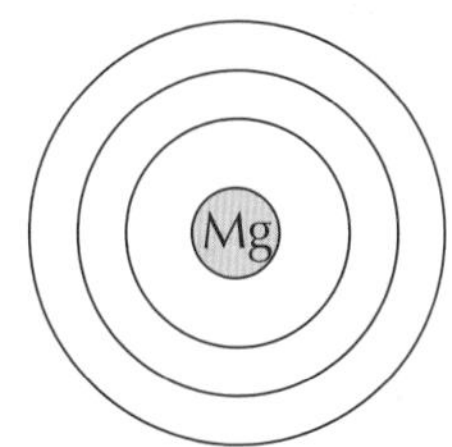

e) Magnesium

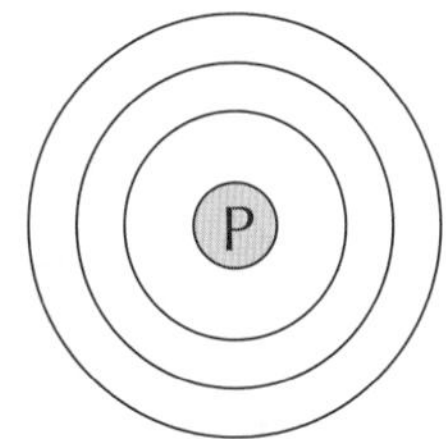

f) Phosphorus

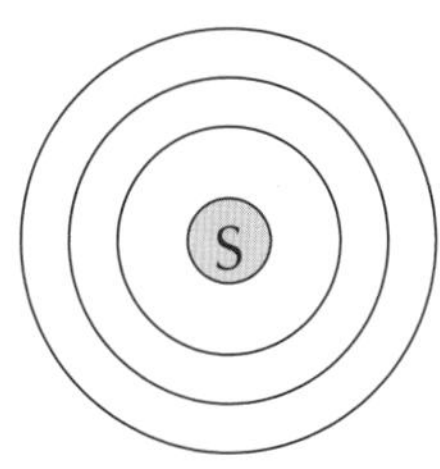

g) Sulfur

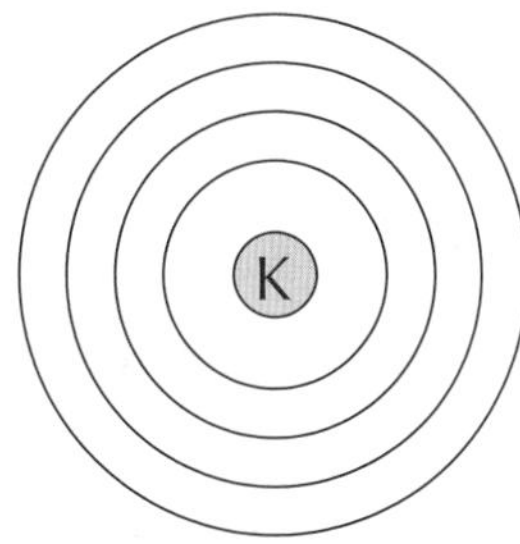

h) Potassium

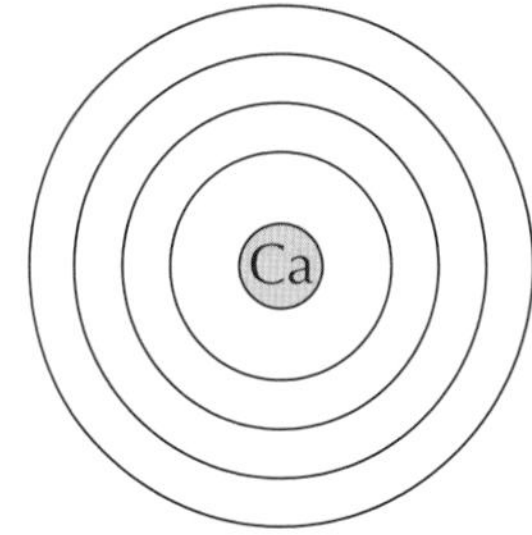

i) Calcium

Top Tips: Once you've learnt the 'electron shell rules' these are pretty easy — the first shell can only take 2 electrons, and the second and third shells a maximum of 8 each. Don't forget it.

Compounds

Q1 Indicate whether each statement is **true** or **false**.

		True	False
a)	Covalent bonding involves sharing electrons.	☐	☐
b)	Atoms react to gain a full outer shell of electrons.	☐	☐
c)	In ionic bonding, atoms lose or gain electrons.	☐	☐
d)	Ions with opposite charges attract each other.	☐	☐

Q2 Use the words below to fill in the blanks in the passage.

positive ionic molecules ions negative covalent attracted

A compound which is formed from a metal and a non-metal consists of .... The metal atoms lose electrons to form .... ions and the non-metal atoms gain electrons to form .... ions. The opposite charges of the ions mean that they're strongly .... to each other — called an .... bond. A compound formed from non-metals consists of .... Each atom shares an electron with another atom — called a .... bond.

Q3 Use the **diagram** to answer the following questions.

Na
Cl
Na
Cl
+
−

a) What kind of chemical **bond** is shown in the diagram? ....

b) How many **electrons** does **chlorine** need to gain to get a full outer shell of electrons? ....

c) What is the **charge** on a **sodium ion**? ....

d) What is the chemical formula of **sodium chloride**? ....

Q4 Why do some atoms **share** electrons? What **type** of bond do they make?

....

....

Balancing Equations

Q1 Which of the following equations are **balanced** correctly?

		Correctly balanced	Incorrectly balanced
a)	$H_2 + Cl_2 \rightarrow 2HCl$	☑	☐
b)	$CuO + 2HCl \rightarrow CuCl_2 + H_2O$	☐	☑
c)	$3N_2 + 3H_2 \rightarrow 2NH_3$	☐	☑
d)	$CuO + H_2 \rightarrow Cu + H_2O$	☑	☐
e)	$CaCO_3 \rightarrow CaO + CO_2$	☑	☐
f)	$CO_2 + H_2O \rightarrow H_2CO_3$	☑	☐

Q2 Here is the equation for the formation of carbon **mon**oxide in a poorly ventilated gas fire. It is **not** balanced correctly.

$$C + O_2 \rightarrow CO$$

Circle the **correctly balanced** version of this equation.

$$C + O_2 \rightarrow CO_2$$ ✗

$$C + O_2 \rightarrow 2CO$$

$$2C + O_2 \rightarrow 2CO$$ (circled)

Q3 In a book, this is the description of a reaction: "**methane** (CH_4) can be burnt in **oxygen** (O_2) to make **carbon dioxide** (CO_2) and **water** (H_2O)".

a) What are the **reactants** and the **products** in this reaction?

Reactants: .... Products: ....

b) Write the **word equation** for this reaction.

....

c) Write the **balanced symbol equation** for the reaction.

....

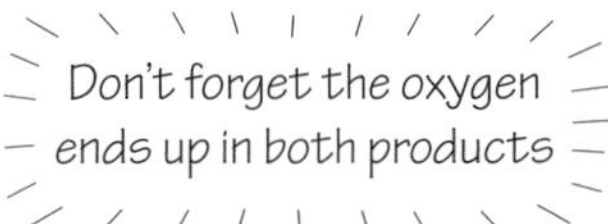

Top Tips: The most important thing to remember with balancing equations is that you can't change the **little numbers** — if you do that then you'll change the substance into something completely different. Just take your time and work through everything logically.

Balancing Equations

Q4 Write out the balanced **symbol** equations for the unbalanced picture equations below.

a) 

\+ Cl Cl → 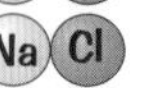

You can draw more pictures to help you balance the unbalanced ones.

....

b) Li + O O  Li O Li

....

c) 

\+ H Cl  

\+ 

 + 

....

d) Li + H O H / H O H → 

\+ H H

....

Q5 Add **one** number to each of these equations so that they are **correctly balanced**.

a) $CuO + HBr \rightarrow CuBr_2 + H_2O$

b) $H_2 + Br_2 \rightarrow HBr$

c) $Mg + O_2 \rightarrow 2MgO$

d) $2NaOH + H_2SO_4 \rightarrow Na_2SO_4 + H_2O$

You need to have 2 bromines and 2 hydrogens on the left-hand side.

Q6 **Balance** these equations by adding in numbers.

a) $NaOH + AlBr_3 \rightarrow NaBr + Al(OH)_3$

b) $FeCl_2 + Cl_2 \rightarrow FeCl_3$

c) $N_2 + H_2 \rightarrow NH_3$

d) $Fe + O_2 \rightarrow Fe_2O_3$

e) $NH_3 + O_2 \rightarrow NO + H_2O$

$Fe_2O_3 + 3CO \rightarrow 2Fe + 3CO_2$

Materials and Properties

Q1 Complete the statements below by circling the correct words.

a) A **weak / strong** material is good at resisting a force.

b) You can tell how strong a material is by gradually applying a force to a sample of the material until it breaks or is **temporarily / permanently** deformed.

c) High tensile strength is when a material can resist **pulling / pushing** forces.

d) Poor compressive strength means low resistance to **pulling / pushing** forces.

e) Climbing ropes need a **low / high** tensile strength, whereas a brick low down in a wall needs a high **tensile / compressive** strength to resist the **weight / mass** of the bricks above it.

Q2 Complete the table by stating if each substance is a **liquid** or a **solid** at room temperature (20 °C).

Substance	Water	Sulfur	Propanone	Sodium chloride
Melting point (°C)	0	115	-95	801
Boiling point (°C)	100	444	56	1413
State at room temperature				

Q3 Answer the following questions about the properties of materials.

a) Explain why it is possible for a bendy material to be strong.

....

b) Steel rods are put inside concrete posts to make them stronger.
Name the most important type of strength that concrete posts need to have.

....

c) Why are diamond tips used on industrial drills?

....

Q4 Use the following densities to answer the questions below.

Gold	19.3 g/cm^3	Iron	7.9 g/cm^3	Concrete	2.6 g/cm^3
Cork	0.25 g/cm^3	Pine	0.5 g/cm^3	Mahogany	0.8 g/cm^3

a) What is the difference between density and mass?

....

b) Which materials from the list will sink when placed in water? (Water density = 1.0 g/cm^3)

....

c) What will happen if a large piece of mahogany is put in a bath of water?

....

Materials, Properties and Uses

Q1 For each of the following questions, choose the most likely letter from the list below.

A diving suit B milk carton C window pane D washing line

a) To which use would you put a low density opaque plastic that is hard and strong? ....

b) To which use would you put nylon fibres that are flexible with high tensile strength? ....

c) To which use would you put neoprene (waterproof, strong, but soft and flexible)? ....

d) To which use would you put polycarbonate (strong, hard and transparent)? ....

Q2 Draw lines to match the following sentences with their correct endings.

Gold is suitable for jewellery because...

Slate is suitable for roofing because...

Stainless steel is suitable for knives and forks because...

Rubber is suitable for car tyres because...

...it is durable.

...it is shiny.

...it is strong but flexible.

...it is non-toxic.

Q3 The properties of different materials make them suitable for different applications.

a) Explain why a tennis racket is made with a **metal frame** and **nylon strings**.

....

....

b) Explain why a saucepan is made with a **metal body** and **wooden handle**.

....

....

Q4 A mystery material has just been discovered. It has a **high melting point**, **high tensile strength** and **low density**, and is also **flexible**, **soft**, **non-toxic** and **flame resistant**.

a) Put a ring around the product that this material would be most suitable for.

knives and forks guttering children's nightwear synthetic candle wax

b) Explain how one of the properties of the 'mystery' substance makes it suitable for your choice.

....

c) For one of the other products give two reasons why the mystery material would **not** be suitable.

1. ....

2. ....

Properties of Metals

Q1 This table shows some of the **properties** of four different **metals**.

Metal	Heat conduction	Cost	Resistance to corrosion	Strength
1	average	high	excellent	good
2	average	medium	good	excellent
3	excellent	low	good	good
4	low	high	average	poor

Use the information in the table to choose which metal would be **best** for making each of the following:

a) Saucepan bases ....

b) Car bodies ....

c) A statue to be placed in a town centre ....

Think about how long a statue would have to last for.

Q2 Use some of the words below to **complete** this passage about corrosion. Some words may be used more than once.

oxygen nitrogen rust carbon dioxide
air metal fatigue aluminium oxide water

Metals corrode when exposed to .... and ....

When iron corrodes, it first gains .... to form iron(III) oxide.

Then .... becomes loosely bonded to the iron(III) oxide to form hydrated iron(III) oxide. Most people call this ....

Q3 The properties of **aluminium** and **copper** make them suitable for different uses.

a) What **properties** does copper have that make it suitable for use in **plumbing**?

....

....

b) Why would an **alloy** of aluminium be more suitable for making **aeroplanes** than pure aluminium?

....

....

Making Metals More Useful

Q1 Most iron is made into the alloy **steel**.

a) Write a definition of the term '**alloy**'.

....

....

b) How is **iron** turned into **steel**?

....

....

Tonight Matthew, I'm going to be... steel.

Q2 Draw lines to connect the correct phrases in each column. One has been done for you.

Metal / Alloy	What has been added	Use
low-carbon steel	nothing	blades for tools
iron from a blast furnace	chromium	cutlery
high-carbon steel	0.1% carbon	car bodies
stainless steel	1.5% carbon	ornamental railings

Q3 Complete the following sentences using some of the metals below.

gold copper platinum titanium nickel iron zinc

a) Nitinol is an alloy that contains .... and ....

b) To make gold hard enough for jewellery it is mixed with metals such as

.... , ... and ....

Getting Metals from Rocks

Q1 This table shows some common **metal ores** and their formulas.

Ore	Formula
Haematite	Fe_2O_3
Magnetite	Fe_3O_4
Pyrites	FeS_2
Galena	PbS
Bauxite	Al_2O_3

a) What is a metal ore?

....

b) Name the two elements that are commonly bonded to metals in ores.

....

Q2 **Gold** is often extracted from ores that contain very **small** percentages of the metal, but iron is only extracted from ores with a **large** percentage of the metal. Explain why.

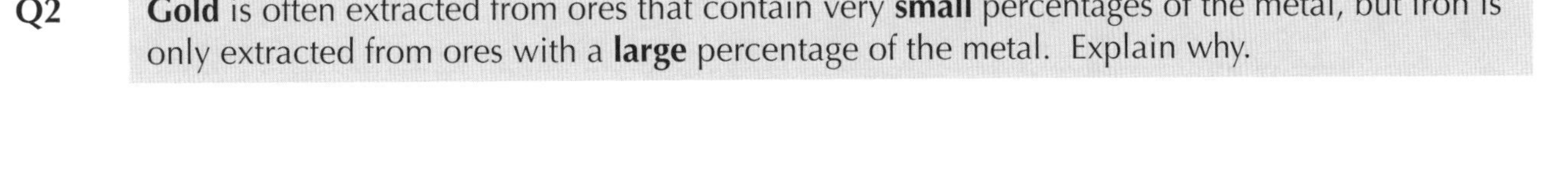

....

....

Q3 The graph shows the average **cost** of extracting aluminium over a ten year period.

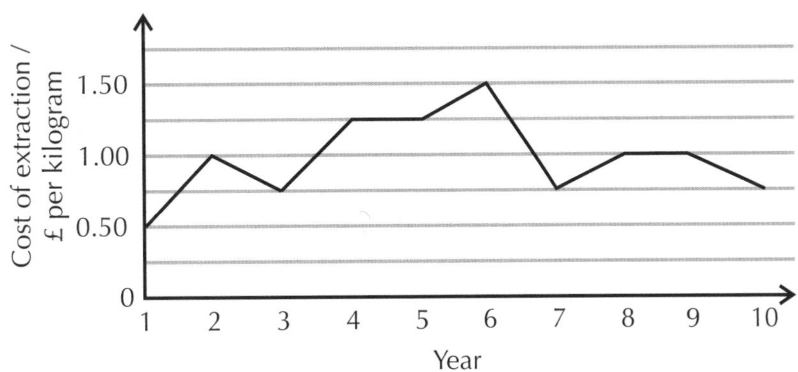

a) In which year was the cost of extracting aluminium **lowest**?

....

b) The cost of mineral extraction per kilogram is 75% of its market value.
In which year was aluminium's market value £2.00 per kilogram?

....

Getting Metals from Rocks

Q4 Explain how improvements in **technology** might affect the economics of metal extraction in future.

....

....

....

Q5 **Copper** is used to make electrical wires.

a) Copper can be extracted from its ore by reduction with carbon. Suggest why copper produced in this way can't be used for electrical wires.

....

b) **i)** How is copper that is suitable for making electrical wires produced?

....

ii) Explain one disadvantage of this method.

....

....

Q6 Use the words below to fill in the blanks to complete the paragraph. Some words may be used more than once.

electrons **electrode** **heat** **liquid** **protons**

positive **negative** **electricity** **copper**

Electrolysis is breaking down a substance using ....

It requires a .... to conduct the

.... During electrolysis, ...

ions move towards the negative ....

Q7 Explain why a substance needs to be either in a **solution** or **molten** for electrolysis to work.

....

....

....

Getting Metals from Rocks

Q8 Why would it **not** be a good idea to carry out the electrolysis of **copper** in an electrolyte that contained **zinc** ions instead of copper ions? Tick the correct box.

- The zinc ions will not conduct an electrical current. ☐
- The copper produced will have zinc impurities in it. ☐
- A poisonous gas would be produced. ☐
- The zinc and copper ions will react with each other. ☐
- The zinc ions will coat the anode. ☐

Q9 The diagram below shows the extraction of **copper** by electrolysis.

a) Identify the labels A to C on the diagram.

Choose from the options in the box.

copper ions	copper atoms	copper sulfate solution
electrodes	batteries	

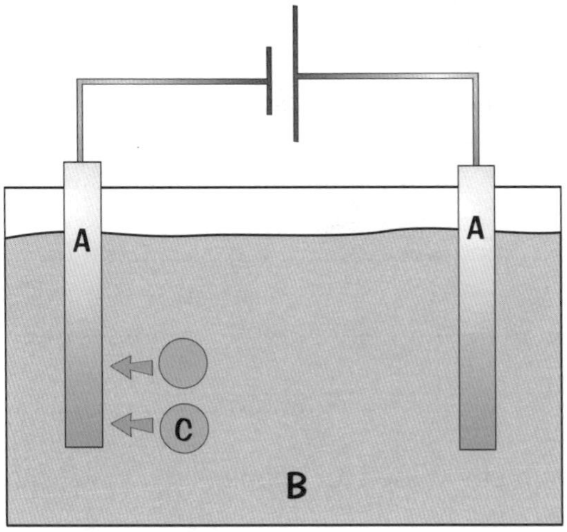

A ....

B ....

C ....

b) When copper is purified by electrolysis, **impure sludge** simply falls to the bottom. It does **not** move to the cathode. Explain why this happens.

....

....

Top Tips: Electrolysis — just remember, electrons are taken away by the positive electrode (the anode) and they're given away by the negative electrode (the cathode). A bit like the arrangement between me and my brother — he takes things away from me, and I give things away to him.

Getting Metals from Rocks

Q10 If scrap iron is heated with copper sulfate this reaction happens:

iron + copper sulfate → copper + iron sulfate

a) Why does this reaction take place? ....

b) Would it be possible to produce iron sulfate by reacting iron with aluminium sulfate? ....

Explain your answer. ....

....

Q11 Copper objects such as old pipes can be **recycled**.
Give **two** reasons why it is important to recycle copper.

1. ....

2. ....

Q12 Scientists are researching **alternative** methods of extracting copper.
Bioleaching is one alternative method which can be used.

a) **Explain** how bioleaching can be used to extract **copper** from copper sulfide.

....

....

....

....

b) Give **another** example of an alternative extraction method used for copper.

....

c) Explain why these alternative extraction methods are so important.

....

....

....

....

Impacts of Extracting Metals

Q1 New mines always have **social**, **economic** and **environmental** consequences. Complete this table to show the effects that a new mine can have.

Social	Economic	Environmental
Services, e.g. health care may be improved because of influx of people.		Pollution from traffic.

Remember to include both positive and negative effects.

Q2 Wherever possible, every scrap of gold is **recycled**. We also recycle **aluminium** as much as possible, even though it is the most common metal in the Earth's crust. Explain the reasons why we **recycle** these two metals.

....

....

....

....

Top Tips: Remember that metals are finite resources — there's a set amount on Earth and once we've extracted them all there won't be any more. We need to be able to get metals out of low-grade ores (ones that only contain small amounts of metal) to get enough to go round.

Nanotechnology

Q1 Nanotechnology is the branch of technology dealing with the making and use of **nanoparticles**.

a) What **size** of particle is considered a nanoparticle? Circle the correct answer.

1 – 100 nanometres   1 nanometre   100 – 1000 nanometres

b) Give an example of a naturally occurring nanoparticle.

....

c) Some nanoparticles have been designed for use in tennis rackets.
Suggest **two** properties of these nanoparticles that could make them suitable for this purpose.

....

....

Q2 Nanoparticles are added to fabrics used for surgical masks.

a) Name the type of nanoparticle used in surgical masks. ....

b) Explain why this type of nanoparticle is used.

....

Q3 Circle the letter of the statement(s) about nanotechnology that are **true**.

A Nanoparticles have the same properties as larger particles of the same material.

B Nanoparticles have a large surface area to volume ratio. This can affect the properties of the material.

C Nanoparticles show different properties to larger particles of the same material.

D Nanoparticles have a very small surface area to volume ratio because of their small size.

Q4 Explain why some people are concerned about the effects of nanoparticles on **human health**.

....

....

....

....

Mixed Questions — Section 4

Q1 Complete the diagram to show the electron structure of **calcium**.

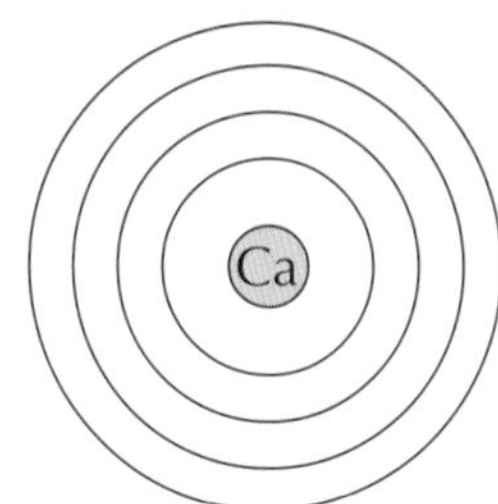

Q2 Metals make up about 80% of all the elements in the periodic table.

a) Shade the area where **metals** are found on this periodic table:

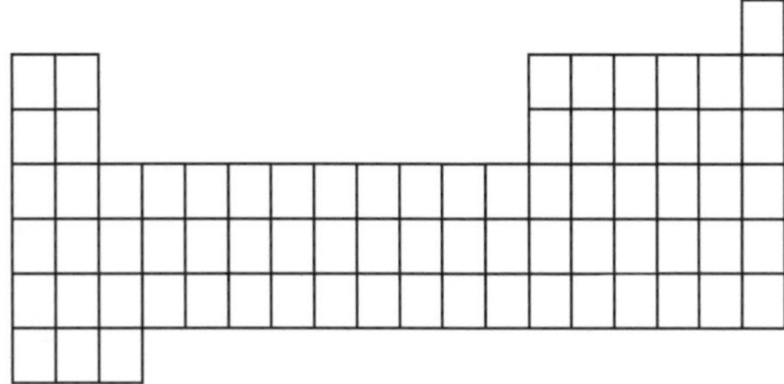

b) Read each of the following statements about metals. If the statement is **true**, tick the box.

- [ ] Metals are generally strong but also malleable.
- [ ] All metals are corrosion-resistant.
- [ ] Metals conduct electricity well.
- [ ] Generally, metals are poor conductors of heat.
- [ ] Properties of a metal can be altered by mixing it with another metal to form an alloy.

c) Look at the information in the table below. R, S, T and U are all metals.

Material	Strength	Cost (£)	Density (g/cm^3)	Melting Point (°C)
R	High	100	3	1000
S	Medium	90	5	150
T	High	450	8	1200
U	Low	200	11	1070

Explain in detail which material would be most suitable to build an **aeroplane body**.

....

....

....

....

Mixed Questions — Section 4

Q3 The metals **aluminium**, **copper** and **iron** can be extracted from their ores.

a) Metal ores are often described as 'finite resources'. Explain the term '**finite resource**'.

....

b) The table shows the **reactivity** series of metals and **dates of discovery**.

i) What pattern can be seen in the data?

....

....

ii) Suggest an explanation for this.

....

....

....

....

metal	discovery
potassium	AD 1807
sodium	AD 1807
calcium	AD 1808
magnesium	AD 1755
aluminium	AD 1825
carbon	
zinc	about AD 1400
iron	about 2500 BC
tin	about 2000 BC
lead	about 3500 BC
hydrogen	
copper	about 4200 BC
silver	about 4000 BC
gold	about 6000 BC
platinum	before 1500 BC

most reactive ↑ ↓ least reactive

c) **i)** Complete the word equation for the reduction of iron ore with carbon.

iron(III) oxide + ... → **iron** + ...

ii) Write a **balanced symbol equation** for this reaction. (The formula of iron(III) oxide is Fe_2O_3.)

....

d) Copper metal can be extracted from its ore by **reduction** using carbon then purified by electrolysis.

i) Explain why electrolysis is used to produce copper metal for **electrical wiring**.

....

ii) Give **two** physical properties of copper that make it suitable for use in **electrical wiring**.

1. ....

2. ....

e) One of the most common elements present in the Earth's crust is aluminium.
Explain why aluminium metal can only be extracted using **electrolysis**.

....

....

....

The Earth's Structure

Q1 Look at the diagram showing the boundary between the African and Arabian plates.

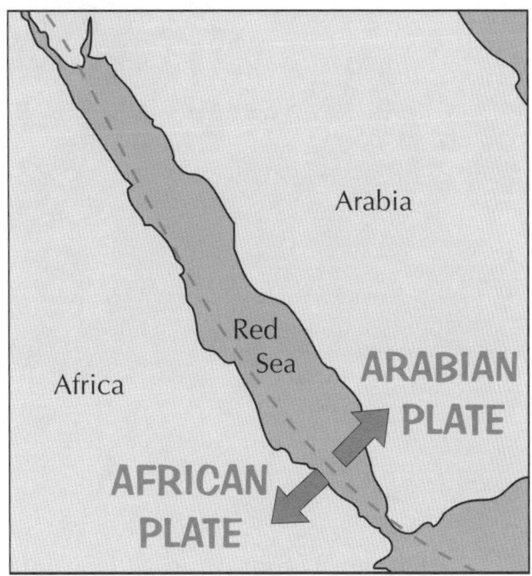

The Red Sea is widening at a speed of 1.6 cm per year.

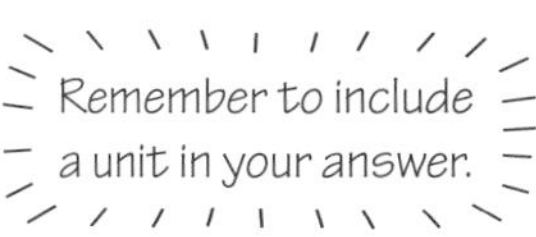

a) If the sea level remains the same, how much will the Red Sea widen in 10 000 years?

....

b) The Red Sea is currently exactly 325 km wide at a certain point. If the sea level remains the same, how wide will the Red Sea be at this point in 20 000 years' time?

....

....

Don't forget to make sure your distances are in the same unit.

Q2 The map below on the left shows where most of the world's earthquakes take place.

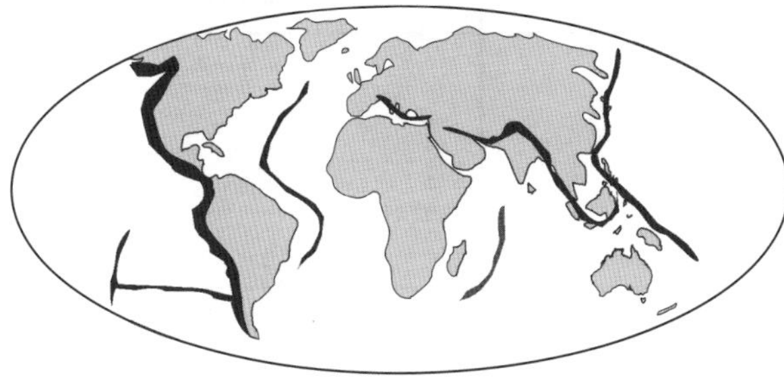

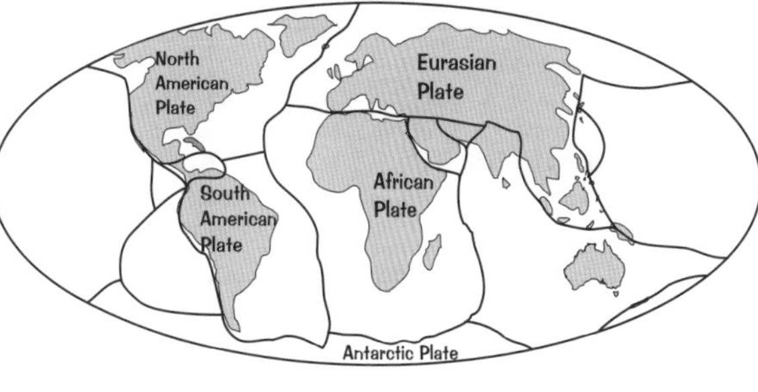

= main earthquake zones

Compare this map to one showing the tectonic plates.
What do you notice about the main earthquake zones?

....

....

The Earth's Structure

Q3 Draw a simple diagram of the Earth's structure.
Label the crust, mantle and core and write a brief description of each.

Q4 Match up the description to the key phrase or word.

Crust	Hot spots that often sit on plate boundaries
Mantle	Caused by sudden movements of plates
Convection current	Caused by heat from radioactive decay in the mantle
Tectonic plates	Thinnest of the Earth's layers
Earthquakes	Large pieces of crust and upper mantle
Volcanoes	Slowly flowing semi-solid layer that plates float on

Q5 How do scientists predict volcanic eruptions and earthquakes?
Complete the table to show what **evidence** can be collected, and comment on its **reliability**.

	Evidence	How reliable is it?
Earthquake		
Volcanic eruption		

Top Tips: That's the problem with "evidence" predicting earthquakes and volcanic eruptions — it's nowhere near 100% reliable. There are likely to be shed-loads of people living near a volcano or on a fault line — it'd be impossible to evacuate them all every time scientists thought there might possibly be an eruption or an earthquake some time soon — it just wouldn't work.

Plate Tectonics

Q1 Wegener studied astronomy at Berlin University in 1904. His fascination with observing identical fossils on both sides of the Atlantic led him to produce his theory of **continental drift** in 1914.

Tick the boxes to say whether the following statements are **true** or **false**.

		True	False
a)	Wegener found that each continent had its own unrelated collection of plant and animal fossils.	☐	☐
b)	The Earth's continents seem to fit together like a big jigsaw.	☐	☐
c)	Rock formations are made of layers, which are different on every continent.	☐	☐
d)	The discovery that the sea floor is spreading suggested that the continents are moving apart. This supports Wegener's theory.	☐	☐
e)	Wegener's theory is now widely accepted because it has been discussed and tested by a range of scientists.	☐	☐
f)	Wegener's theory was **not** readily accepted by scientists at the time.	☐	☐

Q2 Use the words below to complete the passage about Wegener's theory of continental drift.

thousand countries tectonics million Alfred continents movement Pangaea

Wegener suggested that 300 .... years ago there was one supercontinent, called .... This supercontinent broke up into smaller chunks — our modern day .... These chunks are still moving apart. He called his idea the theory of continental drift. It is the basis of the modern theory of plate ....

Q3 Wegener's theory is now accepted by scientists because it explains lots of different pieces of **evidence**. Briefly describe three pieces of evidence that support Wegener's theory.

1. ....

....

....

2. ....

....

3. ....

....

The Three Different Types of Rock

Q1 There are three **main types** of rock.

a) Join up each **rock type** with the correct **method of formation**.

ROCK TYPE	METHOD OF FORMATION
igneous rocks	formed from layers of sediment
sedimentary rocks	formed when magma cools
metamorphic rocks	formed under intense heat and pressure

b) Give an example of:

i) an igneous rock ....

ii) a sedimentary rock ....

iii) a metamorphic rock ....

Q2 Erica finds out that the stonework of her local church is made up of **sedimentary rock**.

a) Describe how sedimentary rock is 'cemented' together.

....

....

b) Which is harder? Granite or marble?

....

c) Powdered limestone and powdered marble react with other chemicals, such as hydrochloric acid, in an identical fashion. Explain this.

....

....

d) Describe the differences between limestone and marble.

....

....

Top Tips: You might think that rocks are just boring lumps of.... rock. But you'd be wrong — rocks are actually boring lumps of different kinds of rock. And the kind of rock they are depends on how they're formed — and this is the stuff you need to make sure you know.

Using Limestone

Q1 State the **chemical name** for limestone.

....

Q2 **Carbonates** decompose to form two products.

a) Name the two products formed when limestone is heated.

1. ....

2. ....

b) What solid would you expect to be formed when magnesium carbonate is heated?

....

c) Write a symbol equation for the reaction that occurs when copper carbonate ($CuCO_3$) is heated.

....

d) Sodium is in Group 1 of the periodic table.
Why does sodium carbonate not decompose when heated using a Bunsen burner?

....

Q3 Use the words below to fill the gaps in the passage.

mortar	sodium carbonate	wood	concrete	clay	limestone

Heating powdered .... with clay in a kiln makes cement.
Cement can be mixed with sand and water to make ...., which is used to stick bricks together. When cement is mixed with water, gravel and sand it makes ...., which is a very common building material.

Q4 The hills of Northern England are dotted with the remains of **lime kilns** where **limestone** ($CaCO_3$) was heated by farmers to make CaO.

a) Write a word equation for the reaction that takes place in a lime kiln.

....

b) CaO reacts violently with water to make calcium hydroxide ($Ca(OH)_2$).

What do farmers use calcium hydroxide for?

....

Using Limestone

Q5 Many of the products used to build houses are made with limestone.
Circle the materials that have **no** connection to limestone.

paint

bricks

concrete

granite

cement

Q6 In Norway **powdered limestone** is added to lakes that have been damaged by acid rain.

a) Name the process that takes place when the powdered limestone reacts with the acid in the lake.

....

b) Suggest why powdered limestone is also used in the chimneys at power stations.

....

....

....

Q7 Limestone is a useful rock but **quarrying** it causes some **problems**.

a) Describe two problems that quarrying limestone can cause.

1. ....

2. ....

b) Explain how limestone quarries may benefit the local community.

....

....

Q8 What are the **advantages** of using **concrete** instead of these traditional building materials?

a) Wood: ....

b) Metals: ....

c) Bricks: ....

Salt

Q1 Indicate whether the following statements about obtaining salt are **true** or **false**.

		True	False
a)	In the UK most salt is obtained by evaporation in flat open tanks.	☐	☐
b)	There are massive deposits of rock salt in Cheshire.	☐	☐
c)	Salt can be mined by pumping hot water underground.	☐	☐
d)	Some holes left by mining salt must be filled in, or they could cause subsidence.	☐	☐

Q2 **Circle** the correct answer for the question below.

Two of the products of the electrolysis of brine are reacted together to make household bleach. They are:

Chlorine and hydrogen.

Chlorine and sodium hydroxide.

Hydrogen and sodium hydroxide.

Q3 The diagram shows the **industrial set-up** used to electrolyse concentrated brine.

a) Identify the substances labelled A, B, C and D on the diagram. Choose from the options in the box below.

Na	O_2	Cl_2	H_2
brine	NaOH	H_2O	

A .... B ....

C .... D ....

A

C

B

−

+

Brine + D

b) Write **balanced** half-equations for the reactions that occur during the electrolysis of this salt solution.

Anode: ....

Cathode: ....

Make sure the charges balance.

c) i) State the electrode where oxidation takes place. ....

ii) State the electrode where reduction takes place. ....

d) Why are inert electrodes used?

....

Chlorination

Q1 Complete the passage below using the following words. You may need to use each word more than once.

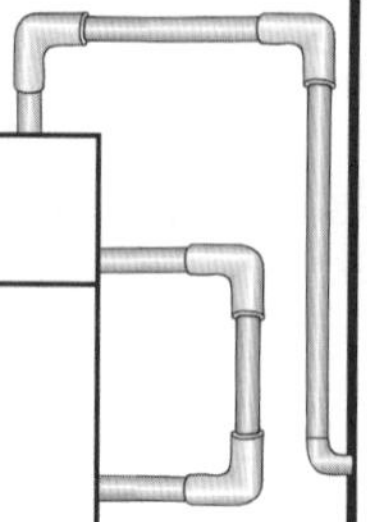

chlorine **water supply** **kills** **microorganisms** **chlorination**

In the UK .... is used to treat the ....

This process is called .... Treating drinking water with

.... has benefited public health because it ....

disease-causing .... that spread through the ....

Q2 Chlorine can be produced by **electrolysing** brine.

a) Suggest **one** other way of producing chlorine.

....

b) Explain why adding sodium chloride to water does not kill microorganisms.

....

....

Q3 The graph below shows how the number of typhoid cases in Unwelland has changed over the last 100 years.

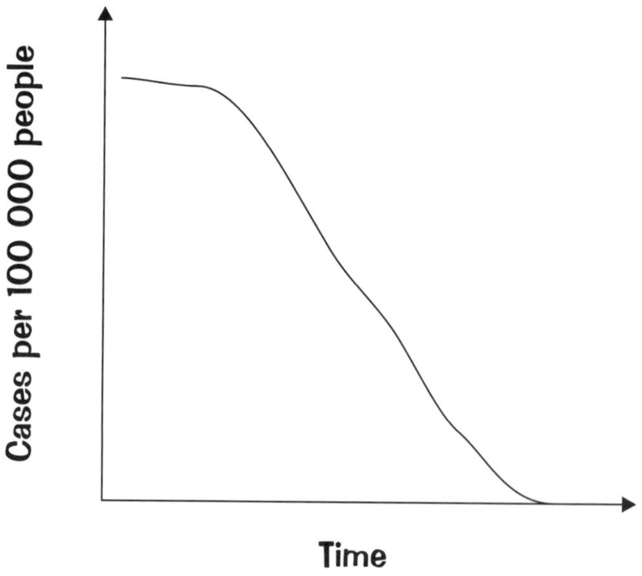

a) Draw a line on the graph to show when you think chlorination of drinking water was introduced in Unwelland.

b) Explain you answer to part **a)**.

....

....

....

....

Cases per 100 000 people

Time

c) Give **one** possible health problem caused by using chlorine to treat water.

....

....

Impacts of Chemical Production

Q1 PVC is a material that is used in a wide variety of products, e.g. window frames and electrical wiring.

a) What type of material is PVC? Tick the correct answer.

☐ monomer ☐ plasticiser ☐ polymer

b) Circle the **three** elements that PVC is made of from the list below.

carbon phosphorus hydrogen chlorine vanadium oxygen

c) Plasticisers are often added to improve the properties of PVC.

Describe **one problem** caused by using plasticisers.

....

....

Q2 Pollutants from the chemical industry can find their way into food chains like the one shown below.

Algae → Water louse → Dragonfly nymph → Water shrew → Kestrel

a) If the stream is polluted by a chemical, which of the organisms in the food chain is most likely to suffer?

....

b) Explain your answer to part **a)**.

....

....

....

....

Q3 Mark is investigating the safety of the plastics and components used to make computer monitors. His friend Emma tells him that there's **no risk** to the environment or human health from any of the components in the monitors.

Do you think Emma is correct? Explain your answer.

....

....

....

Hazard Symbols, Acids and Bases

Q1 Draw lines to match the **symbols** below with their **meanings** and **hazards**.

a)		toxic	can cause death if swallowed, inhaled or absorbed through the skin
b)		corrosive	causes reddening or blistering of the skin
c)		highly flammable	provides oxygen which allows other materials to burn more fiercely
d)		irritant	attacks and destroys living tissue
e)		harmful	like toxic, but not quite as dangerous
f)		oxidising	catches fire easily

Q2 Universal indicator is used to **estimate pH**.

a) Draw lines to match the **universal indicator colour** to its **pH** value and **acid/alkali strength**.

	UNIVERSAL INDICATOR COLOUR	pH	ACID/ALKALI STRENGTH
i)	purple	5/6	strong alkali
ii)	yellow	8/9	weak alkali
iii)	dark green/blue	14	weak acid
iv)	red	7	neutral
v)	green	1	strong acid

b) Suggest why universal indicator only gives an **estimate** of pH.

....

Reactions of Acids

Q1 Fill in the blanks to complete the word equations for **acids** reacting with **metal oxides**, **metal hydroxides** and **metal carbonates**.

a) hydrochloric acid + lead oxide → lead chloride chloride + water

b) nitric acid + copper hydroxide → copper nitrate + water

c) sulfuric acid + zinc oxide → zinc sulfate + water

d) hydrochloric acid + nickel oxide → nickel chloride + water

e) nitric acid + copper carbonate → copper nitrate + water + ...

f) phosphoric acid + sodium hydroxide → sodium phoride + water

Q2 a) Put a tick in the box next to any of the sentences below that are **true**.

i) Alkalis are bases which can't dissolve in water. ☐

ii) Acids react with metal oxides to form a salt and water. ☐

iii) Hydrogen gas is formed when an acid reacts with an alkali. ☐

iv) Salts and water are formed when acids react with metal hydroxides. ☐

v) Sodium hydroxide is an acid that dissolves in water. ☐

b) Use the formulas below to write **symbol equations** for two acid / base reactions.

H_2O HCl $NaCl$ $NaOH$ H_2O H_2SO_4 $CuSO_4$ CuO

1. ....

2. ....

Q3 **Ammonia** can be neutralised by **nitric acid** to form **ammonium nitrate**.

a) Circle the correct formula for ammonia below.

NH_4NO_3 NH_4Cl NH_3 NH_2 NH_4

b) Write down the symbol equation for the reaction between ammonia and nitric acid.

....

c) How is this neutralisation reaction different from most neutralisation reactions?

....

The Evolution of the Atmosphere

Q1 Tick the boxes next to the sentences below that are **true**.

When the Earth was formed, its surface was molten. ☐

The Earth's early atmosphere is thought to have been mostly oxygen. ☐

When oxygen started building up in the atmosphere, all organisms began to thrive. ☐

The early atmosphere was mostly made up of gases that had escaped from inside the Earth during volcanic eruptions. ☐

Q2 The amount of **carbon dioxide** in the atmosphere has changed over the last 4.5 billion or so years.

Describe how the level of carbon dioxide has changed and explain why this change happened.

....

....

....

....

Q3 Draw lines to put the statements in the **right order** on the timeline. One has been done for you.

Present

NOT TO SCALE

4500 million years ago

- The Earth cooled down slightly. A thin crust formed.
- Water vapour condensed to form oceans.
- The Earth formed. There was lots of volcanic activity.
- More complex organisms evolved.
- Plant life appeared.
- The atmosphere is about four-fifths nitrogen and one-fifth oxygen.
- Oxygen builds up in the air as plants photosynthesise.

Don't get confused — 4500 million is the same as 4.5 billion.

The Evolution of the Atmosphere

Q4 The pie chart below shows the proportions of different gases in the Earth's atmosphere today.

a) Add the labels '**Nitrogen**', '**Oxygen**', and '**Carbon dioxide and other gases**'.

Earth's Atmosphere Today

b) Give the approximate percentages of the following gases in the air today:

Nitrogen ....

Oxygen ....

Carbon dioxide ....

Earth's Atmosphere 4500 Million Years Ago

Carbon dioxide

Ammonia

Other gases

Water vapour

c) This pie chart shows the proportions of different gases that we think were in the Earth's atmosphere 4500 million years ago.

Describe the main differences between today's atmosphere and the atmosphere 4500 million years ago.

....

....

d) Explain why the amount of water vapour has decreased.

What did the water vapour change into?

....

....

e) Explain how oxygen was introduced into the atmosphere.

....

f) Give two effects of the oxygen levels in the atmosphere rising.

1. ....

....

2. ....

....

g) Explain why the percentage of nitrogen gas in the air has increased so much.

....

....

....

Life and the Atmosphere Today

Q1 Air is a source of **resources** that can be used in industry.

a) Put numbers in the boxes to show the order of the stages in the fractional distillation of air.

☐ Air is filtered to remove dust.

☐ Air is cooled to -200 °C.

☐ Liquefied air enters the fractionating column and is heated slowly.

☐ Carbon dioxide freezes and is removed. Water vapour condenses and is removed.

b) Fill in the gaps with the words below to explain why air can be separated by fractional distillation.

compound	boiling points	vapour	mixture	weights	fractions

Air is a .... of gases with different ....

c) Give two gases used in industry that the fractional distillation of air produces.

....

Q2 There are many theories of how life on Earth was formed.

a) Briefly describe the '**primordial soup**' theory.

....

....

....

....

b) Describe the experiment that was carried out by Miller and Urey to try and prove this theory.

....

....

c) Describe what happened in the experiment. What does this suggests about the theory?

....

....

Mixed Questions — Section 5

Q1 **Calcium carbonate** ($CaCO_3$), in the form of the rock **limestone**, is one of the most important raw materials for the chemical and construction industries.

a) Limestone can be processed to produce calcium hydroxide.

i) Complete the flow diagram to show how limestone can be processed.

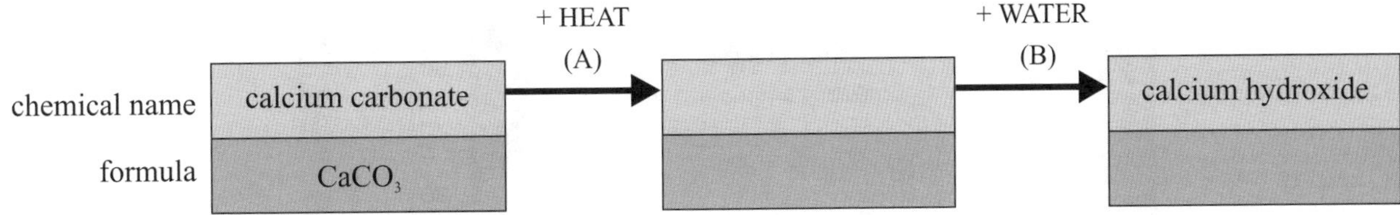

ii) Write a balanced symbol equation for reaction A.

.... → .... + ...

b) Limestone can be processed to form useful building materials. Complete the flow diagram.

c) Give two reasons why limestone is more likely to be used as a building material than wood.

1. ....

2. ....

d) Limestone is also used in the manufacture of mortar.
Name the other main ingredients of mortar.

....

e) Complete the following word equation for **hydrochloric acid** reacting with **calcium carbonate**.

Calcium carbonate + hydrochloric acid →

.... + ... + ...

Q2 People used to think that the Earth's surface was all one piece. Today, we think it's made up of **separate plates** of rock.

a) What is thought to cause the **movement** of the plates?

....

b) Name **two** kinds of natural disasters that can occur at the boundaries between plates.

.... and ....

Mixed Questions — Section 5

Q3 The graphs below give information about the Earth's atmosphere millions of years ago and today.

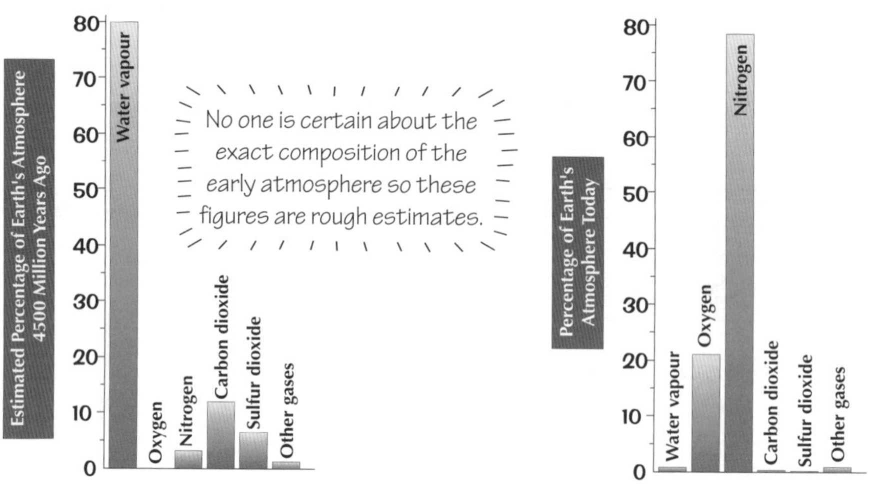

a) Could the early atmosphere **support life** as we know it? Explain your answer.

....

....

b) i) Which **organisms** caused an increase in oxygen and a decrease in carbon dioxide?

....

ii) What else caused a decrease in carbon dioxide?

....

c) Tick the correct boxes to indicate whether each statement is **true** or **false**.

	True	False
i) 78% of the atmosphere is nitrogen.	☐	☐
ii) Very early in Earth's history volcanoes gave out gases.	☐	☐
iii) Scientists are good at predicting volcanoes and earthquakes.	☐	☐

Q4 Increasing carbon dioxide level is causing global warming. Describe and explain the effect that the increasing level of carbon dioxide is having on the **oceans**.

....

....

....

Fractional Distillation of Crude Oil

Q1 Circle the correct words to complete these sentences.

a) Crude oil is a **mixture / compound** of different molecules.

b) Most of the compounds in crude oil are **carbohydrate / hydrocarbon** molecules.

c) The molecules in crude oil **are / aren't** chemically bonded to each other.

d) Physical methods **can / can't** be used to separate out the molecules in crude oil.

Q2 The molecules listed below are in the order of **smallest** to **largest** from left to right. Label this diagram of a **fractionating column** to show where these substances can be collected.

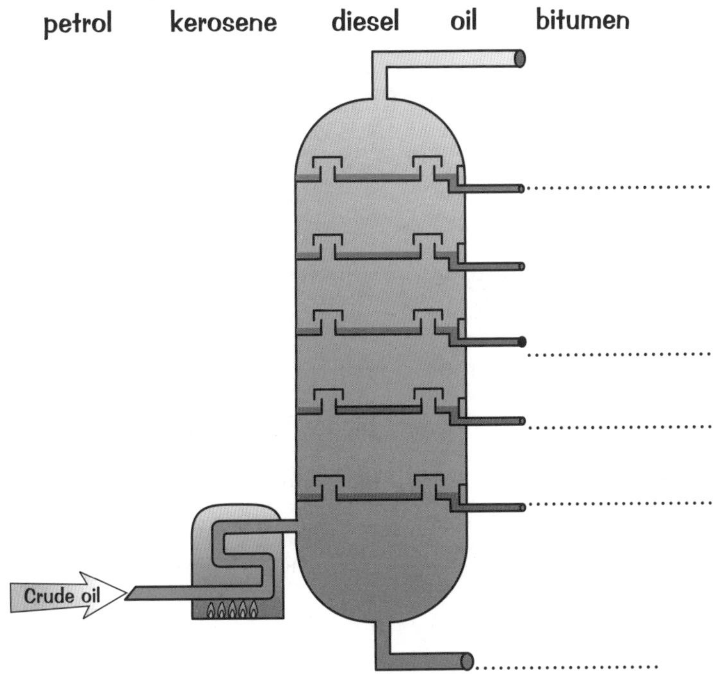

Q3 What is the connection between the **size** of the **molecules** in crude oil and their **condensing** (or **boiling**) points?

....

....

Q4 Explain why distillation is a good way to **separate** the liquids in crude oil.

....

....

....

Properties and Uses of Crude Oil

Q1 **Crude oil** is a mixture of **hydrocarbons**. These **hydrocarbons** are mostly **alkanes**.

a) Draw the structures of the first three alkanes and name each alkane you have drawn.

1. 2. 3.

....

b) Which of these alkanes would you expect to have the highest boiling point?

....

Q2 There are some basic **trends** in the way that **alkanes** behave.
Circle the correct words to complete these sentences.

a) The longer the alkane molecule the **more / less** viscous (gloopy) it is.

b) The shorter the alkane molecule the **lower / higher** its boiling point.

c) The shorter the alkane molecule the **more / less** flammable it is.

Q3 a) What is the **general** formula for **alkanes**?

If you can't remember it you can work it out by looking at the diagrams you have drawn at the top of the page.

....

b) **Eicosane** is a hydrocarbon that can be used to make candles. Each molecule of eicosane contains **20 carbon** atoms. What is the **chemical formula** for eicosane?

....

Q4 Each hydrocarbon molecule in engine oil has a **long** string of carbon atoms.

a) Explain why this type of oil is good for using as a **lubricant** in an engine.

....

....

b) Engines get very **hot** when they are in use. Why would oil molecules with short carbon chains be unsuitable for use as lubricants?

....

....

Cracking Crude Oil

Q1 Fill in the gaps with the words below.

high	shorter	long	catalyst	cracking	diesel	molecules	petrol

There is more need for .... chain fractions of crude oil such as .... than for longer chains such as ....

Heating .... hydrocarbon molecules to .... temperatures with a .... breaks them down into smaller .... This is called ....

Q2 Diesel is **cracked** to produce products that are more in demand.

a) Suggest three useful substances that are produced when diesel is cracked.

....

b) What type of reaction is cracking?

....

Q3 After cracking both **alkenes** and **alkanes** are present.

a) Bromine water is used to test whether a substance is an alkane or alkene. Alkenes decolourise bromine water, but alkanes don't.

Which of the following would decolourise bromine water?

☐ propane ☐ ethene ☐ ethane

b) Put the steps of the cracking process in the correct order by writing numbers in the boxes.

☐ The vapour is passed over a catalyst at a high temperature.
☐ The long-chain molecules are heated.
☐ The molecules are cracked on the surface of the catalyst.
☐ They are vaporised (turned into a gas).

Q4 Change this diagram into a **word equation** and a **symbol equation**.

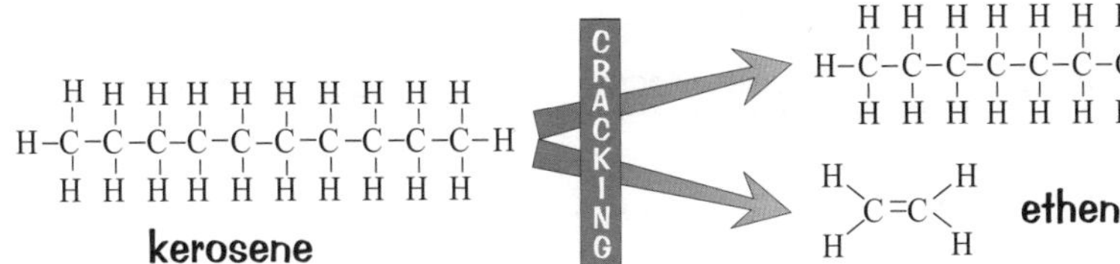

a) Word equation: .... → .... + ...

b) Symbol equation: .... → .... + ...

Alkenes and Ethanol

Q1 Complete this table showing the molecular and displayed formulas of some alkenes.

Alkene	Formula	Displayed formula
Ethene	**a)** C_2H_4	**b)** H H | | C=C | | H H
c) Propene	C_3H_6	**d)** H H H | | | C=C–C | | | H H H

The displayed formula just shows how all the atoms are arranged.

Q2 The general formula for alkenes is $\mathbf{C_nH_{2n}}$. Use it to write down the formulas of these alkenes.

a) pentene (5 carbons) C_5H_{10}

b) hexene (6 carbons) C_6H_{12}

c) octene (8 carbons) C_8H_{16}

d) dodecene (12 carbons) $C_{12}H_{24}$

Q3 True or false?

		True	False
a)	Alkenes have double bonds between the hydrogen atoms.	☐	☑
b)	Alkenes are unsaturated.	☑	☐
c)	Alkenes are not very useful.	☑	☐
d)	Ethene has two carbon atoms.	☑	☐

Q4 Fill in the gaps with the words below. You might need to use some words more than once.

orange	bromine water	colourless	decolourise

You can test for alkenes by adding them to bromine water.

An alkene will decolourise the bromine water, turning it from orange to colourless.

Alkenes and Ethanol

Q5 There are two ways of making ethanol:

Method A	Sugar → ethanol + carbon dioxide
Method B	Ethene + steam → ethanol

a) Which of the methods describes making ethanol by **fermentation**? ....

b) Draw lines to match up the boxes.

Method A	Uses a catalyst
Method B	Uses yeast

c) Ethanol can be used as a fuel. In some countries the fermentation method is often used to produce it. Give two reasons why this method is chosen.

1. ....

2. ....

d) Give a disadvantage of the fermentation method.

....

....

Q6 Explain why producing ethanol from ethene could become **problematic** in the future.

....

....

....

....

Top Tips: It's a cracking idea getting alkenes from crude oil because they're pretty useful for making things, like ethanol. You probably wouldn't want to drink the ethanol you get from reacting ethene with steam though. On the other hand, the ethanol you get from fermenting sugar is pretty multipurpose — it's good for anything from your old man's pint to fuelling his car.

Burning Fuels

Q1 Answer the following questions about **burning hydrocarbons**.

a) Write a **word equation** for the complete combustion of a hydrocarbon.

hydrocarbon + oxygen ⟶ carbon dioxide + water

b) Circle the correct words from each pair in the sentences below.

When a hydrocarbon is burnt, the carbon and hydrogen are **oxidised / reduced**.

The reaction **gives out / takes in** energy

Q2 When choosing fuels there are a number of **factors** which must be taken into consideration. Give three factors that are important when choosing a fuel to be used in a car engine.

1. ....

2. ....

3. ....

Q3 Answer the following questions about **hydrocarbons**.

a) Underline the two correct formulae for the products of the complete combustion of a hydrocarbon.

H_2S CH_4 CO_2 SO_2 H_2O

b) Suggest why a fuel might not burn completely.

....

....

Partial combustion is the same as incomplete combustion.

Q4 **Partial combustion** can cause problems.

a) Fill in the blanks to complete the word equation for the partial combustion of hydrocarbons.

hydrocarbon + oxygen → .... + ...

\+ .... + ...

b) Why is it dangerous if partial combustion occurs in household gas appliances?

....

....

Using Crude Oil as a Fuel

Q1 As crude oil is a **non-renewable** resource people are keen to find **alternative** energy sources. Suggest a problem with each of these ways of using alternative fuels.

a) **Solar** energy for cars: ....

b) **Wind** energy to power an oven: ....

c) **Nuclear** energy for buses: ....

Q2 Forty years ago some scientists predicted that there would be no oil left by the year 2000, but obviously they were **wrong**. One reason is that modern engines are more **efficient** than ones in the past, so they use less fuel. Give two other reasons why the scientists' prediction was wrong.

....

....

Q3 Using oil products as fuels causes some **environmental** problems. Explain the environmental problems that are associated with each of the following:

a) **Transporting** crude oil across the sea in tankers.

....

b) **Burning** oil products to release the energy they contain.

....

....

....

Q4 Write a short paragraph summarising why crude oil is the most **common source** of fuel even though **alternatives** are available.

....

....

....

....

....

Environmental Problems

Q1 Tick the boxes to indicate whether each statement is **true** or **false**.

		True	False
a)	Burning fossil fuels releases gases and particles.	✓	
b)	Oxides of nitrogen cause acid rain by forming dilute nitric acid in clouds.		✓
c)	Oxides of nitrogen form if a fuel burns at low temperatures.	✓	
d)	Soot forms if a fuel contains sulfur.	✓	

Q2 Draw lines to link the correct parts of these sentences.

The main cause of acid rain is	acid rain
Acid rain kills trees and	sulfuric acid.
Sulfur dioxide is produced by burning fuels which contain	acidifies lakes.
Limestone buildings and statues are affected by	sulfur dioxide.
In clouds sulfur dioxide reacts with water to make	sulfur.

Q3 Give **two** ways that the amount of **acid rain** can be reduced.

1. ....

....

2. ....

....

Q4 What is **global dimming** and what is thought to **cause** it?

....

....

Top Tips: The best way to prevent acid rain damage is to reduce the amount of sulfur dioxide that we release into the atmosphere. When acid rain does fall there are some ways of reducing the amount of damage it causes, such as adding powdered limestone to affected lakes.

Carbon Dioxide in the Atmosphere

Q1 Underline the statements below about the greenhouse effect that are **true**.

- Greenhouse gases act like an insulating layer around the Earth.
- Greenhouse gases include carbon dioxide and methane.
- Human activity isn't affecting the amount of greenhouse gases.
- Increasing amounts of greenhouse gases are causing global warming.

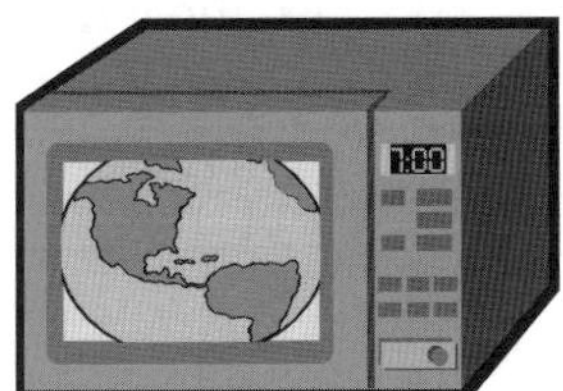

Q2 Here is a diagram of the **carbon cycle**.

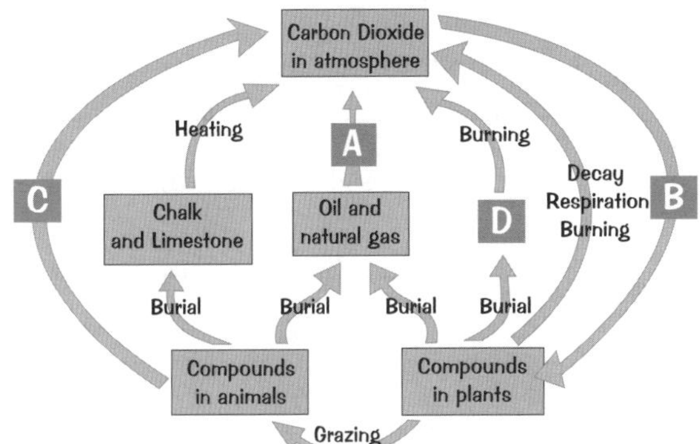

a) What is process A? ....

b) What is process B? ....

c) Process C could be decay. What else could it be?

....

d) What is substance D? ....

Q3 The graph shows the average temperature of the Earth between **1961** and **1990**, and how the temperature has differed from it over the last **150 years**.

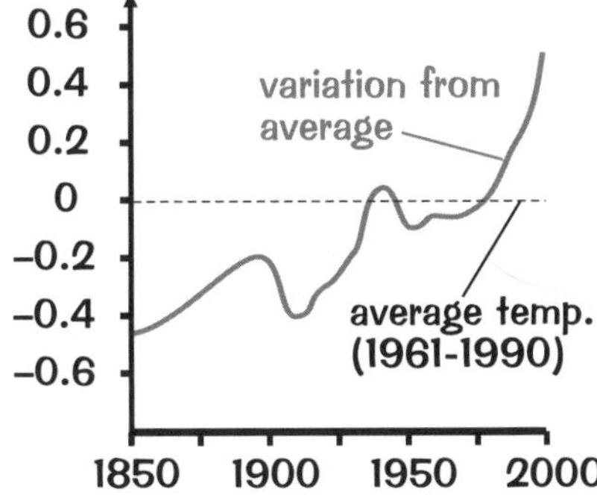

a) Describe what trend the graph shows.

....

....

....

b) There's a consensus among scientists that this temperature change was due to an increase in atmospheric CO_2 level. Describe two ways in which deforestation has caused this increase in CO_2.

1. ....

2. ....

c) Name one other human activity that's been causing this increase in atmospheric CO_2 level.

....

Reducing Carbon Dioxide in the Atmosphere

Q1 Scientists are researching new ways to **remove** CO_2 from the atmosphere.

a) Use the words below to fill the gaps in the passage.

high	photosynthesis	seeding	hydrocarbons	phytoplankton	injecting

Iron ………………………… involves ………………………… iron into the upper ocean to encourage blooms of ………………………… . These blooms remove CO_2 from the atmosphere during ………………………… and so could help to restore the balance. Converting carbon dioxide into ………………………… using ………………………… temperature and pressure, and a catalyst, is another method being researched by scientists.

b) Give **one** possible disadvantage of **one** of the methods described in the passage above.

……

……

Q2 **Hydrogen** is often talked about as the 'fuel of the future'.

a) What is the **only product** produced when **hydrogen** is burned?

……

b) Why is it better for the **environment** if we burn hydrogen rather than petrol?

……

……

c) Currently, most of the vehicles that can use hydrogen as a fuel are demonstration vehicles that are being developed by scientists. Explain the problems that will have to be overcome before the public will be able to use hydrogen-powered vehicles on a large scale.

Think about storage of hydrogen and the costs involved.

……

……

……

Q3 Biodiesel is a fuel made from vegetable oil.
A litre of biodiesel contains **90%** of the energy found in a litre of normal diesel.

Normal diesel contains 37 megajoules (37 000 000 J) of energy per litre.
How much energy does a litre of biodiesel contain?

……

Using Alkenes to Make Polymers

Q1 Tick the box next to the **true** statement below.

- [x] The monomer of poly(ethene) is ethene.
- [ ] The polymer of poly(ethene) is ethane.
- [x] The monomer of poly(ethene) is ethane.

We bring you gold, frankincense... and poly-myrrh

Q2 Polymers have many uses, for example, in LYCRA® fibre for tights.

Give three other uses of polymers.

1. ....

2. ....

3. ....

Q3 Most polymers are **not** biodegradable.

Biodegradable means that something can rot.

a) What problems does this cause for the environment?

....

....

b) How can you minimise this environmental problem when using objects made from polymers?

....

c) Things are often made from plastics because they are cheap. Why might this change in the future?

....

....

....

Think about what plastics are made from.

Using Alkenes to Make Polymers

Q4 The equation below shows the polymerisation of ethene to form **poly(ethene)**.

$$n\left(\begin{array}{cc} H & H \\ | & | \\ C & = C \\ | & | \\ H & H \end{array}\right) \longrightarrow \left(\begin{array}{cc} H & H \\ | & | \\ -C & - C- \\ | & | \\ H & H \end{array}\right)_n$$

many ethene molecules — poly(ethene)

Draw a similar equation below to show the polymerisation of propene (C_3H_6).

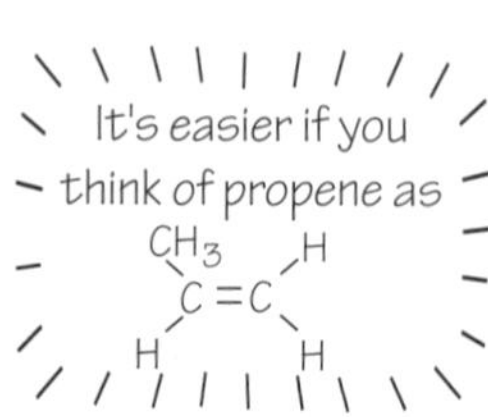

Q5 Plastic bags made just from polymers don't biodegrade.

Name two materials that can now be combined to make biodegradable plastic bags.

1. ....

2. ....

Q6 Fractional distillation of crude oil produces useful fractions and not-so-useful fractions. The not-so-useful ones are **cracked** to form alkenes. Alkenes can be **polymerised** to make plastics.

Write down the differences between cracking and polymerisation.

....

....

....

....

Top Tips: It's amazingly easy to name polymers. You just take the name of the monomer (the little molecules that are joined together) stick it in brackets, and write the word 'poly' in front of it. And Bob's your uncle (except if his name's Mike or anything else that's not Bob).

Structure and Properties of Polymers

Q1 Complete the following passage by circling the correct words.

Polymer chains are held **together** / **apart** by forces between the chains. If these forces are weak, the chains **cannot** / **can** slide over each other easily. This makes the polymer **inflexible** / **flexible** and gives it a **low** / **high** melting point. The stronger the forces between the polymer chains, the **more** / **less** energy is needed to break them apart, and the **lower** / **higher** the melting point.

Q2 Polymers can be **modified** to give them different properties.

a) In what four ways can polymers be modified to change their properties?

1. .... 2. ....

3. .... 4. ....

b) How could you lower the melting point of a polymer?

....

c) Describe how a polymer's properties would change if its chain length was increased.

....

....

d) Explain how adding cross-linking agents affects the properties of a polymer.

....

....

Q3 uPVC is strong, durable and rigid. When another chemical is added to the uPVC, it becomes stretchy, soft and easier to shape. It can then be used as **synthetic leather**.

a) What is the general name given to chemicals that can be added to polymers to make them softer and more pliable?

....

b) Explain how these chemicals make the polymer softer.

....

....

Plant Oils

Q1 Oil can be extracted from some **fruits** and **seeds**.

a) Name two fruits and two seeds which are good sources of oil.

Fruits: .... and ....

Seeds: .... and ....

b) Give two uses of plant oils.

1. ....

2. ....

c) Why is the use of high pressure an important part of the oil extraction process?

....

Q2 Write out a **correct version** of this sentence.

Vegetable oils provide loads of energy, but are not nutritious.

....

....

Q3 Tick the boxes to show whether these statements are true or false.

		True	False
a)	Vegetable oils have lower boiling points than water.	☐	☐
b)	Vegetable oils help food cook faster.	☐	☐
c)	Cooking with vegetable oils reduces the energy content of food.	☐	☐
d)	Flavours come from chemicals that are soluble in oil.	☐	☐
e)	Food cooked in oils has less flavour.	☐	☐

Q4 Vegetable oils can be turned into **fuels**.

a) Explain why vegetable oils are suitable for processing into fuels.

....

b) Name one fuel made from vegetable oil.

....

Plant Oils

Q5 Ben and Martin both planned an experiment to identify saturated and unsaturated oils.

Ben's Method

1. Put some oil in a test tube.
2. Add some bromine water.
3. Shake vigorously.
4. Repeat for next oil.
5. When all the oils are done, write down the results.

Martin's Method

1. Put 2 ml of oil into a test tube.
2. Label the test tube with the name of the oil sample.
3. Add 5 drops of bromine water.
4. Record any colour change.
5. Repeat for each oil.

Whose experimental method is better? Give reasons for your answer.

....

....

....

Q6 Margarine is usually made from partially hydrogenated vegetable oil.

a) Describe the process of hydrogenation.

....

....

b) How does hydrogenation affect the melting points of vegetable oils?

....

c) Explain why some vegetable oils are only partially hydrogenated.
Give an example of a partially hydrogenated vegetable oil.

....

....

Q7 Some types of fats are considered bad for your heart.

a) Which type of fats are **less healthy**? Underline your answer.

Saturated **Unsaturated**

b) Explain why this type of fat is bad for your heart.

....

....

Emulsions

Q1 Each of these sentences has an error. Write out a **correct version** of each sentence.

a) Emulsions are always formed from oil suspended in water.

....

b) The thicker an emulsion, the less oil it contains.

....

c) Emulsions can be combined with air, but it makes them runnier.

....

Air is whipped into cream to make a topping for a trifle.

d) Emulsions are only found in foods.

....

Q2 **Lecithin** is added to chocolate drinks to prevent the oils separating out from the water. The diagram shows a molecule of lecithin.

a) Label the **hydrophilic** part and the **hydrophobic** part of the lecithin molecule.

b) Explain how this molecule keeps the oil and water parts of chocolate drinks from separating into two different layers. Include a diagram to help explain your answer.

....

....

....

....

....

....

Q3 Adding emulsifiers to foods has **advantages** and **disadvantages**.

a) Explain why emulsifiers increase the shelf-life of food.

....

b) Why can adding emulsifiers to food sometimes be problematic?

....

....

Mixed Questions — Section 6

Q1 The general formula for an alkene is C_nH_{2n}.

a) **Explain** what this general formula means.

b) The displayed structure for ethene is shown to the right. **Draw** the displayed structure for propene in the other box.

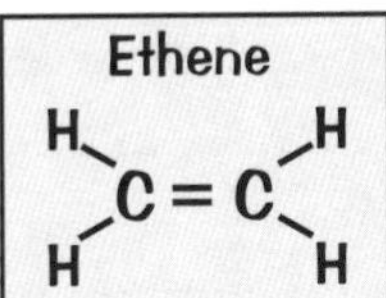

Propene

c) How do alk**e**nes differ from alk**a**nes?

Q2 Octane is heated and passed over a catalyst. It **thermally decomposes** as shown to the right.

octane → hexane + ethene

a) What is the process of splitting up long-chain hydrocarbons by thermal decomposition called?

b) Describe how ethene can be used to make **ethanol**.

c) Suggest **one** other way to make ethanol. What is the advantage of making it this way?

Q3 Ethene molecules can join together in a **polymerisation** reaction.

a) **Explain** the term '**polymerisation**'.

b) Styrene molecules can also join together to form a polymer. **Name** this polymer and **draw** a diagram of part of it below.

Styrene

Mixed Questions — Section 6

Q4 **Petrol** and **diesel** are two commonly used fuels for cars.

a) Diesel has longer molecules than petrol.
List **three** differences you would expect in physical properties between petrol and diesel.

1. ....

2. ....

3. ....

b) **Ethanol** is an alternative fuel to petrol and diesel.
Why is ethanol a more environmentally friendly fuel?

....

Q5 **Lubricating oils** in car engines keep moving metal surfaces apart. Viscous oils do this better than runny oils, but if they're too viscous they don't lubricate the moving parts properly.

The following experiment was set up to find which of two oils was the more viscous.
The time taken for each oil to run through the burette was noted at two temperatures.

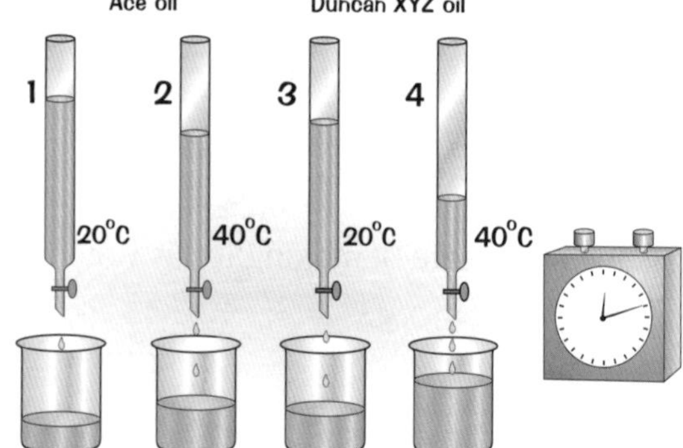

Burette	Temperature (°C)	Time for 50 cm^3 of oil to flow through (s)
1	20	90
2	40	53
3	20	64
4	40	28

Use the table of results to answer the following questions:

a) Which oil is **more viscous** at 20 °C? ....

b) Temperatures in an engine are much higher than 40 °C.
What will happen to the viscosity of these oils at engine temperature?

....

c) How could you **improve** the experiment to find out which oil would be more viscous when used in an engine?

....

d) Which oil would you expect to be tapped off closer to the top of a fractionating column?

....

Heat, Temperature and Kinetic Theory

Q1 Complete these sentences by **circling** the correct word from each pair.

Heat is a measure of **hotness** / **energy**.

Temperature is a measure of **hotness** / **energy**.

Heat travels from a **hot** / **cold** place to a **hot** / **cold** place.

When a substance is heated its particles vibrate **more** / **less** quickly.

Q2 The pictures below show the **arrangement** of particles in a **solid**, a **liquid** and a **gas**. Draw lines to match each picture and description to the correct word.

GAS

LIQUID

SOLID

There are weak forces of attraction between the particles.

There are almost no forces of attraction between the particles.

There are strong forces of attraction holding the particles close together.

Q3 Tick the correct boxes below to show whether the sentences are **true** or **false**.

		True	False
a)	The particles in a **liquid** are free to move at **high** speeds.	☐	☐
b)	The particles in a gas have **more** energy than those in liquids and solids.	☐	☐
c)	In a solid, the particles can only **vibrate** about a fixed position.	☐	☐
d)	In a liquid, the particles form **irregular** arrangements.	☐	☐
e)	The particles in a liquid have **less** energy than those in a solid.	☐	☐

Q4 If you keep **heating** a solid, it will eventually **melt** and turn into a liquid. Explain why this happens, in terms of **particles**.

....

....

....

....

....

Conduction and Convection

Q1 Tick to show whether the sentences are true or false.

		True	False
a)	Conduction involves **energy** passing between **vibrating particles**.	☐	☐
b)	Some **metals** are very **poor** conductors.	☐	☐
c)	**Solids** are usually better **conductors** of heat than liquids and gases.	☐	☐
d)	**Plastic** is a **poor** conductor because it contains **free electrons**.	☐	☐

Q2 George picks up a piece of **wood** and a **metal spoon**. Both are at the same temperature: **20 °C**.

Explain why the metal spoon feels **colder** to the touch than the piece of wood.

....

....

Q3 Match each observation with an explanation by joining them together with lines.

The very bottom of a hot water tank stays cold...

Warm air rises...

A small heater can send heat all over a room...

because water isn't a good heat conductor.

because heat flows from warm places to cooler ones.

because it is not so dense.

Q4 Sam uses the apparatus shown to investigate **heat transfer** in water.

He heats the middle of the tube with a Bunsen flame.
The ice at the top of the tube melts quickly,
but the ice at the bottom does not melt.

What does this experiment show about conduction and convection in water? Explain your answer.

....

....

....

Q5 Great Aunt Marjorie knits blankets for babies. She says that a blanket **with holes** in keeps a baby **warmer** than a blanket without holes in. Why is this?

....

....

Heat Radiation

Q1 Tick the correct boxes below to show whether the sentences are true or false.

		True	False
a)	The amount of heat radiation absorbed by a surface depends only on its colour.	☐	☐
b)	The hotter a surface is, the more heat it radiates.	☐	☐
c)	All objects are constantly absorbing and emitting heat radiation.	☐	☐
d)	Solar hot water panels use black pipes to reflect the heat.	☐	☐
e)	Silver survival blankets help the body to absorb heat.	☐	☐

Q2 Complete the following sentences by circling the correct words.

a) Dark, matt surfaces are **good** / **poor** absorbers and **good** / **poor** emitters of heat radiation.

b) The best surfaces for radiating heat are **good** / **poor** absorbers and **good** / **poor** emitters.

c) The best materials for making survival blankets are **good** / **poor** absorbers and **good** / **poor** emitters.

d) The best surfaces for solar hot water panels are **good** / **poor** absorbers and **good** / **poor** emitters.

Q3 Sue makes a cup of **tea**. At first, it is too hot to drink so she leaves it to **cool**.

a) What can you say about the amount of heat **emitted** compared to the amount of heat **absorbed** by the tea, as it cools down?

....

....

b) Sue forgets to drink the tea. The tea cools until it reaches room temperature. The temperature of the tea then stays **constant**. What can you say about the amount of heat **absorbed** and **emitted** by the tea now?

....

c) Draw a line to match the beginning and end of each sentence below.

A system that's at a constant temperature...	...radiates more power than it absorbs.
A system that's warming up...	...radiates less power than it absorbs.
A system that's cooling down...	...radiates the same average power that it absorbs.

Top Tips: The amount of radiation an object absorbs or emits depends on its colour, its texture and how hot it is compared to its surroundings. Now then, after all that I think we deserve a cup of tea.

Condensation and Evaporation

Q1 Complete the passage using the words given below. You will not have to use all the words.

kinetic energy **heats up** **liquid** **attractive** **light energy** **solid** **repulsive** **cools**

Condensation is when a gas turns into a .... As a gas ...., the particles in the gas slow down and lose .... The particles are pulled closer together by the .... forces between the particles. If the particles get close enough together, then condensation takes place.

Q2 a) Tick the boxes to show whether the sentences are true or false.

	True	False
i) Evaporation is when particles escape from a liquid.	☐	☐
ii) Particles can only evaporate from a liquid at temperatures above the liquid's boiling point.	☐	☐
iii) Only the speed of a particle affects whether it can escape a liquid.	☐	☐

b) Write a correction for each false sentence.

....

....

Q3 Explain how **sweating** more **cools you down** when you get hot. You should talk about **particles** in your answer.

....

....

....

....

....

Q4 List **two** factors that would **increase** the **rate** of each of the following:

a) evaporation of a liquid.

....

....

b) condensation of a gas.

....

....

Rate of Heat Transfer

Q1 **Radiators** are used to **transfer heat** to their surroundings.

a) Why do radiators have a large surface area?

....

b) Explain why a radiator would transfer heat quicker to a **metal spoon** in contact with it, than to the **air** surrounding it.

....

....

Q2 List four features of a **vacuum flask** that reduce non-useful heat transfers. State whether each reduces conduction, convection or radiation.

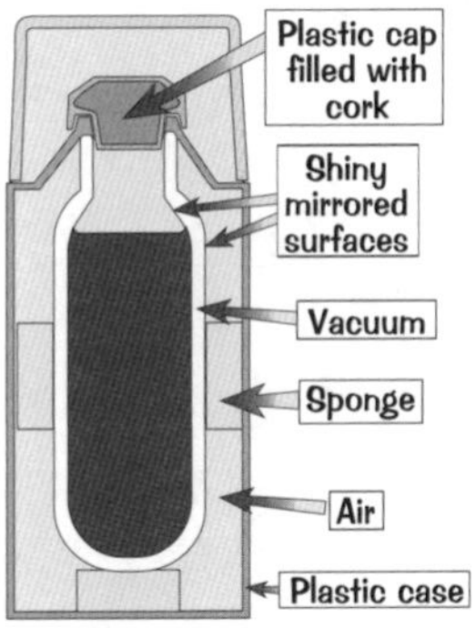

1..

2..

3..

4..

Q3 Mr Pink has a copper hot water tank with an electric **immersion heater** in it. The hot water tank **loses heat** from its **walls** by radiation, conduction and convection. Complete the table below, showing how to **reduce non-useful** heat transfers from the tank's walls.

Type of Transfer	Suggested improvements to reduce heat loss
Radiation	
Conduction	
Convection	

Which fluid will move and carry heat away? Where will it go, and how could you stop it?

Energy Efficiency in the Home

Q1 Fill in the blanks in the passage below using the words in the box.

windows	efficient	sinks	radiators	sources	insulate

Things that emit energy are called ...., e.g. ....

Things that transfer and waste energy are called ...., e.g. ....

To save energy, you can .... your house so the sinks 'drain' less energy.

You can also make sources and sinks more .... so they waste less energy.

Q2 Heat is lost from a house through its **roof**, **walls**, **doors** and **windows**.

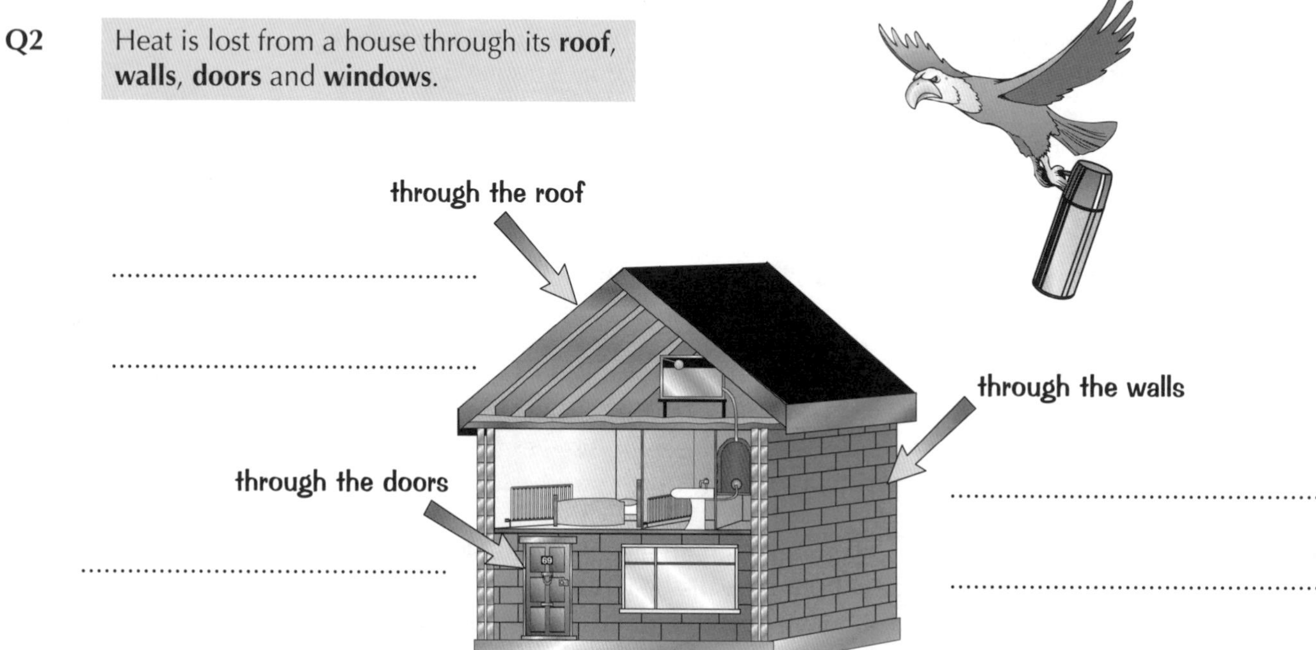

a) In the spaces on the diagram, write down at least one measure that could be taken to reduce heat losses through each part of the house.

b) Miss Golightly has just bought a new house which has very large windows. Suggest three ways she could reduce heat loss through the windows of her new house.

1. ....

2. ....

3. ....

Top Tips: If you want to build a new house, there are regulations about making it energy efficient — that's one reason why a lot of new houses have quite small windows. If you live in an old house, you can sometimes get a grant to cover the cost of installing extra insulation.

Energy Efficiency in the Home

Q3 Mr Tarantino wants to buy a **hot water tank jacket** to save on his heating bills, but his friend tells him that **loft insulation** would save him money **sooner**.

	Hot water tank jacket	Loft insulation
Initial Cost	£60	£200
Annual Saving	£15	£100
Payback time	4 years	

a) Calculate the **payback time** for loft insulation and write it in the table.

b) Is the friend's advice correct? Give reasons for your answer.

....

....

Q4 Explain how the following types of **insulation** work.

a) Cavity wall insulation:

....

....

b) Loft insulation:

....

....

c) Double glazing:

....

....

Q5 Gary is choosing between two brands of **loft insulation** material.
Brand A has a U-value of **0.15 W/m²K**. Brand B has a U-value of **0.2 W/m²K**.

a) What do U-values measure?

....

b) If both brands are the same price, which brand should Gary buy? Explain your answer.

....

....

Specific Heat Capacity

Q1 a) What is **specific heat capacity**?

....

b) Agatha has 1 kg samples of two substances — A and B. Substance **A** has a **higher** specific heat capacity than substance B. Both samples cool down by 10 °C. Which will release more heat — A or B? Circle the correct answer.

Substance A

Substance B

Q2 To the right is a table with a list of **materials** and their **specific heat capacities**. Use the information in the table to help you answer the questions below.

Material	Specific heat capacity (J/kg°C)
Concrete	880
Oil	2000
Mercury	139
Water	4200
Copper	380

a) Which of the materials is used in storage heaters?

....

b) Which material is usually used to transfer heat around central heating systems? Explain why this material is the best one to use.

....

....

Q3 Mildred thinks she could make her hot water bottle more efficient by filling it with **mercury**, which has a specific heat capacity of **139 J/kg°C**. The specific heat capacity of water is **4200 J/kg°C**.

Work out the **difference** in energy released by two litres of mercury cooling from 70 °C to 20 °C and two litres of water cooling from 70 °C to 20 °C. (2 l of mercury has a mass of 27.2 kg. 2 l of water has a mass of 2 kg.)

Don't try this at home — mercury's toxic at any temperature.

....

....

....

....

Q4 A piece of copper is heated to **90 °C** and then lowered into a beaker of water which is at **20 °C**. The copper transfers **3040 J** of energy to the water before it is removed. The temperature of the copper after it is removed is **50 °C**. The specific heat capacity of copper is **380 J/kg°C**.

Calculate the **mass** of the copper. ....

....

....

Energy Transfer

Q1 Use the words below to fill in the gaps.

dissipated **transferred** **created** **conservation**

The Principle for the .... of Energy says:

Energy can be .... usefully from one form to another, stored or

.... — but it can never be .... or destroyed.

Q2 Complete the following **energy transfer diagrams**. The first one has been done for you.

A solar water heating panel: ......light energy...... → ......heat energy......

a) A gas cooker: .... → ......heat and light energy......

b) An electric buzzer: ......electrical energy...... → ....

c) A television screen: .... → ....

Q3 The diagram shows a **steam locomotive**.

Oil lamp

Coal

a) What form(s) of energy are there in the:

i) coal ....

ii) hot steam (which powers the engine) ....

b) Describe two **energy transfers** which take place on the locomotive.

1..

2..

Q4 Bruce is practising **weightlifting**.

a) When Bruce holds the bar still, above his head, what kind of energy does the weight have?

....

b) Bruce had porridge for breakfast. Describe how the chemical energy in his porridge is transferred into the energy of the weight identified in part **a)**.

....

....

c) When Bruce lets go of the weight, what happens to its energy?

....

Efficiency of Machines

Q1 Tick the boxes to show whether these statements are **true** or **false**.

		True	False
a)	The **total energy supplied** to a machine is called the **input**.	☐	☐
b)	The **useful output** of a machine is never more than its total input.	☐	☐
c)	The **energy output** of a machine is the **useful energy** it delivers.	☐	☐
d)	The more **efficient** a machine is, the more energy it **wastes**.	☐	☐

Q2 Here is an **energy flow diagram** for an electric lamp. Complete the following sentences.

a) The **total energy input** is .... J

b) The **useful energy output** is .... J

c) The amount of energy **wasted** is .... J

d) The **efficiency** of the electric lamp is ....

Q3 Use the **efficiency formula** to complete the table.

Efficiency = Useful Energy Output ÷ Energy Input

Total Energy Input (J)	Useful Energy Output (J)	Efficiency
2000	1500	
	2000	0.50
4000		0.25
600	200	

Q4 Tina was investigating a model **winch** — a machine that uses an electric motor to lift objects.

Tina calculated that, in theory, **10 J** of electrical energy would be needed to lift a **boot** 50 cm off a table. She then tried lifting the boot with the winch and found that **20 J** of electrical energy was used.

Why did the winch use so much electrical energy in practice?
In your answer, include an explanation of what happened to the 'extra' 10 joules.

....

....

....

Energy Transformation Diagrams

Q1 Professor Bean is testing a new **high-efficiency** car engine.
He finds that for every 100 J of energy supplied to the engine, 75 J are transformed into **kinetic energy** in the moving car, 5 J are wasted as **sound energy** and the rest is turned into **heat energy**.

On the grid below, draw an **energy transformation (Sankey) diagram** to illustrate his results.

Q2 The Sankey diagram below is for a **winch** — a machine which **lifts** objects on hooks and cables.

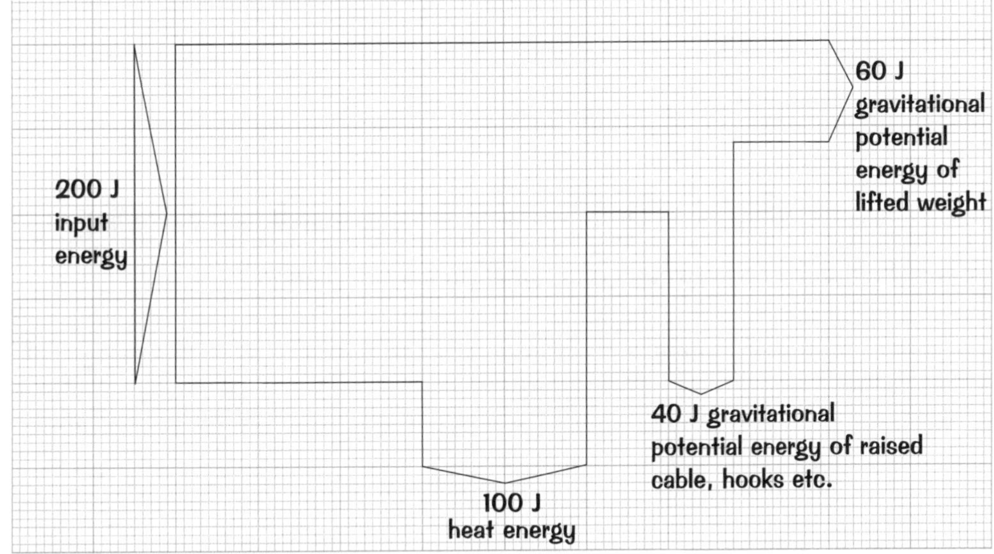

a) What is the total amount of energy **wasted**? .... J

b) How much useful **gravitational energy** is produced? .... J

c) Calculate the **efficiency** of the winch. Give your answer as a decimal.

Efficiency = Useful Energy Output ÷ Energy Input

....

....

Power Stations and Nuclear Energy

Q1 Use the words in the following list to complete the paragraph below.

non-renewable **kinetic** **chemical** **electrical** **fossil** **heat**

Most power stations use .... sources of energy, such as coal, oil or gas.

These .... fuels are initially burnt in a boiler.

This converts the .... energy in the fuel to .... energy.

A turbine then converts this energy into .... energy,

which in turn is converted to .... energy by a generator.

Q2 Which of these statements are **true** and which are **false**?

		True	False
a)	In nuclear power stations heat is produced by nuclear fusion.	☐	☐
b)	Nuclear power stations take the longest of all types of power stations to start up.	☐	☐
c)	Nuclear fuels are renewable energy sources.	☐	☐

Q3 Is the method of **electricity** generation in a **nuclear** power station any different from the method of electricity generation in a **coal-fired** power station? Explain your answer.

....

....

....

Q4 We can be affected by radiation in two ways — **contamination** and **irradiation**.

a) Explain the difference between contamination and irradiation.

....

....

....

b) State which is worse for you and explain why.

....

....

Top Tips: Nuclear fuel can provide millions of times more energy than the same mass of fossil fuel. Given the current concerns about CO_2 emissions from burning fossil fuels, you can see why many people see nuclear fuel as an attractive alternative. Nuclear waste is really dangerous though.

Wind and Solar Energy

Q1 People often **object** to wind turbines being put up near to where they live.

a) List three reasons why they might object.

1)..

2)..

3)..

b) List three arguments **in favour** of using wind turbines to generate electricity.

1)..

2)..

3)..

Q2 Geoff wanted to find out how much electricity he could generate using a small wind turbine. Each night he used a wind-powered generator to charge a battery. On each following day, he timed how long the battery could keep a lamp lit. His results are shown in the table below.

Day	Mon	Tues	Wed	Thu	Fri	Sat	Sun
Time lamp stays lit (mins)	45	50	2	25	60	35	42

a) Why did Geoff time how long the lamp stayed lit?

....

b) Suggest a reason why the lamp only stayed lit for 2 minutes on Wednesday.

....

Q3 Explain the advantages and disadvantages of using **solar cells** to generate electricity.

....

....

....

....

Wave and Tidal Energy

Q1 In a wave power station, there are several steps involved in making electricity. Number these steps in the right order.

☐ The air makes the turbine spin.

☐ Electricity is produced by the generator.

☐ A wave forces air through a turbine.

☐ The spinning turbine drives a generator.

Q2 Tick the boxes to show whether each statement applies to **wave** power or **tidal** power or **both**.

		Wave	Tidal
a)	Doesn't need steam to drive the turbine.	☐	☐
b)	Suitable for small-scale use.	☐	☐
c)	Is a reliable way to generate electricity.	☐	☐
d)	The amount of energy generated depends on the weather.	☐	☐
e)	The amount of energy generated depends on the time of the month and year.	☐	☐

Q3 **Tidal barrages** can be used to generate electricity.

Give two reasons why people might object to a **tidal barrage** being built.

1. ....

2. ....

Q4 **Wave-powered generators** can be very useful around islands, like Britain.

a) Give two **advantages** of using wave power to generate electricity.

1. ....

2. ....

b) Give two possible **problems** with using wave power.

1. ....

2. ....

Biofuels, Geothermal and Hydroelectricity

Q1 Use the words below to complete the following paragraph.

woodchips | fossil fuels | ethanol | water | steam | turbines | methane

Biofuels are used to generate electricity in a similar way to ....

Biofuels are burnt to heat .... and make ....

which is used to drive .... to power generators and make electricity.

Biofuels can be solids (e.g. ....), liquids (e.g. ....)

or gases (e.g. ....) .

Q2 Tick the boxes to show whether these statements about **geothermal** energy are true or false.

		True	False
a)	Set-up costs are low.	☐	☐
b)	It is possible in any country in the world.	☐	☐
c)	There are lots of associated environmental problems.	☐	☐
d)	Geothermal power stations use steam to drive turbines.	☐	☐

Q3 Describe how electricity is generated using **geothermal** energy.

....

....

....

Q4 Geothermal energy is **renewable** and has very few **environmental problems**.

Give two **disadvantages** of using geothermal energy.

1. ....

....

2. ....

....

Biofuels, Geothermal and Hydroelectricity

Q5 At a public meeting, people are sharing their views about **hydroelectric** power.

We should use hydroelectric power more — it doesn't cause any pollution.

Brian

And it gives us loads of free energy.

Hillary

But it makes a terrible mess of the countryside.

Sue

At least it's reliable — it always gives us electricity when we need it.

Liz

Say whether you agree or disagree with each person's view, and explain your reasons.

a) I **agree** / **disagree** with Brian because ....

....

b) I **agree** / **disagree** with Hillary because ....

....

c) I **agree** / **disagree** with Sue because ....

....

d) I **agree** / **disagree** with Liz because ....

....

e) Outline two **advantages** of hydroelectric power which were not mentioned at the public meeting.

1)...

2)...

f) Outline two **disadvantages** of hydroelectric power not mentioned at the meeting.

1)...

2)...

Top Tips: Biofuels, geothermal energy and hydroelectricity are all renewable energy sources. One uses steam coming from hot rocks underground, one uses rainwater trapped behind a dam, and the other is burning stuff like wood and cow muck. How lovely.

Energy Sources and the Environment

Q1 Draw lines to match up each environmental problem below with something that causes it.

Problem	Cause
Acid rain	Releasing CO_2 by burning fossil fuels
Global warming	Coal mining
Dangerous radioactive waste	Sulfur dioxide formed by burning oil and coal
Spoiling of natural landscapes	Using nuclear power

Q2 **Lisa** says: "Using **nuclear** power to make electricity is too dangerous."
Ben says: "Using **fossil fuels** is even more dangerous in the long run."

Who do you think is right? Explain your answer.

....

....

....

....

Q3 Biofuels are often described as being '**carbon neutral**'.

Explain why burning biofuels is 'carbon neutral'.

....

....

....

Q4 '**Carbon capture**' reduces the impact of burning fossil fuels on the environment.

a) Describe what is meant by the term 'carbon capture'?

....

....

b) Give an example of how the captured carbon dioxide can be stored.

....

Comparison of Energy Resources

Q1 Which of the following fossil fuel power stations has the **shortest start-up time**? Circle your answer.

Coal **Oil** **Gas**

Q2 The city of Fakeville decides to replace its old coal-fired power station. They have to choose between using **gas**, **nuclear**, **wind** or **geothermal**.

Give one **disadvantage** of each choice:

a) **Gas** ....

....

b) **Nuclear** ....

....

c) **Wind** ....

....

d) **Geothermal** ....

....

Q3 This is part of a leaflet produced by the pressure group '**Nuclear Is Not the Answer**' (NINA).

Read the extract and answer the questions on the next page.

> Imagine life without electricity. No lights, no computers, no TV... no kettles, no tea? Unthinkable. But that's what could happen when the oil and gas run out — because in the UK we generate about 75% of our electricity from power stations running on fossil fuels.
>
> The Government has decided to build more nuclear power stations.
> At NINA, we believe that nuclear is not the answer.
>
> Nuclear power stations generate power, yes, but they also generate huge piles of highly radioactive waste. No one has any idea how to get rid of this waste safely. So should we really be making more of it? Radioactive waste stays dangerous for hundreds of thousands of years. Would you be happy living near a nuclear fuel dump? That's not all — nuclear power stations, and the lethal waste they create, are obvious targets for terrorists. And, last but not least, building more nuclear power stations would cost the taxpayer billions.
>
> The good news is, we don't need nuclear power. There are safer, cleaner ways to produce electricity — using renewable energy. Many people argue that renewables are unreliable — the wind doesn't always blow, for instance. Well, true, but tidal power is reliable — and we have hundreds of miles of coastline with tides washing in and out twice every day.
>
> If you don't want your children to grow up in a nuclear-powered world, join NINA today.

Comparison of Energy Resources

a) Explain clearly why the author thinks that we could find ourselves without electricity.

....

....

b) Give two reasons why the author thinks nuclear power is **dangerous**.

1..........

2..........

c) Nuclear power stations are the most expensive type of power plant to **decommission**.

Explain what is meant by the term decommission.

....

....

d) The author suggests that tidal power is a **plentiful** and **reliable** source of energy. Do you agree? Explain your answer.

I **agree** / **disagree** because ....

....

....

e) Give two other arguments **in favour** of tidal power.

1..........

....

2..........

....

Mixed Questions — Section 7

Q1 Electricity is generated in **power stations**.

a) In a gas-fired power station, gas is burned and its chemical energy is converted into heat energy.

i) Describe how this heat energy is then converted into electrical energy.

....

....

ii) If the power station is 38% efficient, how much energy is **wasted** for every 1000 J of electrical energy **produced**?

....

....

b) Natural gas is a fossil fuel. Burning it releases carbon dioxide and contributes to climate change.

Suggest two alternative types of fuel which could be used to produce heat in power stations without contributing to climate change.

.... and ....

Q2 A group of farmers live on a remote island, growing potatoes and farming llamas. They decide to put **solar cells** on the roofs of their houses and **wind turbines** in their fields.

a) Suggest why the farmers have chosen to use:

i) solar power ....

....

ii) wind power ....

....

....

b) Name one other renewable source of energy the farmers could use.

....

c) Explain why few households in the UK could rely on these technologies for their electricity supply.

....

....

Mixed Questions — Section 7

Q3 Steve has bought a new fridge-freezer.

a) Steve's new fridge-freezer has its freezer compartment above the refrigerator.
How does this arrangement encourage **convection currents** in the main body of the fridge?

....

....

b) Steve makes some ice cubes in his new fridge-freezer. Explain how the arrangement and energy of the water particles are different in the ice cubes than in the liquid water.

....

....

....

Q4 In one coal-fired power station, for every **1000 J** of energy input to the power station, 100 J is wasted in the **boiler**, 500 J is wasted in the **cooling water** and 50 J is wasted in the **generator**.

a) What **type** of energy is contained in the **coal**? ....

b) On the grid below, draw a detailed energy transformation diagram for this power station.

c) Calculate the **efficiency** of the power station.

....

....

Mixed Questions — Section 7

Q5 Eric investigates ways of **saving energy** in his grandmother's house. He calculates the annual savings that could be made on his grandma's fuel bills, and the cost of doing the work.

Work needed	Annual Saving (£)	Cost of work (£)
Hot water tank jacket	15	15
Draught-proofing	65	70
Cavity wall insulation	70	560
Thermostatic controls	25	120

a) Which of these energy-saving measures has the shortest **payback time**?

....

b) Which of the options in the table would save Eric's grandma the most money **over 5 years**? Show your working.

....

....

....

c) Eric's grandma likes to have a hot bath in the evenings. How much energy is needed to heat 90 kg of water from 14 °C to 36 °C ? (The specific heat capacity of water is 4200 J/kg°C.)

....

....

....

Q6 A council are discussing plans to build a new **power station**.

a) Suggest three issues they need to consider when choosing an energy resource for the power station.

1. ....

2. ....

3. ....

b) Some council members are concerned about the effect fossil-fuel power stations have on the environment. How does carbon capture and storage technology help reduce these effects?

....

....

Generating Electricity

Q1 Use the words in the box to **fill in the blanks** in these two paragraphs about generating electricity.

moving electromagnetic magnet coil induction
alternating voltage reverses magnetic complete

You can create a .... across an electrical conductor by .... a magnet near the conductor. This is called ....

In generators, this is usually achieved by rotating a .... near a .... of wire. The generator produces an .... current when it is connected up to a .... circuit. The current alternates since the direction of the .... field .... every time the magnet rotates by half a turn.

Q2 The diagram on the right shows the trace produced when a **coil** is connected to a cathode ray oscilloscope and a **magnet** is **rotated nearby**.

a) On the diagram, draw what the trace would look like if the magnet was rotated **faster**.

The amplitude **and** the frequency would change.

b) Apart from rotating the magnet faster, what **three other things** could you do to make the maximum voltage **larger**?

1. ....

2. ....

3. ....

Q3 The lights on Sebastian's bicycle are powered by a **dynamo**. Explain why the bicycle lights dim as he slows down.

....

....

....

Top Tips: You can tell why people thought electricity was magic in the olden days — wave a magnet near some wire and hey presto... you get some electricity. Make sure you know what to change to make the voltage generated change and you'll generate lots of marks.

Electricity and the National Grid

Q1 Number these statements 1 to 5 to show the order of the steps that are needed to deliver energy to Mrs Miggins' house so that she can boil the kettle.

	An electrical current flows through power cables across the country.
	Mrs Miggins boils the kettle for tea.
	Electrical energy is generated in power stations.
	The voltage of the supply is raised.
	The voltage of the supply is reduced.

Q2 Electricity can be transmitted by either **overhead** or **underground cables**. Tick the appropriate box to answer each of the following questions:

	Overhead cables	Underground cables
a) Which **cost** more to set up?	☐	☐
b) Which require the most **maintenance**?	☐	☐
c) Which are the easiest to **repair**?	☐	☐
d) Which are most affected by **weather**?	☐	☐
e) Which are most **reliable**?	☐	☐
f) Which are the **easiest** to install?	☐	☐
g) Which cause the most disturbance to **land**?	☐	☐

Q3 Using **high voltages** to transmit electricity means you need some **expensive** equipment, like power cables.

a) List the three other types of equipment you need for **high voltage transmission**.

1. ....

2. ....

3. ....

b) Explain why it is still **cheaper** to use **high voltages** for transmission.

....

....

Electricity and the National Grid

Q4 Each of the following sentences is incorrect. Write a correct version of each.

a) The National Grid transmits energy at **high voltage** and **high current**.

....

b) A step-up transformer is used to **reduce the voltage** of the supply before electricity is transmitted.

....

c) Using a **high current** makes sure there is not much energy **wasted**.

....

Q5 The **National Grid** distributes electricity from power stations to the consumers.

a) Explain what is meant by the 'supply and demand' of electricity.

....

....

b) Describe **one** problem the National Grid faces concerning supply and demand.

....

c) Suggest **two** ways the National Grid can increase the supply of electricity.

....

....

d) Suggest **two** ways in which consumers can help reduce demand for electricity.

....

....

Top Tips: The key thing to remember is that high voltage means low current, which means the cables don't get so hot — so less energy is wasted. And while you're at it, the ways of matching supply with demand are really important to learn too. You might get asked about all this stuff in the exam, which is why we put it in our book. It wasn't just for fun. If you did have fun — good for you.

Power and the Cost of Electricity

Q1 The **current** an appliance draws depends on its **power** rating. Complete the table below, showing the power rating and current drawn by various appliances at mains voltage — **230 V**.

Appliance	Power (W)	Current (A)
Kettle	2600	
Radio	13	
Laptop computer		3.2
Lamp		0.17

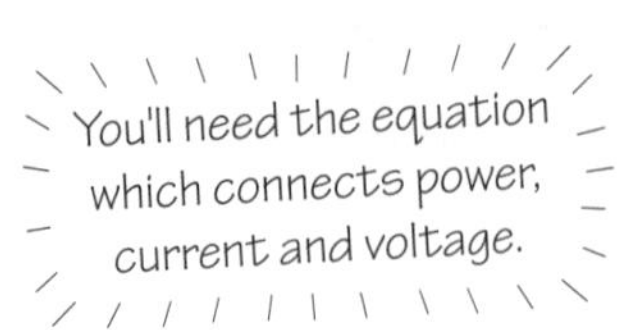

Q2 Boris puts his **2 kW** electric heater on for 3 hours.

a) Calculate how many **kilowatt-hours** of electrical energy the heater uses.

.... kWh.

b) Boris gets his electricity supply from Ivasparkco. They charge 7p per kilowatt-hour. Work out the **cost** of the energy calculated in part **a)**.

....

....

c) Boris's wife grumbles at him for leaving a 60 W lamp on overnight — about 9 hours every night. Boris says his wife uses **more energy** by using an 8 kW shower for 15 minutes every day.

Is Boris right? Calculate how much energy each person uses and compare your results.

....

....

....

Q3 Mr Havel recently received his **electricity bill**. Unfortunately, he tore off the bottom part to write a shopping list.

Customer : Havel, V

Date	Meter Reading
11 06 06	34259
10 09 06	34783

Total Cost @ 9.7p per Unit

a) How many **Units** of energy did Mr Havel use in the three months from June to September?

....

b) What would the bill have said for 'total cost'?

....

....

Power and the Cost of Electricity

Q4 **Off-peak electricity** is sometimes **cheaper** than electricity at peak times.

a) Give an example of an electrical appliance designed to use off-peak electricity.

....

b) i) Give one advantage for the consumer of using off-peak electricity:

....

ii) Give one advantage for the electricity generating company of using off-peak electricity:

....

....

Q5 **Pumped storage** power stations work by using **off-peak** electricity to pump water into a holding reservoir at night. In the daytime they release water from the reservoir to generate electricity, which is then sold to the National Grid at **peak rate** prices. The table below shows data for a typical pumped storage power station.

	Night time (input)	Daytime (output)
Running time	7 hours	5 hours
Power	275 MW	288 MW
Cost per kWh	3.7p	7.2p

Be careful — watch out for units.

a) Calculate the cost of electricity used in the night time operation.

....

....

b) Calculate the value (in £) of the electricity generated in the daytime operation.

....

....

Q6 A tumble drier operating on a **230 V household supply** uses a current of **10 A**.

a) Calculate the power rating of the tumble drier in kW.

....

b) Peak time electricity costs 11.3p/Unit. Off peak electricity costs 6.0p/Unit. Calculate the **money saved** if a tumble drier is operated for 2 hours during off peak hours rather than at peak time.

....

....

Choosing Electrical Appliances

Q1 Two different types of **power drill** and some of their features are shown below.

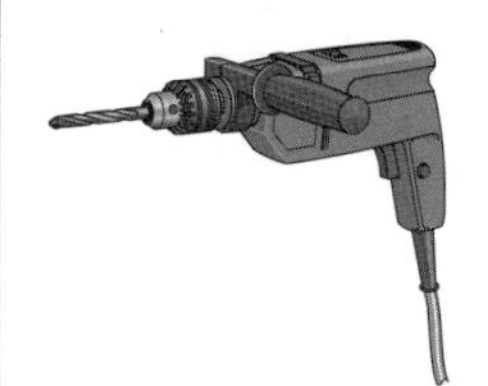

Mains Powered Drill

Power output: 1.2 kW

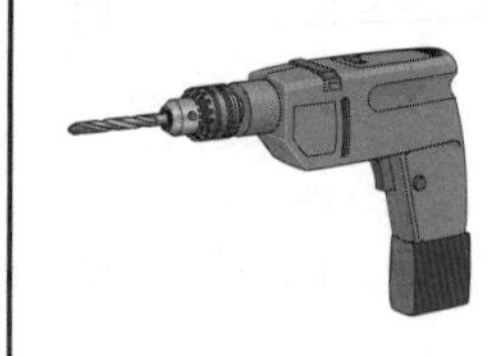

Battery Powered Drill

Power output: 200 W

Battery Life: 8 hours

Suggest **two** reasons someone might choose to buy the battery powered drill instead of the mains powered drill.

....

....

Q2 A **battery powered lamp** takes **6 hours** to charge fully when connected to a **400 W** power supply. This gives the lamp enough energy for **8 hours** of use. A **mains powered** lamp has a power rating of **1.6 kW**.

a) If both lamps are used for 8 hours, calculate the difference in the amount of energy used. Give your answer in kWh.

....

....

....

b) If the cost of electricity is 12p per kWh, calculate the difference in cost of using both lamps for 8 hours.

....

c) Suggest why somebody going on a camping trip might choose to buy a wind-up lamp instead of the mains powered or battery powered lamps described above.

....

....

Q3 **Access to electricity** can improve people's **standard of living** in developing countries.

Give two examples of how electricity can help improve **public health** in developing countries.

1. ....

2. ....

Wave Basics

Q1 Complete the sentence below by circling the correct word in each pair.

Waves transfer **energy / matter** without transferring any **energy / matter.**

Q2 There are **two ways** in which you can make waves on a **slinky** spring.

a) Which diagram shows a **transverse** wave, and which one shows a **longitudinal** wave?

Transverse: ....

Longitudinal: ....

①

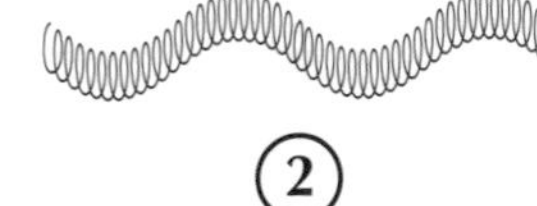

②

b) Write down one difference between these two types of wave.

....

....

Q3 Diagrams **A**, **B** and **C** represent electromagnetic waves.

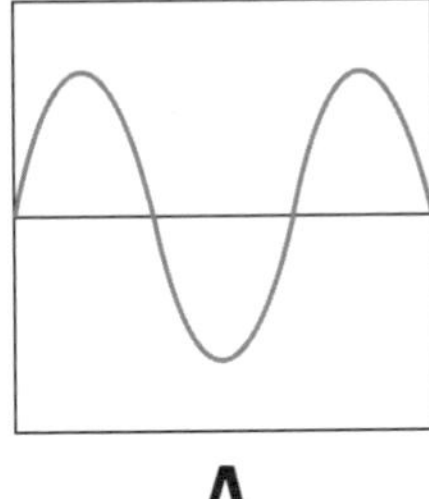

A

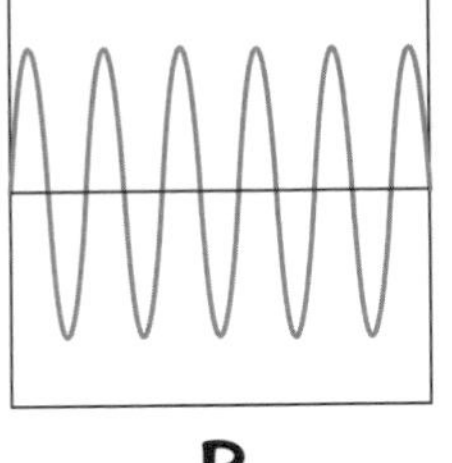

B

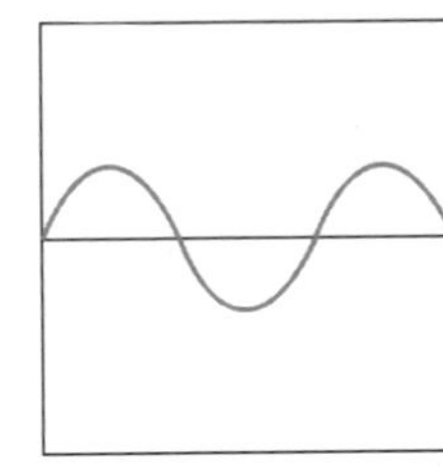

C

a) Which two diagrams show waves with the same **frequency**? .... and ....

b) Which two diagrams show waves with the same **amplitude**? .... and ....

c) Which two diagrams show waves with the same **wavelength**? .... and ....

Q4 Which of the phrases below relate to **transverse** waves and which to **longitudinal**? Write '**T**' for transverse, and '**L**' for longitudinal.

- ☐ vibrations are at 90° to the direction of energy transfer
- ☐ electromagnetic radiation
- ☐ sound waves
- ☐ vibrations are along the same direction as the energy transfer
- ☐ produced by a slinky spring whose end is wiggled at 90° to the spring itself
- ☐ ripples on water
- ☐ produced by a slinky spring whose end is pushed and pulled towards and away from the rest of the spring

Wave Basics

Q5 
All waves have a **frequency** and a **wavelength**.

a) What units are used to measure wavelength? ....

b) What does it mean to say that "the frequency of a wave is 25 hertz"?

....

c) The diagram shows a waveform.
Which of A, B or C is the length of one whole wave?

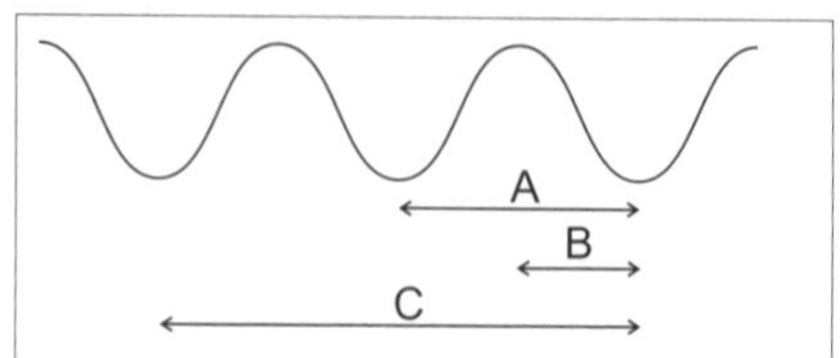

....

Q6 There are six equations below, some of which are **incorrect**.
Draw a big thick line through the ones that are incorrect.

$\text{Frequency} = \text{Speed} \times \text{Wavelength}$

$\text{Frequency} = \dfrac{\text{Wavelength}}{\text{Speed}}$

$\text{Wavelength} = \dfrac{\text{Speed}}{\text{Frequency}}$

$\text{Speed} = \dfrac{\text{Frequency}}{\text{Wavelength}}$

$\text{Speed} = \text{Frequency} \times \text{Wavelength}$

$\text{Frequency} = \dfrac{\text{Speed}}{\text{Wavelength}}$

Q7 **Green light** travels at 3×10^8 m/s and has a wavelength of about 5×10^{-7} m.

Calculate the **frequency** of green light. Give the correct unit in your answer.

....

....

Q8 Jason draws the graph on the right to show a wave with an **amplitude** of **4 m** and a **wavelength** of **2 m**.

a) What has Jason done wrong?

....

....

b) On the same set of axes, draw a wave with a **wavelength** of **5 m** and an **amplitude** of **3 m**.

Q9 An ultraviolet wave has a frequency of 4.6×10^{15} Hz. It travels at a speed of 3×10^8 m/s.

Calculate the **wavelength** of the wave.

....

....

Wave Properties

Q1 Harriet spends at least an hour looking at herself in a **mirror** every day. The image she sees is formed from light reflected by the mirror.

a) What is meant by a "normal" when talking about reflection?

....

....

b) Complete the diagram to show an incident ray of light being reflected by the mirror. Label the **angle of incidence**, **i**, the **normal**, and the **angle of reflection**, **r**.

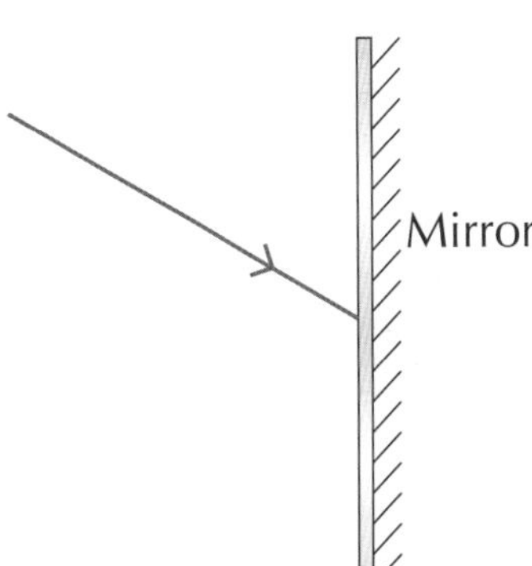

Q2 The diagram below shows a pencil being reflected in a **plane mirror**. Some of the rays have already been drawn in.

a) On the diagram, draw in the rays showing how light is reflected to form an image of the **top** of the pencil.

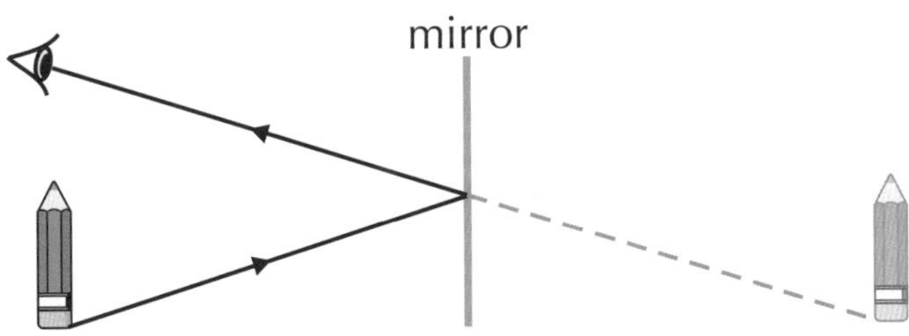

b) Is the image in a plane mirror real or virtual? ....

c) Is the image inverted or upright? ....

d) The image of the pencil is **laterally inverted**. Explain what this means.

....

....

Top Tips: If you get asked a question about constructing ray diagrams, remember the important rule for drawing reflections in a plane mirror: angle of incidence = angle of reflection. Always use a ruler to draw your ray diagrams too — examiners love a line drawn with a ruler.

Diffraction and Refraction

Q1 An important property of waves is **diffraction**.

a) Explain what 'diffraction' means.

....

....

b) A ripple tank is used to study the behaviour of waves as they pass through gaps. The gap in diagram 1 is about the **same size** as the wavelength. The gap in diagram 2 is **much bigger**. Complete both diagrams to show what happens to the waves after they pass through the gaps.

1

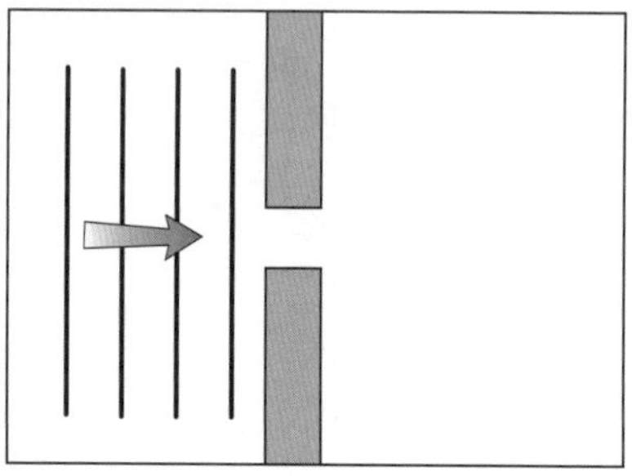

2

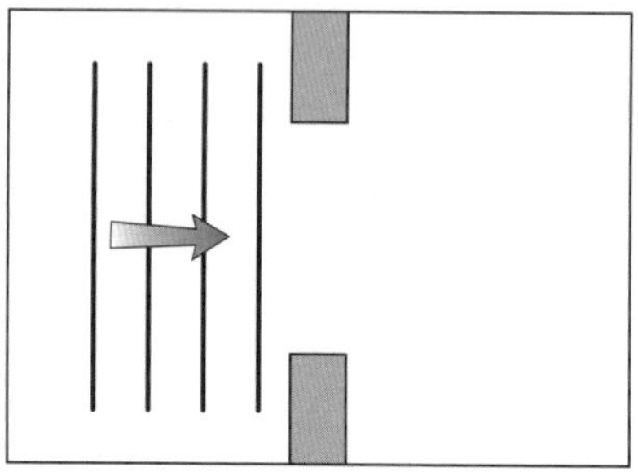

Q2 Diagrams A and B show waves travelling from a **less dense** medium to a **denser** medium.

A
Denser
Less Dense

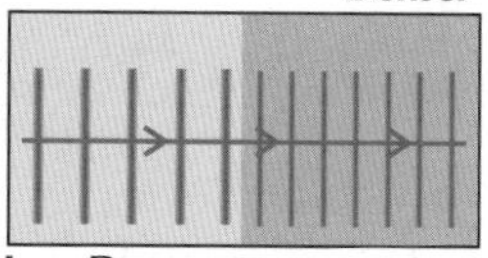

B
Denser
Less Dense

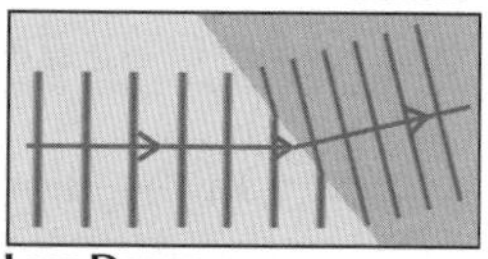

a) Which diagram shows the waves being **refracted**? ....

b) Why does refraction **not happen** in the other diagram?

....

c) What happens to the **wavelength** of the waves as they pass into the denser medium?

....

d) What happens to the **frequency** of the waves as they pass into the denser medium?

....

e) What happens to the **velocity** of the waves as they pass into the denser medium?

....

f) Imagine that the wave in the denser medium in diagram B passes into a **less dense** medium again. What would you expect to happen to the wave?

Think about wavelength, frequency and speed.

....

....

Sound Waves

Q1 Sound waves are caused by **vibrations**.

Put the following sentences in the correct order to describe how the sound of a drumbeat is made and reaches our ears.

A The vibration of the drum sets the air molecules next to it vibrating too.

B We hear the sound when the vibrations in the air reach our ears.

C When someone beats a drum, the skin on top of the drum vibrates.

D A series of compressions and decompressions travel outwards through the air (or other medium) as a longitudinal wave.

Correct order: .... , ... , ... , ...

Q2 Choose from the words below to fill in the spaces in the passage.

high **low** **vibrate**

A sound wave makes air molecules .... If there are many vibrations per second the frequency or pitch of the sound is .... If there are only a few vibrations per second the pitch of the sound is ....

Q3 Complete the sentences below by circling the correct word in each pair.

The bigger the **amplitude / frequency** of a sound wave, the **louder / quieter** the sound.

Q4 A bell is vibrating with a **frequency** of **2 kHz**. How many times a **second** is it vibrating?

....

Q5 Most humans can **hear** sounds in the frequency range **20 Hz to 20 000 Hz**.

1 MHz = 1 000 000 Hz

a) What is the frequency of a sound wave that has 30 compressions in one second?

....

b) Put the following frequencies in order, from the lowest frequency to the highest.

3 MHz, 8 kHz, 630 Hz, 400 kHz, 5 Hz, 21 kHz

....

c) Give the term for sounds which have:

i) frequencies higher than 20 000 Hz. ....

ii) frequencies lower than 20 Hz. ....

Analogue and Digital Signals

Q1 Fill in the blanks, choosing from the words below.

digital	analogue	amplified	weaken	interference	noise

All signals .... as they travel. To overcome this, they can be .... Signals may also suffer .... from other signals or from electrical disturbances. This causes .... in the signal. When signals are amplified, the noise is also amplified, but it's much harder to remove noise from a(n) .... signal.

Q2 Sketch: A 'clean' digital signal. A 'noisy' digital signal. A 'noisy' analogue signal.

Q3 a) Explain why it is better to send **digital** signals to a computer rather than analogue ones.

....

b) Explain why digital signals suffer less from **noise** than analogue signals.

....

....

c) State one other advantage of using digital signals for communication.

....

Q4 The diagrams opposite show magnified views of the surfaces of a **compact disc** and an old-fashioned **record**.

The CD is read by a laser, along the path shown by the arrow. The record is read by a needle which follows the grooves.

Both devices produce an electrical signal, which is then converted into sound.

For each device, sketch the **type** of trace you would expect to see on a monitor.

Compact disc

Old-fashioned record

Compact Disc

Record

EM Waves and Communication

Q1 The different types of **EM waves** form a spectrum.

a) Use the words below to complete the table to show the seven types of EM waves:

Infrared X-rays Gamma rays Radio waves Ultraviolet Microwaves

			VISIBLE LIGHT			
1 m-10^4 m	10^{-2} m (1 cm)	10^{-5} m (0.01 mm)	10^{-7} m	10^{-8} m	10^{-10} m	10^{-15} m

b) In which direction does the **energy** of the electromagnetic radiation **increase** across the table? Tick the box next to the correct answer.

- ☐ The energy of the waves **increases** from **left to right** across the table.
- ☐ The energy of the waves **increases** from **right to left** across the table.

Q2 a) Tick the correct boxes to show whether each of the following statements is true or false.

	True	False
i) Visible light travels faster in a vacuum than both X-rays and radio waves.	☐	☐
ii) Microwaves have the highest energy of all EM waves.	☐	☐
iii) Radio waves have the shortest wavelength of all EM waves.	☐	☐
iv) All EM waves can travel through space.	☐	☐

b) Write a correction for each false sentence.

....

....

....

....

Q3 Circle the letter next to the statements below that are true.

A Long waves such as radio waves are good for transmitting information over long distances.

B Some wavelengths of radio wave are reflected by the ionosphere and come back to Earth.

C Short-wave radio waves can be diffracted around hills.

D To receive TV signals, you must be in the direct line of sight of the transmitter.

EM Waves and Communication

Q4 Complete the sentences below by circling the correct word in each pair.

EM waves with higher frequencies have **shorter / longer** wavelengths.

The **higher / lower** the frequency of an EM wave, the greater the energy of the wave.

Q5 The house shown below receives radio signals from a nearby transmitter, even though there is a **mountain** between the house and the transmitter.

Use the words below to fill in the blanks in the passage.

ionosphere **short-wave** **long-wave** **FM**

The house can receive .... signals because they can diffract around the mountain. It also receives .... signals because they are reflected by the .... However .... signals are not received at the house as the transmitter is not in direct line of sight of the house.

Q6 Red and violet are at opposite ends of the spectrum of **visible** light. Describe two things they have in common and two ways in which they differ.

....

....

....

....

Top Tips: You may have realised by now that radio waves are really important for communication. I don't want to panic you, but you're more than likely being hit by loads of radio waves right now, there's pretty much nowhere to hide. Luckily radio waves are harmless, and they'll only affect you if you can't remember all about them in your exams. So get learning.

Microwaves

Q1 Gabrielle in Britain and Carwyn in Canada are talking by **mobile phone**. The mobile phone signals are sent via a **communications satellite**.

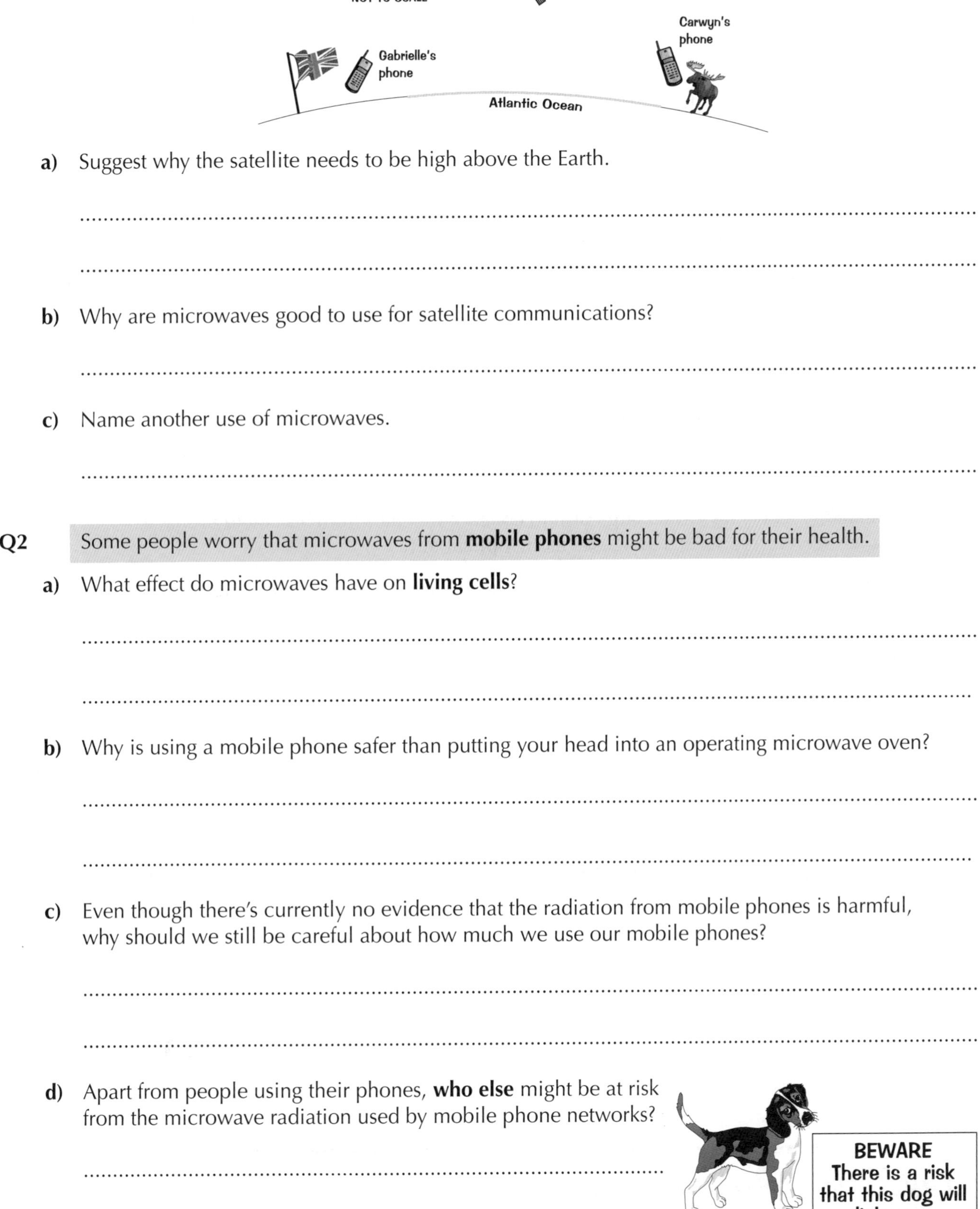

a) Suggest why the satellite needs to be high above the Earth.

....

....

b) Why are microwaves good to use for satellite communications?

....

c) Name another use of microwaves.

....

Q2 Some people worry that microwaves from **mobile phones** might be bad for their health.

a) What effect do microwaves have on **living cells**?

....

....

b) Why is using a mobile phone safer than putting your head into an operating microwave oven?

....

....

c) Even though there's currently no evidence that the radiation from mobile phones is harmful, why should we still be careful about how much we use our mobile phones?

....

....

d) Apart from people using their phones, **who else** might be at risk from the microwave radiation used by mobile phone networks?

....

....

Infrared and Visible Light

Q1 Tick the boxes to show whether these statements are **true** or **false**.

		True	False
a)	Infrared radiation can be used for wireless communication.	☐	☐
b)	Infrared is too dangerous to be used in the home.	☐	☐
c)	Infrared radiation is known as heat radiation.	☐	☐
d)	Cold objects emit more infrared radiation than hot objects.	☐	☐
e)	Infrared radiation can be used to cook food.	☐	☐

Q2 All **hot objects** give out infrared radiation.

Describe **one** use of infrared that relies on this property.

....

....

Q3 A **cable TV** company uses a large dish to collect TV signals from a satellite in space. It then sends these signals to houses along **optical fibres**.

a) What type(s) of EM waves could be used to send the signals along the optical fibres?

....

b) Describe how the EM radiation is transmitted down the optical fibre.

....

Q4 Visible light is used for **photography**.

Briefly describe how a camera uses visible light to take a photo.

....

....

....

Top Tips: There are four main types of electromagnetic radiation used in communications technology — microwaves, radio waves, visible light and infrared radiation. Make sure you know the uses of each. Then as a reward, practice using infrared radiation by channel hopping with your remote.

X-Rays and Gamma Rays

Q1 Indicate whether the following statements about X-rays are **true** or **false**.

		True	False
a)	X-rays can be used to look inside objects.	☐	☐
b)	Medical X-ray photographs show "shadows of our bones".	☐	☐
c)	Flesh is more dense than bone so it lets X-rays through more easily.	☐	☐

Q2 Some rocks in the Earth's crust give out ionising radiation.

a) Circle the correct word below to show whether this statement is **true** or **false**.

Ionising radiation is emitted all the time from radioactive sources. **True / False**

b) Name three types of EM radiation that can cause ionisation.

1. .... 2. .... 3. ....

c) Explain what is meant by the term '**ionising radiation**'.

....

....

Q3 Complete the following paragraphs on radiotherapy using the words provided.

ill centre normal kill cells focused cancer dose radiotherapy
High doses of gamma radiation will .... living .... Because of this, gamma radiation is used to treat .... Gamma rays are .... on the tumour using a wide beam. Damage to .... cells can make the patient feel very .... This damage is minimised by directing the radiation at the tumour and using the minimum .... possible.

Q4 Describe two ways in which X-rays are used in **airports**.

1. ....

....

2. ....

....

UV Radiation and Ozone

Q1 Prolonged exposure to the Sun is linked to an increased risk of **skin cancer**.

a) Which part of the radiation from the Sun causes the damage? ....

b) How are human cells affected by this radiation?

....

Q2 Marie has **darker skin** than her friend, so she has slightly more protection from harmful radiation.

a) **How** does darker skin give this protection?

....

....

b) Suggest two ways you can **reduce** your exposure to harmful radiation from the Sun.

1. ....

2. ....

c) Marie uses a sun cream with '**SPF 25**' on the label. What does 'SPF 25' mean?

....

Q3 The **ozone layer** helps protect life on Earth.

a) Where is the ozone layer? ....

b) How does the ozone layer help protect life on Earth?

....

c) Name one group of pollutant gases which break up ozone molecules.

....

Q4 Scientists discovered a '**hole**' in the ozone layer over **Antarctica**.

a) How do scientists verify their findings?

....

....

b) Describe one way that the international community responded to the discovery of the 'hole'.

....

The Greenhouse Effect

Q1 The diagram below shows how the 'greenhouse effect' keeps the Earth warm. Use the descriptions **A** to **E** to label the diagram. The first one has been done for you.

A The Earth absorbs radiation from the Sun.

B The greenhouse gases emit some heat towards Earth.

C The greenhouse gases emit some heat radiation into space.

D The Earth emits heat radiation.

E Greenhouse gases absorb radiation from Earth.

A

Q2 Tick the boxes next to any **greenhouse gases** below.

nitrogen ☐ water vapour ☐ carbon dioxide ☐

oxygen ☐ methane ☐ helium ☐

Q3 Which of the statements below is the best description of the **greenhouse effect**? Circle A, B, C or D.

A Global warming caused by man's impact on the environment.

B A process which keeps the Earth warmer than it would otherwise be.

C A chemical reaction in the atmosphere which releases heat energy.

D The natural heating effect of the Sun.

Q4 Over the last 200 years or so the atmospheric concentration of some **greenhouse gasses**, like CO_2 and methane, has increased.

a) i) Give one natural source of atmospheric CO_2.

....

ii) Describe two ways in which humans have contributed to the increase in atmospheric CO_2.

....

....

b) List some natural and man-made sources of methane.

....

....

Global Warming and Climate Change

Q1 Complete the passage by choosing from the words below.

fallen clouds carbon pressures greenhouse
temperatures increased butterfly sulfur sea

Global .... have .... in recent years.
This is due to an increased .... effect caused by 'too much'
.... dioxide in the atmosphere.

Q2 Tick the boxes to show which statements are **descriptions of data** and which are possible **explanations of data**.

		Description of Data	Explanation of Data
a)	Global temperatures are steadily increasing.	☐	☐
b)	Carbon dioxide levels in the atmosphere are steadily increasing.	☐	☐
c)	The rise in atmospheric carbon dioxide concentration is causing a rise in global temperatures.	☐	☐
d)	There are more extreme weather events every year.	☐	☐
e)	The Earth's increasingly extreme weather is caused by global warming.	☐	☐

Q3 **Climate** means the **general long-term weather conditions** in a region. E.g. Ireland has a wet climate — it gets lots of rain throughout the year, and it's been like this for hundreds of years.

a) If Ireland's climate changed to become drier, suggest how this might affect farmers in Ireland.

....

....

b) Many scientists think that climate change will also involve more cases of **extreme weather**.

i) Give two examples of 'extreme weather' events.

....

ii) Central Africa has a generally very **dry** climate. Farmers rely on heavy rains during one part of the year to provide enough water for their crops and animals.

Suggest one way that climate change might affect people living here.

....

....

....

Top Tips: You need to know about the possible consequences of global warming and climate change. It's not just so you can pass exams — serious changes could happen in your lifetime.

Seismic Waves

Q1 Read the following sentences and underline the correct word from each highlighted pair.

Disturbances in the Earth produce **EM / seismic** waves, which can travel **through / along** the Earth.

These waves can be recorded on a seismograph, which draws a **seismologist / seismogram**.

Q2 Earthquakes can produce both **S-waves** and **P-waves**.

a) Which of these two types are **longitudinal** waves? ....

b) Which of these two types travels **faster**? ....

c) Which type of wave **cannot** travel through the **outer core** of the Earth? ....

Q3 Circle the letters next to any of these statements which are **true**.

A Both P- and S-waves can travel from the North Pole to the South Pole.

B A longitudinal wave travels in the same direction as the force which causes it.

C Transverse waves travel at right angles to the force which causes them.

D P-waves travel more slowly through the inner core.
This suggests that it is made of solid material.

Q4 Both P- and S-waves **curve** as they travel through the Earth.

a) Why do they curve?

....

b) P-waves can change direction abruptly as they travel through the Earth. Explain why this happens.

....

....

c) **i)** Which type of wave doesn't reach the opposite point of the Earth to the site of an earthquake?

....

ii) What does this tell seismologists about the structure of the Earth's interior?

....

Top Tips: No less significant than P- and S-waves is the Mexican Wave. This has been known to trigger earthquakes centred on large sports stadiums all over the world. The scientific consensus is that human behaviour is responsible and that the long term effects of the Mexican Wave are unknown.

Mixed Questions — Section 8

Q1 Waves A, B and C represent **infrared**, **visible light** and **ultraviolet** radiation (not in that order). They are all drawn to the same scale.

a) Which of the waves has the greatest amplitude? ....

b) Which of the waves represents UV radiation? ....

c) Describe one way in which human activities have caused an increase in our exposure to UV radiation from sunlight.

A

B

C

....

....

Q2 Jemima is using an **electric sander** which has a power rating of **360 W**.

a) The electricity supply in Jemima's house is at 230 V. Calculate the **current** the sander draws.

....

b) Jemima's electricity supplier charges **15.2p per kWh**. Jemima has the sander on for 45 minutes. How much does this cost (to the nearest penny)?

....

....

Q3 A pebble is dropped into still water. Waves move out across the surface of the water. The wavelength is **2 cm** and the waves are generated at a rate of **10 per second**.

a) What is the **wavelength** in metres?

....

b) What is the **frequency** of the wave in Hz?

....

c) What is the **speed** of the wave?

....

Q4 My landline telephone is connected to the telephone exchange by **optical fibres**.

a) What **type** of EM wave might be sent from the exchange? ....

b) Draw a labelled diagram to show how an optical fibre works.

Mixed Questions — Section 8

Q5 Infrared radiation is used by TV **remote controls**. Jake shows Peter that he can change the TV channel by pointing the remote control at a mirror on the opposite wall.

a) What property of EM rays has Jake demonstrated? Circle the correct answer.

reflection **refraction** **diffraction**

b) Draw a ray diagram below to show the path of the radiation emitted from the remote control to the TV.

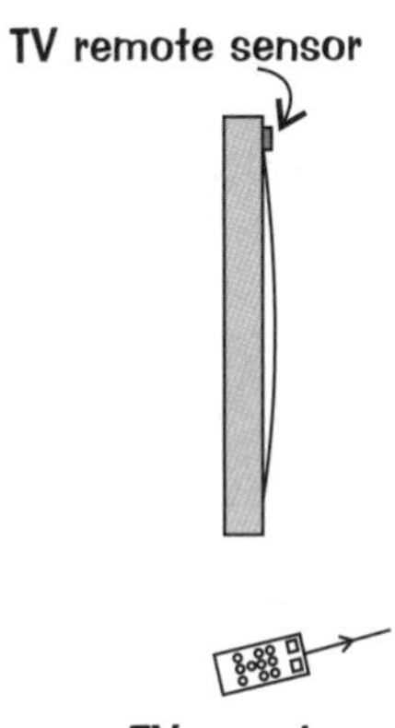

Q6 Radio Roary transmits **long-wave** signals with a wavelength of **1.5 km**.

a) Calculate the **frequency** of Radio Roary's transmission. (Use speed = 3×10^8 m/s.)

....

....

b) Mr Potts is on holiday in the Scottish Highlands. The cottage he's staying in has a TV and radio.

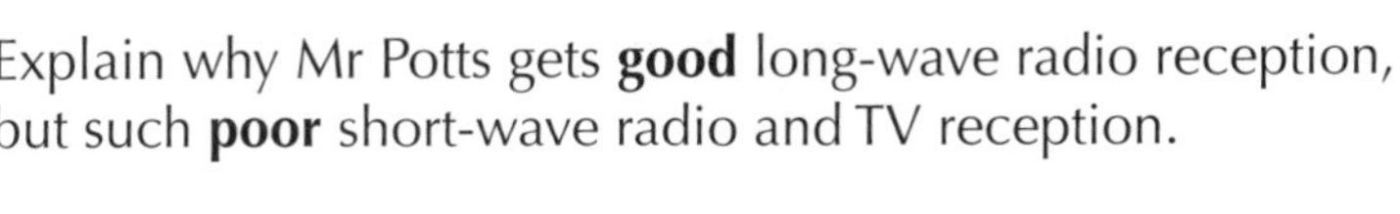

Mr Potts has a favourite show on a short-wave radio station, but finds that he can only get long-wave radio reception. TV reception is also very poor, so he can't watch his favourite cookery and gardening shows.

Explain why Mr Potts gets **good** long-wave radio reception, but such **poor** short-wave radio and TV reception.

....

....

c) Radio Roary broadcasts **analogue** signals, but Radio Piracy broadcasts **digital** signals.

Why might Radio Piracy have better sound quality than Radio Roary?

....

....

....

Galileo and Copernicus

Q1 Circle the correct word in the following sentences.

a) The planets all orbit the Earth in a **geocentric** / **heliocentric** model.

b) **Galileo** / **Copernicus** introduced a heliocentric model in 1543.

c) The Copernican model states that the planets all orbit the **Sun** / **Milky Way**.

d) The orbits of the planets in the Copernican model are all perfect **circles** / **ellipses**.

e) In the Copernican model the Sun is at the centre of the **Universe** / **Solar System**.

f) We now know that the planets actually have **circular** / **elliptical** orbits.

An egocentric model.

Q2 **Galileo** made some observations of **Jupiter** that helped to provide evidence for the **Copernican model** of the Solar System.

a) What technological advance helped Galileo to look at Jupiter?

....

b) Briefly describe what Galileo saw when making his observations of Jupiter and Venus.

....

....

....

....

c) Explain how Galileo's observations helped provide evidence for the Copernican model.

....

....

....

d) Why were Galileo's ideas controversial at the time?

....

....

Top Tips: For as long as humans have looked at the sky they've tried to find an explanation for how it all works — it takes a long time and technological advances for some ideas to change. Make sure you know what Copernicus' great idea was, and what Galileo saw that showed it might be right.

The Solar System

Q1 This diagram shows the major bodies in the Solar System. It **isn't to scale**.

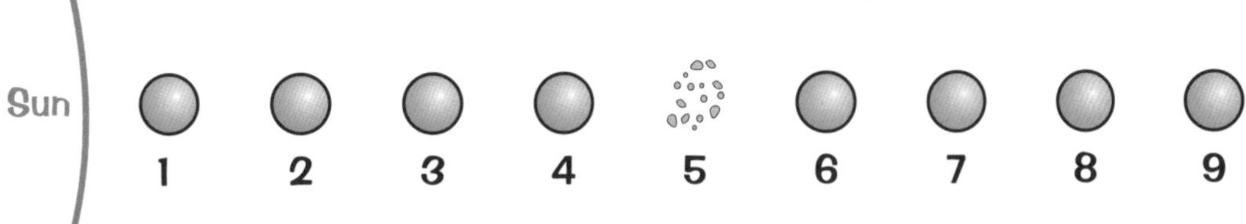

In the table below, write the correct number under each name to show its position in the Solar System.

Body	Mars	Jupiter	Asteroids	Venus	Saturn	Neptune	Earth	Mercury	Uranus
Number									

Q2 When Robert looks up into the night sky, he sees **stars** and **planets** (as long as it's a clear night).

Give three ways in which the planets that Robert sees are different from the stars he sees.

1. ....

2. ....

3. ....

Q3 As well as planets, there are **asteroids** and **comets** orbiting the Sun.

a) Why haven't the asteroids clumped together to form a single planet?

....

....

....

b) **i)** What are comets made of?

....

ii) What causes the comet to have a 'tail'?

....

....

Beyond the Solar System

Q1 Fill in the blanks in the sentences below using some of the words from the list.

asteroids comets Sun big galaxy halfway arms thousands millions galaxies stars

a) Our Sun is one of .... of .... of stars which form the Milky Way .... The Sun is about .... along one of the spiral .... of the Milky Way.

b) The distance between .... is usually millions of times more than the distance between ....

Q2 Some stars look **brighter** than others in the night sky.

Write down two factors that affect how bright a star looks to us from Earth?

1. ....

2. ....

Q3 The **light year** is a unit of distance.

a) If the speed of light in a vacuum is 3.0×10^8 m/s, show that 1 light year is approximately equal to 9.5×10^{15} m.

Start by working out the number of seconds in a year.

....

....

b) The most distant objects that the Hubble Space telescope has seen are about 13 billion light years away. Approximately how many metres are there in 13 billion light years?

....

Q4 The diagram shows two photographs of the same part of the night sky. The photographs were taken 6 months apart.

A B

5th January

A B

5th July

a) Two of the stars (labelled A and B) appear to have moved, while the rest have stayed in the same places. What does this tell us about stars A and B, and why?

....

....

b) Which of the two stars is closer to Earth — star A or star B? Give a reason for your answer.

....

Looking into Space

Q1 When observing the light from stars, astronomers often complain of **light pollution**.

What is light pollution and why is it a problem?

....

....

Q2 Telescopes have been developed that use EM radiation other than visible light.

a) Give two other types of electromagnetic radiation that can be detected by telescopes.

1. ....

2. ....

b) Give **one** example of something can be seen using electromagnetic waves outside the visible spectrum.

....

Q3 **Telescopes** are improving all the time.

a) How do we benefit from modern telescopes having improved magnification?

....

b) Advances in telescopes and computers mean we are now able to collect and analyse more data than ever before. Explain the impact of this on our understanding of the Universe.

....

....

....

Q4 When we look into space, we see things as they were in the **past**.

a) Explain why we are seeing stars as they were in the past.

....

b) SETI is an organisation that searches for extraterrestrial intelligence by looking for **radio signals** transmitted from other planets. Explain why aliens living **200 light-years** away would be unable to detect **us** yet using the same technique.

The world's first radio station began broadcasting in 1897.

....

....

The Life Cycle of Stars

Q1 A star in its **stable** phase **doesn't get bigger or smaller**, even though there are forces tending to make it expand and forces trying to make it contract.

a) What causes the outward pressure on the star?

....

b) What is the force pulling the star inwards? ....

c) Why doesn't the star expand or contract?

....

d) What is another name for a star in its stable phase? ....

Q2 Stars are formed from clouds of dust and gas called **nebulas**.

a) **Why** does the material come together?

....

b) Where does the **heat and light energy** emitted by a star come from?

....

Marilyn was nearing the end of her stable phase

Q3 Old stars eventually turn into **red giants**.

a) What causes a star to become a red giant? ....

....

b) Why is a red giant red? ....

....

Q4 Complete the passage below to describe what eventually happens to red giants.

A star with a similar mass to the Sun will eject gas and dust as a

..., leaving a dense core called a ....

A bigger star will explode as a ...., leaving a very dense core called

a .... The biggest stars will form a

... instead.

Due to printing restrictions, red giants are currently unavailable.

The Life of the Universe

Q1 Francesca is standing by a busy street when an ambulance rushes past, with its sirens blaring.

a) As the ambulance moves away, how will the siren sound different to Francesca? Underline the correct answer.

It will sound higher pitched　　　　It will sound lower pitched

b) What is the name of this effect?

....

c) As the ambulance moves away, what happens to the wavelength of the sound waves heard by Francesca?

....

d) How would the frequency of the sound wave Francesca heard have changed as the ambulance approached her?

....

Q2 Brian set up a microphone at his local railway station to record his favourite **train noises**. He attached the microphone to an oscilloscope.

An express train passed through the station at a constant speed. Diagram A below shows the trace on the monitor at 11:31:07, as the train **approached** Brian's microphone.

On diagram B, sketch the trace Brian might have seen as the train **left** the station.

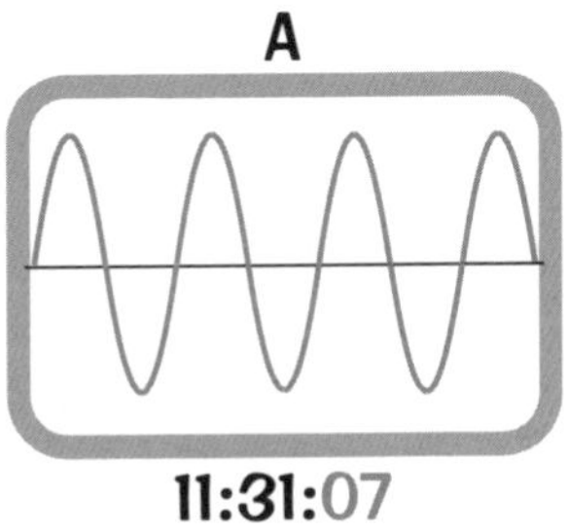

A

11:31:07

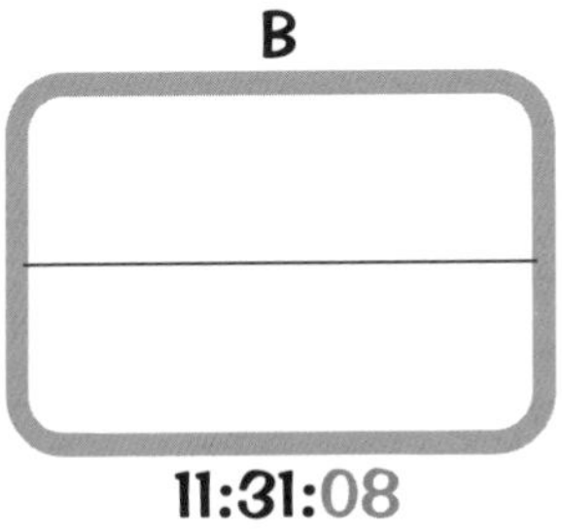

B

11:31:08

Q3 What evidence is there to support the idea that the Universe is expanding? Include a brief explanation of **red-shift** in your answer.

....

....

....

....

The Life of the Universe

Q4 Many cosmologists believe that the Universe began with a **Big Bang**.

a) Briefly describe the Big Bang theory.

....

....

....

....

b) According to the Big Bang theory, what is happening to space itself?

....

Q5 The Big Bang theory is currently the only theory that can explain the existence of **cosmic microwave background radiation** (CMBR).

a) What is cosmic microwave background radiation?

....

....

b) How does the Big Bang theory explain CMBR?

....

....

....

Q6 The Big Bang theory can't explain everything about the Universe. Describe **one** limitation of the Big Bang theory.

....

....

....

Top Tips: Crikey, the question of how the Universe started is a pretty big question. Make sure you know all about the Big Bang theory and the evidence that supports it. It's interesting stuff, I reckon.

Mixed Questions — Section 9

Q1 The Sun consists mainly of **hydrogen**. It also contains **helium**.

a) In a few million years time, the Sun will contain **more helium** and **less hydrogen** than it does now. Explain why.

....

....

b) It takes about 500 seconds for light from the Sun to reach us. If light travels at 300 000 km/s, how far away is the Sun?

....

Q2 **Astronomers** watch the night sky to find out about **stars** and **galaxies**.

a) How can **parallax** be used to determine the distance to nearby stars?

....

....

The diagram shows a **light wave** from Cygnus A — a galaxy 700 million light years from Earth.

b) On the diagram, redraw the wave to show how it might appear to us on Earth because the light is **red-shifted**.

c) Explain how red-shifts from distant and nearer galaxies provide evidence for the Big Bang theory.

....

....

....

Q3 Describe the main features of the **Solar System**. Include a **sketch** of the Solar System in your answer.

....

....

....

....

....

....

Section 1 — Nerves and Hormones

Section 1 — Nerves and Hormones

Pages 1-2 — The Nervous System

Q1 E.g. so they can react/respond to the changes and avoid danger.

Q2 Light receptor cells contain a nucleus, cytoplasm and a cell membrane.

Q3 hearing

Q4 a) Chemical receptor. **Tongue** underlined.
b) Chemical receptor. **Nose** underlined.
c) Sound receptor. **Ears** underlined.
d) Pain receptor. **Skin** underlined.

Q5 a) central nervous system
b) brain and spinal cord
c) neurone/nerve cell

Q6 The information from the receptors in the toe can't complete its normal path through the spinal cord to the brain.

Q7 a) i) fingertip
ii) sole of foot
b) The fingertip. This was the most sensitive part of the body to pressure, so it is likely to contain the most receptors.
c) John and Marc might have been applying different pressures, so any differences the pupils noticed might not have been only due to the number of receptors / John and Marc are different, introducing an extra variable so it was not a fair test.
d) Test each pupil a number of times and find the average. Even better, sometimes prod the pupils with one point and at other times with two. Ask them how many points they feel each time.

Page 3 — Synapses and Reflexes

Q1 a) protect
b) without

Q2 E.g. a reflex reaction happens without you having to take time to think about it.

Q3 a) i) sensory neurone
ii) relay neurone
iii) motor neurone
b) i) electrically
ii) chemically
c) i) effector
ii) It contracts (to pull the finger away).
d) i) synapses
ii) The signal is transferred across the gap by chemicals, which are released when the impulse arrives at one side of the gap. The chemicals diffuse across the gap and trigger a new impulse in the neurone on the other side of the gap.

Page 4 — Hormones

Q1 chemical, glands, blood, target

Q2 a) blood
b) oestrogen
c) FSH
d) glands
e) LH

Q3 Hormones use a chemical signal and nerves use an electrical signal. Responses that are due to hormones happen more slowly and last longer than those that are due to the nervous system. Nerves act on a very precise area, while hormones travel all over the body and can affect more than one area at once.

Q4 a) nervous system
b) hormonal system
c) nervous system
d) nervous system
e) hormonal system

Page 5 — The Menstrual Cycle

Q1 FSH — pituitary gland
oestrogen — ovaries
LH — pituitary gland

Q2 a) 1. Causes an egg to mature in an ovary.
2. Stimulates the ovaries to produce oestrogen.
b) Oestrogen inhibits the production of FSH.
c) It stimulates the release of an egg from the ovary.

Q3 a) & b)

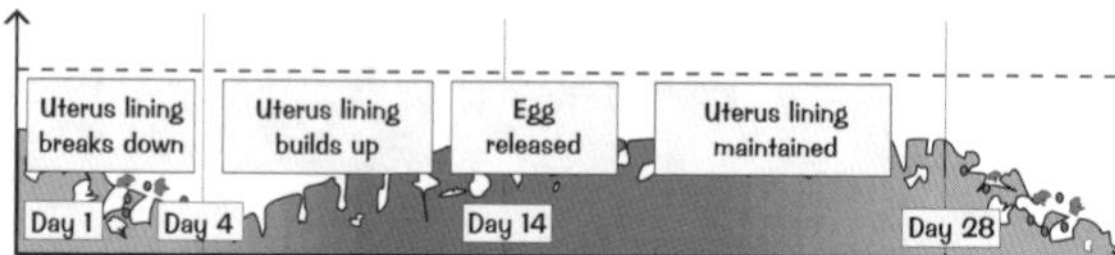

Page 6 — Controlling Fertility

Q1 a) FSH, LH
b) They stimulate egg release in the woman's ovaries.

Q2 a) E.g. it's over 99% effective at preventing pregnancy.
It reduces the risk of getting some types of cancer.
b) Oestrogen is taken every day to give high levels of oestrogen in the blood. This inhibits the release of FSH by the pituitary gland. Eventually egg development in the ovaries stops so that none are released during the menstrual cycle.
c) Because it has fewer side effects.

Q3 a) FSH and LH are given to the woman to increase the number of eggs that develop. The eggs are collected from her ovaries and fertilised outside the body. They're then allowed to develop into embryos. Once the embryos are tiny balls of cells, one or two are then placed back inside the uterus/womb to improve the chance of pregnancy.
b) **Advantages** — It allows infertile couples to have children. It allows screening of embryos for genetic defects.
Disadvantages — There can be reactions to the hormones, e.g. vomiting, dehydration, abdominal pain. There may be an increased risk of some types of cancer. The process can be expensive, and there's no guarantee that it will work.
It may result in multiple births, which can be risky.

Page 7 — Plant Hormones

Q1 a) auxins
b) at the tips of the shoots and roots
c) i) In the shoot, auxin moves towards the lower side of the shoot where it stimulates growth — so the shoot bends upwards, against gravity. The shoot is negatively geotropic.
ii) In the root, auxin moves to the lower side of the root, where it inhibits growth, making the root grow downwards, in the same direction as gravity.
The root is positively geotropic.

Q2 Seedling A: the foil prevents any light reaching the tip, so the auxin is evenly distributed in the tip and no bending occurs.
Seedling C: the mica strip prevents the auxin from moving to the side that's in the shade, so there is even distribution of auxin and no bending occurs.

Section 2 — Diet and Health

Page 8 — Commercial Use of Plant Hormones

Q1 E.g. as selective weedkillers / growing cuttings with rooting powder / controlling the ripening of fruit / controlling dormancy.

Q2 a) E.g. unripe fruit is firmer, so it's less easily damaged during picking and transport.

b) i) E.g. they can be sprayed with a ripening hormone.

ii) During transport to the market.

Q3 a) A period during which seeds will not germinate until they've been through certain conditions.

b) E.g. it would ensure that all the seeds would germinate at the same time. It means that seeds can be made to germinate at times of the year when they wouldn't normally.

Page 9 — Homeostasis

Q1 a) The maintenance of a constant internal environment in the body.

b) They need steady conditions in order to function properly.

c) The nervous communication system

Q2 Negative feedback is a mechanism that keeps the internal environment constant by producing a response that counteracts any change away from the desired level.

Q3 a) opposite, reverses

b)

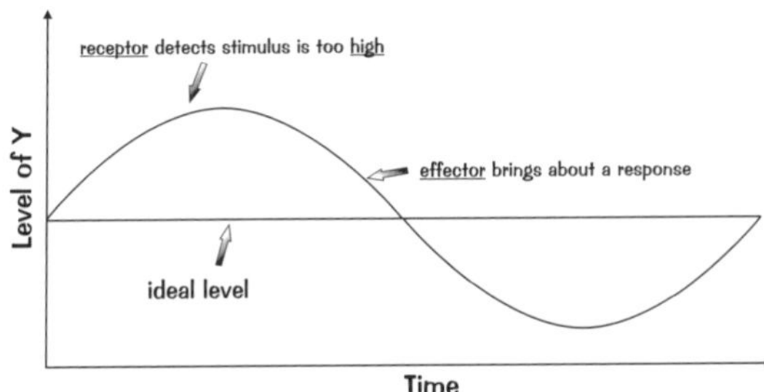

c) the processing centre

Page 10 — Controlling Ions, Temperature and Blood Sugar

Q1 a) the brain / the thermoregulatory centre

b) 37 °C is the optimum temperature for enzymes controlling reactions in the human body. The enzymes don't work as well if the temperature varies too much from the optimum.

Q2 a) When sweat evaporates it uses heat from your skin. This transfers heat from your skin to the environment, cooling you down.

b) i) Vasodilation is the widening of blood vessels. Vasoconstriction is the constriction of the blood vessels.

ii) Vasodilation and vasoconstriction allow the body to control the blood flow near the surface of the skin. This allows the body to lose or retain heat in response to the environmental temperature.

Q3 a) The person might have done some exercise. / The person might not have eaten for a long time.

b) E.g. eating foods that are rich in simple carbohydrates, i.e. sugars.

c) To provide the body's cells with a constant supply of energy.

Page 11 — Controlling Water Content

Q1 hot, sweat a lot, less, dark, less, concentrated.

Q2 More water. The exercise will make him breathe harder, so more water will be lost via the lungs.

Q3 a) a hormone

b)

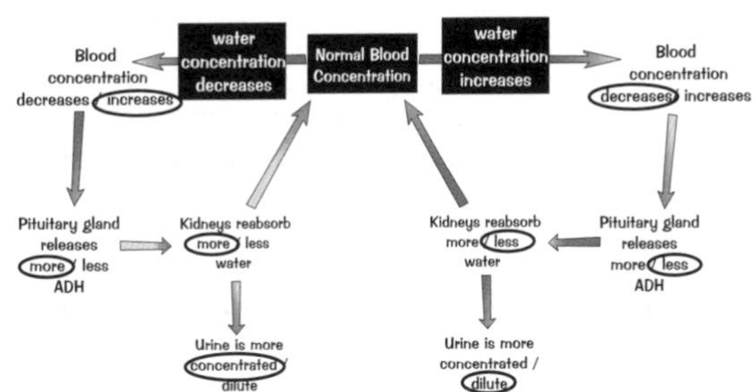

Pages 12-13 — Mixed Questions — Section 1

Q1 a) The sense organs are the ears, and they contain sound and balance receptors.

b) Sensory neurones carry impulses from receptors to the CNS. Motor neurones carry impulses from the CNS to the effectors (muscles and glands).

c) i) E.g. through the skin as sweat, via the lungs in breath, via the kidneys as urine.

ii) If the air is hotter then more water will be lost through sweat so less urine will be produced.

Q2 a) 30 days

b) An egg is released / ovulation.

c) Any from: FSH / LH / progesterone.

d) Oestrogen inhibits the production of FSH, which stops egg development and production.

Q3 The following should be ticked:
Ronald loses salt in his sweat.
Ronald's kidneys remove salt from his blood.
Ronald gets rid of salt in his urine.

Q4 a) In the blood.

b) slow response, response lasts for a long time

c) i) at the tips of shoots, at the tips of roots

ii) In shoots, auxin makes the cells grow faster. In the roots, auxin slows cell growth.

iii) e.g. weedkiller

Section 2 — Diet and Health

Pages 14-15 — Diet and Metabolic Rate

Q1 A diet containing the right balance of different foods and the right amount of energy.

Q2 a) Protein is needed for **growth** and **cell repair/replacement** (in either order).

b) Carbohydrates provide much of your **energy**.

c) Fats are needed to **keep warm** and for **energy** (in either order). Other answers are possible.

d) Vitamins and minerals are needed in **tiny/small** amounts to stay healthy.

Q3 a) The speed at which all the chemical reactions that take place in your body happen.

b) proportion of muscle to fat in the body, inherited factors, amount of exercise

Q4 Wendy needs more carbohydrate and protein in her diet because she is more physically active. She needs more protein for muscle development and more carbohydrate for energy.

Section 2 — Diet and Health

Q5 a) The average man is bigger than the average woman and so needs more energy for metabolic reactions and movement. The average man also has more muscle, which needs more energy than fatty tissue.
b) Cyclists riding in the Tour de France are doing a lot of exercise every day, and active people need more energy. They may also be more muscular than the average man.
Q6 a) Egg
b) In 50 g of bread there are (50 ÷ 100) × 60 = 30 g carbs. In 50 g of milk there are (50 ÷ 100) × 10 = 5 g carbs. 30 – 5 = **25 g more carbohydrate in the bread**.
c) Any fruit or vegetable. This would provide vitamins, minerals and fibre.

Page 16 — Factors Affecting Health

Q1 a) They have an unbalanced diet.
b) A disease caused by a lack of vitamins or minerals.
Q2 You will be 'fit' if you take regular exercise, but if your diet isn't balanced or you're lacking in a certain nutrient, you will be malnourished.
Q3 a) (16 ÷ 50) × 100 = **32%**.
b) E.g. bad diet, overeating and not enough exercise.
c) Heart disease, cancers and type 2 diabetes should be underlined.
Q4 a) E.g. exercise increases the amount of energy used by the body and decreases the amount stored as fat. So people who exercise are less likely to suffer from health problems like obesity.
b) E.g. inherited factors can affect a person's metabolic rate or cholesterol level.

Page 17 — Evaluating Food, Lifestyle and Diet

Q1 less, use, less, increases
Q2 Report B is likely to be more reliable as it was published in a reputable journal, probably conducted by an independent researcher, and used a large sample size.
Q3 a) Burger B is the most unhealthy because it contains a higher proportion of fat (including saturated fat) and carbohydrate than Burger A, and has a higher energy content.
b) Sharon's lifestyle could increase her risk of obesity. This is because she's taking in a lot of energy by eating Burger B regularly, but not using much energy because she doesn't exercise.

Page 18 — The Circulatory System

Q1 vessels, arteries, veins, nutrients/oxygen, oxygen/nutrients, carbon dioxide
Q2 a) The right side of the heart pumps blood to the lungs and the left side pumps blood elsewhere in the body.
b) i) muscle cells
ii) They need a supply of food and oxygen to keep the heart beating continually.
Q3 a) A = Artery, B = Vein, C = Capillary
b) i) Arteries carry blood away from the heart at high pressure so they need to be strong and elastic to withstand this pressure.
ii) Capillaries exchange substances with the body cells via diffusion. Walls that are one cell thick increase the rate of diffusion by decreasing the distance over which it happens.
iii) Veins carry blood back to the heart at low pressure. Valves prevent the blood flowing back in the wrong direction.

Page 19 — Heart Rate and Blood Pressure

Q1 artery, two, higher, relaxes
Q2 The pulsation of an artery is caused by blood being pumped through it by a heart beat, so you can measure your pulse rate to work out your heart rate.
Q3 a) three
b) Because individuals vary.
c) Nigel
d) If a fatty deposit breaks through the lining of the artery a blood clot may form around it and block the artery completely. If an artery that supplies blood to the heart becomes completely blocked, an area of the heart muscle won't receive any oxygen — which would cause a heart attack.

Page 20 — Factors Affecting Heart Disease

Q1 a) Lifestyle
b) Lifestyle
c) Non-lifestyle
d) Lifestyle
e) Lifestyle
Q2 Regular
Q3 People in non-industrialised countries eat less junk food and so have a lower fat diet. Poorer people in non-industrialised countries will have to walk more because they cannot afford cars and so they get more exercise.
Q4 a) Studies that look at the patterns of disease and the factors that affect them.
b) E.g. You could study a group of people who all died from heart disease to look for similarities in their lifestyle that may be linked to heart disease.

Page 21 — Drugs

Q1 a) A chemical that interferes with reactions in your body.
b) i) Your body can't function normally without the drug, leading to cravings and withdrawal symptoms if the drug is not taken.
ii) E.g. heroin
c) To lower the risk of heart and circulatory disease.
Q2 a) E.g. to increase their heart rate.
b) E.g. the athlete may not be fully informed of the serious risks of stimulants. It makes sporting competitions unfair if an athlete gains an advantage by taking stimulants and not just through hard training.
Q3 Some studies have shown a link, but others have not. Results can often be interpreted in different ways, depending on what the researcher wants to show (and who's funding the study).
Q4 a) As a control group.
b) Statins combined with lifestyle changes helps to reduce cholesterol levels more than just lifestyle changes alone.

Page 22 — Testing Medicinal Drugs

Q1 1. Drug is tested on human cells and tissues
2. Drug is tested on live animals
3. Human volunteers are used to test the drug
Q2 a) To check whether the drugs have any unknown side effects, and to find the optimum dose of each drug.
b) To make sure the drug has no harmful side effects when the body is working normally.
Q3 a) For use as a sleeping pill.
b) It relieved morning sickness, but it also crossed the placenta and stunted the growth of the fetus's limbs.
c) e.g. leprosy

Section 2 — Diet and Health

Q4 a) A placebo is a substance that's like a drug being tested but contains no drug.

b) They use a placebo to make sure it is the actual drug which is causing any effects. Some patients will have beneficial effects just because they *think* they are receiving medicine.

c) A double-blind trial is one where neither the scientist doing the test nor the patient knows whether they are getting a drug or a placebo.

Page 23 — Recreational Drugs

Q1 Liver disease, unconsciousness and addiction should be underlined.

Q2 a) Any two from: e.g. for enjoyment / relaxation/stress relief / inspiration.

b) E.g. they can cause problems with the heart / circulatory system.

Q3 a) Stepping stone — using cannabis makes people want to try harder drugs.

b) Gateway drug — people who use cannabis will have access to drug dealers and so will find it easier to try harder drugs.

c) Genetics — some people are just more likely to use drugs, so people that use cannabis are more likely to use all kinds of drugs.

Q4 a) Because so many more people take them.

b) Any two from: The NHS spends large amounts each year on treating patients with smoking- or drinking-related problems. / The cost to businesses of people missing work due to smoking- or drinking-related problems. / The cost of cleaning up the streets, police time, damage to people and property, etc.

Pages 24-25 — Fighting Disease

Q1 A microorganism that causes infectious disease.

Q2 A molecule that causes an immune response.

Q3 a) true

b) false

c) false

d) false

e) true

Q4 small, damaging, toxins, poisons, cells, replicate, damage

Q5 a) Blood clots are used to quickly seal the skin if it's damaged and keep microorganisms out.

b) The air passages are lined with mucus and cilia to trap and remove the bacteria before they reach the lungs.

Q6 a) No — a different antibody is needed to recognise each different species of microorganism.

b) White blood cells can engulf and digest microbes. They produce antitoxins to neutralise any toxins they produce.

Q7 Some white blood cells stay around in the blood after the original chickenpox infection has been fought off — these are called memory cells. When you're infected with chickenpox again, your memory cells will rapidly produce the antibodies to kill it. So you're naturally immune to chickenpox and won't get ill.

Page 26 — Fighting Disease — Vaccination

Q1 causing damage, will

Q2 a) i) true

ii) true

iii) false

iv) true

b) Dead and inactive microorganisms are harmless but the body will still produce antibodies to attack them.

Q3 Any two of, e.g. Some people do not become immune after vaccination. / Others can experience a bad reaction, e.g. swelling at the injection site. / In rare cases there could even be a serious reaction such as seizures.

Q4 John is protected from infection because his white blood cells can make antibodies to the bacteria a lot quicker than James's can. When John was vaccinated, he was given some inactive tuberculosis (TB) pathogens. These had antigens on the surface. John's white blood cells then learnt to make the antibodies specific to these antigens.

Page 27 — Fighting Disease — Drugs

Q1 a) The medicine doesn't kill the virus causing the cold — it just relieves the symptoms.

b) Colds are caused by a virus and antibiotics only kill bacteria.

c) Because viruses reproduce using your own body cells, which makes it very difficult to develop drugs that destroy just the virus without killing the body's cells.

d) Different antibiotics kill different types of bacteria, so a patient needs to be treated with the right antibiotic for it to have an effect.

Q2 a) 2. So if you have an infection, some of the bacteria might be resistant to antibiotics.
3. When you treat the infection, only the non-resistant strains of bacteria will be killed.
4. The individual resistant bacteria will survive and reproduce.
5. The population of the resistant strain of bacteria will increase.

b) E.g. MRSA

Q3 a) E.g. to prevent microorganisms getting in from the air.

b) The flame kills any microorganisms already on the loop.

Page 28 — Fighting Disease — Past and Future

Q1 a) Semmelweis asked all the doctors to wash their hands using antiseptic solution when entering his ward. This killed bacteria on their hands and stopped them from spreading infections to their next patients.

b) Doctors at this time didn't know about bacteria, so they couldn't see any clear reason to stick to Semmelweis's method.

Q2 a) The number of deaths has fallen dramatically.

b) i) E.g. by overusing antibiotics.

ii) They're working on developing new antibiotics that are effective against resistant strains.

Q3 a) The new strain could be resistant to antibiotics, so current treatments would no longer clear an infection. It could be a new strain that we've not encountered before, so no-one would be immune to it.

b) A big outbreak of disease.

c) Vaccines use dead or inactive microorganisms to stimulate an immune response and prepare the body for future infection. If the microorganism then evolves and changes, the immune system won't recognise it any more and won't be prepared for an infection.

Pages 29-30 — Mixed Questions — Section 2

Q1 valves in veins — keep blood flowing in the right direction
permeable walls of capillaries — allow substances to diffuse in and out of the blood
thick, elastic walls of arteries — withstand the high pressure of blood leaving the heart

Section 3 — Genetics, Evolution and the Environment

Q2 a) E.g. to increase muscle size
b) E.g. high blood pressure
Q3 a) The bacteria have been killed by the antibiotic.
b) i) Antibiotic 3.
ii) No, because flu and colds are caused by viruses but antibiotics don't kill viruses.
Q4 a) Vitamins
b) Overeating
c) higher
d) more
e) energy
Q5 a) measles, mumps and rubella
b) E.g. the risk of catching the diseases decreases if more children are vaccinated.
Q6 Heroin is an example of an addictive, illegal drug. Some studies have found a link between cannabis use and mental health problems.
Q7 a) They recognise the antigens on the surface of the pathogen.
b) Yes, because antibodies are always specific so they won't be effective against the new cold pathogen.

Section 3 — Genetics, Evolution and the Environment

Page 31 — Genes, Chromosomes and DNA

Q1 organism, cell, nucleus, chromosome, gene
Q2 a) True
b) True
c) False
d) False
e) True
Q3 a) E.g. collagen
b) E.g. enzymes
Q4 An organism's genotype is all of the genes it has. Its phenotype is the characteristics that it displays.

Page 32 — Reproduction

Q1 a) two
b) gametes
c) identical
d) half as many
e) Sexual
Q2 a) clones
b) sperm
c) fertilisation
Q3 a) The new skin cells came from the existing skin cells around the cut dividing to give new cells.
b) Asexual reproduction produces cells with identical genes to the parent cells.
c) It took time for the cells to divide enough times to cover the cut completely.
Q4 Sexual reproduction involves the production of gametes by each parent. Each gamete has half the normal number of chromosomes. The gametes fuse together and a baby with a full set of chromosomes is produced.

Page 33 — Genetic Diagrams

Q1 a)

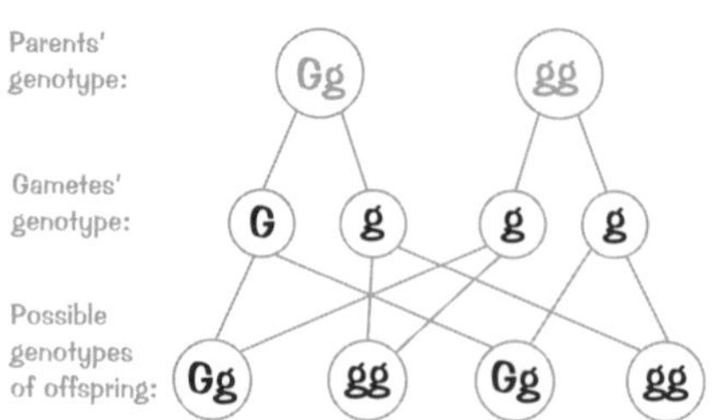

b) 1 : 1 (half grey, half white)
c) 6 grey mice, 6 white mice.
Q2 a)

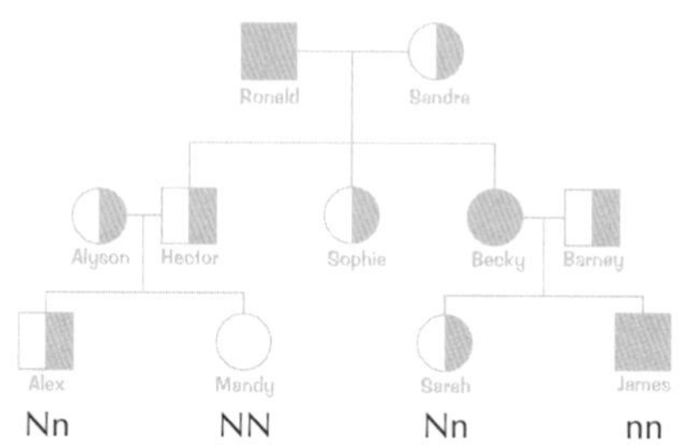

Nn NN Nn nn

b) 25%
c) No. The previous children's type of vision will have no effect on future children.

Page 34 — Genetic Diagrams and Sex Chromosomes

Q1 a)

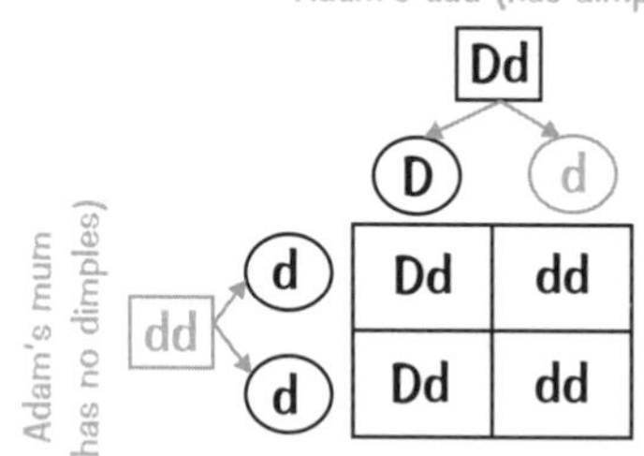

b) 50%
Q2 sex, X, Y, males
Q3 a) The protein causes the development of testes in an embryo. The testes then produce male sex hormones, which bring about development of the male reproductive system. Without the protein, an embryo develops ovaries and the rest of the female reproductive system.
b) On the Y chromosome.

Page 35 — Genetic Disorders

Q1 a) dominant
b) The symptoms don't usually appear until after the age of 40, so many people have had children and even grandchildren before they know they have the disease.
c) Any three from: tremors/shaking, clumsiness, memory loss, mood changes, poor concentration.
Q2 a) This is possible if a person is heterozygous for the recessive allele. You need two copies of the recessive allele to show the symptoms of cystic fibrosis.

Section 3 — Genetics, Evolution and the Environment

b) Any three from: thick sticky mucus, breathing difficulty, chest infections, difficulty in digesting food.

c)

	Carrier	Sufferer
Libby	50%	25%
Anne	50%	0%

Page 36 — Cloning

Q1 Parent plant → Cuttings are taken, each with a new bud on → The cuttings are kept in moist conditions until they are ready to plant → Cloned plant

Q2 removing and discarding a nucleus = **A**
implantation in a surrogate mother = **D**
useful nucleus extracted = **B**
formation of a diploid cell = **C**

Q3 E.g. cloning quickly gets you lots of ideal offspring. But you also get a population with a reduced gene pool — so if a new disease appears, they could all be wiped out. The study of animal clones could improve our understanding of the development of the embryo / of ageing and age-related disorders. Cloning could also be used to help preserve endangered species. However, it's possible that cloned animals might not be as healthy as normal ones. Some people worry that humans might be cloned in the future and any success may follow many unsuccessful attempts, e.g. children born severely disabled.

Page 37 — Genetic Engineering

Q1 a) 1. The gene for the characteristic is selected.
2. The gene is cut from one organism's chromosome using enzymes.
3. Enzymes are used to cut another organism's chromosome.
4. The gene is inserted into the organism's chromosome.

b) E.g. bacteria can be genetically engineered to produce human insulin.

Q2 a) early, fertilisation

b) i) E.g. GM crops can increase the yield of a crop, making more food. / People living in developing nations often lack nutrients in their diets. GM crops could be engineered to contain the nutrient that's missing.

ii) Any two from: e.g. growing GM crops might affect the number of weeds and flowers (and so the population of insects) that live in and around the crops — reducing farmland biodiversity. / Not everyone is convinced GM crops are safe. People are worried they may develop allergies to GM foods. / Transplanted genes may get out into the natural environment.

c) E.g. sheep have been genetically engineered to produce substances, like drugs, in their milk that can be used to treat human diseases. / Scientists are trying to treat genetic disorders like cystic fibrosis by inserting working genes into sufferers. This is called gene therapy. / People living in developing nations often lack nutrients in their diets. GM crops could be engineered to contain the nutrient that's missing.

Pages 38-39 — Adaptations

Q1 a) The kangaroo rat.

b) The polar bear.

c) The polar bear has a rounded body shape, which means it has a small surface area for its volume.

d) Less heat.

e) The kangaroo rat has a large surface area compared to its volume. This helps it to lose more body heat and stops it overheating.

Q2 a) In the desert.

b) i) The cactus has spines instead of leaves, because the small surface area gives less of a surface for water to evaporate from. / The spines help to protect the cactus from being eaten by animals.

ii) The cactus has a thick, fleshy stem where it can store water. / The stem can photosynthesise.

iii) The cactus has shallow but very extensive roots, so it can take in as much water as possible when it rains.

Q3 extremophiles, temperature, pressure (or pressure, temperature)

Q4 a) i) white fur

ii) It provides camouflage (white colour makes it hard to spot against a snowy background).

b) It is a warning colour to scare off predators.

c) E.g. thorns on roses / sharp spines on cacti / the shell of a tortoise / poison in bees / poison in poison ivy.

Q5 a) Reading down the table: 1.5 : 1, 1 : 1, 0.75 : 1, 0.6 : 1.

b) The surface area : volume ratio decreases as the size of the cube increases.

c) The small cube, because it has a small volume where it can hold heat but a relatively large surface over which it can lose it.

d) A mouse is small so it would lose heat quickly. Fur provides a layer of insulation to minimise heat loss.

Page 40 — Variation

Q1 have differences, genes, gametes, Identical twins, hair style, environment, variation

Q2 a) No. Identical twins have exactly the same genes. Features like hair colour are controlled by genes, so you would expect the girls to have the same hair colour.

b) The difference in weight must be due to environment (e.g. eating more or exercising less), because the twins have exactly the same genes.

c) I don't think that birthmarks are caused by genes. Identical twins have exactly the same genes, so if Stephanie had a birthmark then Helen should too if it was genetic.

Q3 a) Sexual reproduction gives new combinations of genes, so the foal might not be genetically suited to racing. / Organisms are affected by their environment as well as their genes.

b) Genes.

Pages 41-42 — Evolution

Q1

	Plant	Animal
Travels to new places		X
Makes its own food	X	
Is fixed to the ground	X	
May be single celled		

Q2 a) Rays and Sharks

b) E.g. they could be in competition.

Q3 There is variation within species caused by differences in their genes
The best adapted animals and plants are most likely to survive.
Some characteristics are passed on through reproduction from parent to offspring.

Section 3 — Genetics, Evolution and the Environment

Q4 1. Ancestors to the buff tip moth showed variation in their appearance. Some had genes that made them look a bit like a stick.
2. Short-sighted birds in poor light didn't spot the stick-like moths.
3. So the stick-like moths were more likely to survive and reproduce.
4. Genes that made the moths look like sticks were more likely to be passed on to the next generation.

Q5 a) E.g. longer legs would help when running away from predators. B has a hoof rather than toes. This makes it more stable when running. The environment may have changed from rocky slopes or swamps (where toes would help with balance) to flat plains (where balance is less important).

b)

A
C
B
D
Modern horse

Q6 A small number of the original bacteria were naturally resistant to the antibiotic. These bacteria survived the antibiotic and reproduced to form the second plaque. All the bacteria in the second plaque inherited the antibiotic resistance.

Page 43 — More About Evolution

Q1 A, E

Q2 Lamarck, more developed, longer, the next generation

Q3 People with dyed blue hair do not have children with blue hair.
Sheep whose tails are cut short give birth to lambs with full-length tails.

Q4 Any two from, e.g. because they have different beliefs / because they have been influenced by different people / because they think differently.

Page 44 — Competition and Environmental Change

Q1 a) Light — Plants
Minerals from the soil — Plants
Space — Plants and Animals
Water — Plants and Animals
Food — Animals
Mates — Animals

b) The two species would have to compete for it.

c) E.g. as a source of food.

Q2 a) Any two from: the temperature of the water increased, the amount of light increased, the amount of nutrients increased, etc.

b) The number of fish in the pond increased rapidly in May (also accept April). Even though the water is warm at this time and there is a lot of light, the number of algae suddenly decreases, so this must be because they are being eaten by fish.

c) Any two from: e.g. a change in the occurrence of infectious diseases. / A change in the availability of food sources. / A change in the number or types of competitors.

Page 45 — Measuring Environmental Change

Q1 a) An indicator species.

b) E.g. collect samples of the same size / in the same way / at the same time of day.

c) Mayfly larvae prefer clean water and sludgeworms prefer water that contains sewage.

d) E.g. sewage is full of bacteria, which use up a lot of oxygen. Animals like mayfly larvae might not have enough oxygen to survive.

e) E.g. using a dissolved oxygen meter to measure the oxygen concentration.

Q2 a) Site 1

b) Advantage: E.g. they allow reliable numerical data to be collected / exact pollutants to be identified.
Disadvantage: E.g. more expensive than living methods

c) i) Lichens

ii) E.g. they aren't always reliable methods for measuring pollution, as factors other than pollution can affect them.

Pages 46-47 — Pyramids of Biomass and Number

Q1 a) algae

b) winkle

c) algae/producers

Q2 a) C

b) The total mass of the organisms decreases at each trophic level as shown by this pyramid.

c) Their energy initially comes from the Sun.

Q3 a) The levels of DDT increase dramatically as you go up the trophic levels.

b) i) 13.8 ÷ 0.04 = **345**

ii) 2.8 ÷ 0.04 = **70**

c) DDT is stored in the tissues of animals and a pyramid of biomass represents the mass of the living tissues.

Q4 a)

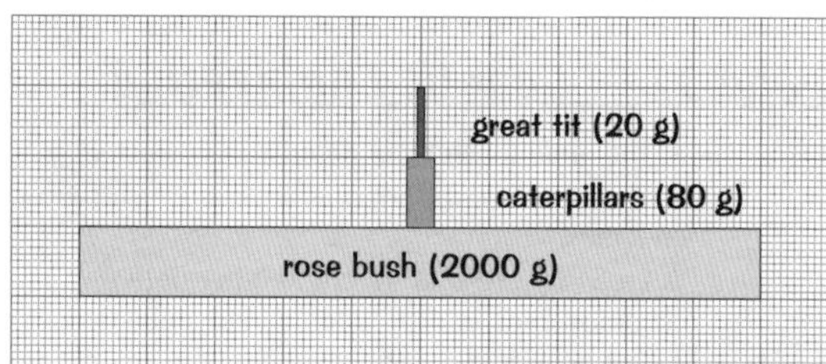

b)

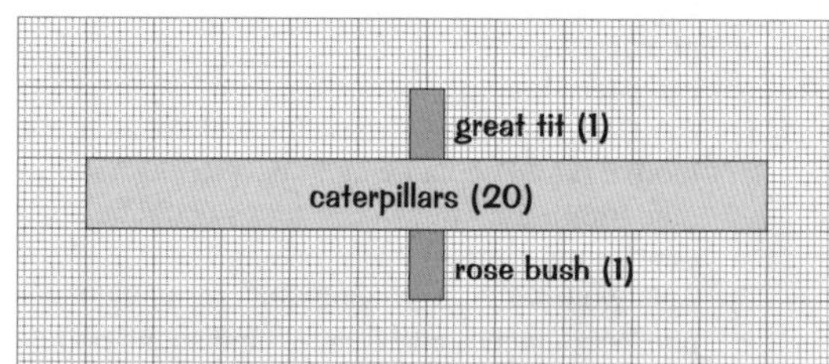

c) The caterpillars bar in the pyramid of numbers is longer than the rose bush because one rosebush can feed lots of caterpillars. But the biomass of the rosebush is much bigger than the biomass of the caterpillars.

Pages 48-49 — Energy Transfer and Decay

Q1 a) true

b) true

c) true

d) true

e) false

f) false

Q2 Any three from:
Decomposers — Adding more decomposers will speed up decay.
Shredded waste — Shredding the waste gives more surface area for the microorganisms to work on.
Base in contact with soil — More microorganisms will have access to the contents of the compost bin.
Mesh sides — These allow contact with the air, so plenty of oxygen is available to help the microorganisms work faster.
Open top — This allows contact with the air, so plenty of oxygen is available to help the microorganisms work faster.

Q3 a) energy
b) plants, photosynthesis
c) eat
d) respiration
e) lost, movement
f) inedible, hair

Q4 2. Plants use minerals and the products of photosynthesis to make complex nutrients.
3. Nutrients in plants are passed to animals through feeding and used in respiration to provide energy.
4. Energy released in respiration is lost by decay, heat and movement and the production of waste.
5. Waste and dead tissues are decayed by microorganisms.
6. Materials are recycled and returned to the soil by decay.

Q5 a) i) E.g. carbon, nitrogen, oxygen, hydrogen
ii) From the soil, air, water or eating other plants and animals.
b) When animals die or produce waste, microorganisms cause these materials to decay. The process of decay releases the elements back to the soil, air or water again for plants to use. The plants are then eaten by animals.

Q6 a) not stable
b) stable
c) not stable
d) stable

Q7 a) $(2070 \div 103\ 500) \times 100 =$ **2%**
b) $2070 \div 10 = 207$
$207 - (90 + 100) =$ **17 kJ**
c) E.g. heat loss / movement / excretion.
d) So much energy is lost at each stage of a food chain that there's not enough left to support more organisms after about five stages.

Page 50 — The Carbon Cycle

Q1 carbon dioxide, photosynthesis, respiration, microorganisms, eating, carbohydrates, waste, detritus

Q2 Plants use — carbon dioxide to build complex molecules.
Microorganisms release — carbon dioxide by decaying waste and dead tissue.
Animals and plants release — carbon dioxide through respiration.
Animals take in — carbon through feeding.
Plants take in — carbon by photosynthesis.

Q3 a) fossil fuel (accept coal or oil)
b) combustion / burning

Page 51 — The Nitrogen Cycle

Q1 Plants — By absorbing nitrates from the soil
Animals — By eating other organisms
Decomposers — By breaking down dead organisms and animal waste

Q2 a) Decomposers — Decompose proteins and urea into ammonia.
b) Nitrifying bacteria — Turn ammonia into nitrates which plants can use.
c) Denitrifying bacteria — Turn nitrates back into nitrogen gas.
d) Nitrogen-fixing bacteria — Turn nitrogen gas into nitrogen compounds that plants can use.

Q3 a) Lightning converting nitrogen from the air into nitrogen compounds in the soil.
b) Denitrifying bacteria converting nitrates in the soil into nitrogen gas.

Q4 a) Legume plants have root nodules that contain nitrogen-fixing bacteria. These bacteria convert nitrogen gas into nitrogen compounds, which plants can use.
b) Plants use the nitrogen compounds in the soil to make proteins for growth. More nitrogen compounds in the soil would mean increased plant growth.

Pages 52-53 — Mixed Questions — Section 3

Q1 a) i) It increased.
ii) It stayed constant.
b) The goat.
c) Because they lose too much water, and water is scarce in the desert.
d) natural selection

Q2 a) Donkeys have 62 chromosomes and horses have 64 chromosomes, so mules will have 63 chromosomes.
b) Ligers have chromosomes that can all pair up, because lions and tigers have the same number of chromosomes. Mules have one chromosome that can't pair up, so their chromosome pairs can't split up to make normal gametes.

Q3 a) Egg A. The parents of egg A provided the genetic material that was inserted into egg B, so the toad inherited its features from these parents.
b) Dolly was a clone because she was produced using genetic material from a single sheep. The fertilised cell used in the toad experiment contained a mixture of genes from two parents, so was not a clone.
c) Species that are sensitive to slight changes in their environment (so can be used to indicate environmental conditions).

Q4 a) Yes. If both parents were heterozygous then they would both carry the allele for long hair. This means they could have offspring that are homozygous for the long hair allele.
b) No. To be long haired the guinea pigs would have to be homozygous, so neither would be carrying the short hair allele.

Section 4 — Atoms, Elements and Compounds

Page 54 — Atoms and Elements

Q1 a) zero
b) ion
c) protons, electrons (in either order)
d) negatively

Q2

Particle	Charge
Proton	+1
Neutron	0
Electron	-1

Q3 a) nucleus
b) electron
c) proton
d) neutron
e) proton

Section 4 — Atoms, Elements and Compounds

Q4

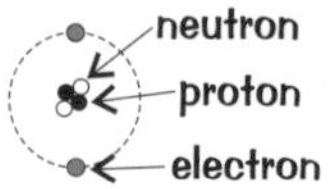

Diagram should be correctly labelled as above

Q5 copper and oxygen should be circled

Page 55 — The Periodic Table

Q1 a) A group in the periodic table is a **vertical** line of elements.
b) Most of the elements in the periodic table are **metals**.
c) There are about 100 different **elements** in the periodic table.
d) Non-metals are on the **right-hand** side of the periodic table.
e) Elements in the same group have **similar** properties.
f) The symbol for chlorine is **Cl** and the symbol for potassium is **K**.

Q2 a)

b) 11
c) 11
d) 23 – 11 = **12**

Q3 a) The following should be ticked: **A** and **D**
b) Sodium and potassium are both in Group I, so they both contain the same number of electrons in their outer shell. The properties of elements are decided by the number of electrons they have in their outer shell.

Q4 a) false
b) false
c) true
d) true
e) true

Pages 56-57 — Electron Shells

Q1 a) i) true
ii) false
iii) false
iv) false
b) ii) The lowest energy levels are always filled first.
iii) Atoms are most stable when they have full outer shells.
iv) Reactive elements have partially filled outer shells.

Q2 E.g. The inner most electron shell should be filled first / there should be two electrons in the inner shell; The outer shell contains too many electrons, it only holds a maximum of 8 electrons.

Q3 a) 2,2
b) 2,6
c) 2,8,4
d) 2,8,8,2
e) 2,8,3
f) 2,8,8

Q4 a) Noble gases are unreactive elements because they have full outer shells of electrons.
b) Group I metals are reactive elements, because they have an incomplete outer shell of electrons.

Q5 a) 2,8,7
b)

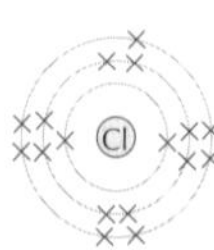

c) Its outer shell isn't full (it's keen to get an extra electron).

Q6 a) C b) N c) F d) Na e) Mg f) P g) S h) K i) Ca

Page 58 — Compounds

Q1 a) true
b) true
c) true
d) true

Q2 Missing words are: ions, positive, negative, attracted, ionic, molecules, covalent.

Q3 a) ionic
b) 1
c) +1
d) NaCl

Q4 Sharing electrons allows both atoms to achieve the stable 'full outer shell' of electrons. They form covalent bonds.

Pages 59-60 — Balancing Equations

Q1 a) Correctly balanced
b) Incorrectly balanced
c) Incorrectly balanced
d) Correctly balanced
e) Correctly balanced
f) Correctly balanced

Q2 The third equation should be circled.

Q3 a) The reactants are methane and oxygen, and the products are carbon dioxide and water.
b) methane + oxygen → carbon dioxide + water
c) $CH_4 + 2O_2 \rightarrow CO_2 + 2H_2O$

Q4 a) $2Na + Cl_2 \rightarrow 2NaCl$
b) $4Li + O_2 \rightarrow 2Li_2O$
c) $MgCO_3 + 2HCl \rightarrow MgCl_2 + H_2O + CO_2$
d) $2Li + 2H_2O \rightarrow 2LiOH + H_2$

Q5 a) $CuO + \mathbf{2}HBr \rightarrow CuBr_2 + H_2O$
b) $H_2 + Br_2 \rightarrow \mathbf{2}HBr$
c) $\mathbf{2}Mg + O_2 \rightarrow 2MgO$
d) $2NaOH + H_2SO_4 \rightarrow Na_2SO_4 + \mathbf{2}H_2O$

Q6 a) $\mathbf{3}NaOH + AlBr_3 \rightarrow \mathbf{3}NaBr + Al(OH)_3$
b) $\mathbf{2}FeCl_2 + Cl_2 \rightarrow \mathbf{2}FeCl_3$
c) $N_2 + \mathbf{3}H_2 \rightarrow \mathbf{2}NH_3$
d) $\mathbf{4}Fe + \mathbf{3}O_2 \rightarrow \mathbf{2}Fe_2O_3$
e) $\mathbf{4}NH_3 + \mathbf{5}O_2 \rightarrow \mathbf{4}NO + \mathbf{6}H_2O$

Page 61 — Materials and Properties

Q1 a) strong
b) permanently
c) pulling
d) pushing
e) high, compressive, weight

Section 4 — Atoms, Elements and Compounds

Q2

Substance	Water	Sulfur	Propanone	Sodium chloride
Melting point (°C)	0	115	-95	801
Boiling point (°C)	100	444	56	1465
State at room temperature	liquid	solid	liquid	solid

Q3 a) Some bendy materials can go back to their original shape / are not permanently deformed.
b) compressive strength
c) Diamond is very hard and so can cut through most materials.
Q4 a) Density is a material's mass per unit volume.
b) gold, iron, concrete
c) Mahogany is less dense than water so it will float (providing there's enough water in the bath).

Page 62 — Materials, Properties and Uses

Q1 a) B
b) D
c) A
d) C
Q2 Gold is suitable for jewellery because — it is shiny.
Slate is suitable for roofing because — it is durable.
Stainless steel is suitable for knives and forks because — it is non-toxic.
Rubber is suitable for car tyres because — it is strong but flexible.
Q3 a) The metal frame gives the racket strength and stiffness. Nylon is flexible, can be spun into fibres and has good tensile strength.
b) The metal body has strength and stiffness and conducts heat. The wooden handle has stiffness and strength and insulates the user from heat.
Q4 a) children's nightwear
b) E.g. softness because it will be next to the skin / high tensile strength so it can be made into fibres and is hard-wearing / low density so clothes are lightweight / non-toxic because children might chew their clothes / flame resistant for safety near fires.
c) E.g. any two from: Knives and forks — they shouldn't be soft or flexible. / Guttering — it shouldn't be soft or too flexible (low density). / Candle wax — it shouldn't have a high melting point or be flame resistant.

Page 63 — Properties of Metals

Q1 a) Metal 3 (because it has the best heat conduction, and is strong and resistant to corrosion).
b) Metal 2 (because it is the strongest, isn't too expensive and won't corrode too much). (Accept metal 3.)
c) Metal 1 (because it is most resistant to corrosion so it will last a long time).
Q2 Missing words are: air/water, water/air, oxygen, water, rust.
Q3 a) Copper would be suitable to make pipes as it can be bent. It also doesn't react with water.
b) Materials to make a plane would need to be strong. Some alloys of aluminium are much stronger than pure aluminium so they would be a more suitable material.

Page 64 — Making Metals More Useful

Q1 a) A mixture of two or more metals or a mixture of a metal and a non-metal.
b) By adding small amounts of carbon and sometimes other metals to the iron.
Q2 low-carbon steel — 0.1% carbon — car bodies
high-carbon steel — 1.5% carbon — blades for tools
stainless steel — chromium — cutlery
Q3 a) nickel, titanium
b) zinc, copper or nickel

Pages 65-68 — Getting Metals from Rocks

Q1 a) A metal ore is a mineral which contains enough metal to make it worthwhile extracting the metal from it.
b) oxygen and sulfur
Q2 Gold is less common than iron, which makes it expensive and this means that it is worth extracting it from low-grade ores. Iron is less valuable, and more common, so it is only economic to extract it from high-grade ores.
Q3 a) Year 1
b) cost of extraction = 75/100 x £2.00 = £1.50
The cost of mineral extraction was **£1.50** in year 6.
Q4 As technology improves, it becomes possible to extract more metal from a sample of rock than before. So it might now be worth extracting metal that wasn't worth extracting in the past.
Q5 a) Any one from:
e.g. it is too impure to conduct electricity well. /
The impurities make it too brittle to be used for wires.
b) i) Impure copper (obtained e.g. by reduction with carbon) is purified using electrolysis.
ii) E.g. electrolysis is expensive because it uses a lot of energy.
Q6 Missing words are: electricity, liquid, electricity, positive, electrode.
Q7 Electrolysis is the breaking down of substances using electricity. A molten substance or solution has free ions which conduct the electricity.
Q8 The copper produced will have zinc impurities in it.
Q9 a) A — electrodes
B — copper sulfate solution
C — copper ions
b) The impurities are not charged (i.e. they are neutral) so they are not attracted to the cathode.
Q10 a) Because iron is more reactive than copper.
b) No, because iron is less reactive than aluminium so it wouldn't be able to push the aluminium out and bond to the sulfate.
Q11 Any two from, e.g. there is a limited supply of copper. There is an increasing demand for copper. Mining new copper is damaging to the environment.
Q12 a) Bioleaching uses bacteria to separate copper from copper sulfide. The bacteria get energy from the bond between copper and sulfur, separating out the copper from the ore in the process. The leachate (the solution produced by the process) contains copper, which can be extracted, e.g. by filtering.
b) Phytomining.
c) The supply of copper-rich ores is limited and the demand for copper is growing. These alternative methods can extract copper from low-grade ores and from the waste that is currently produced when copper is extracted.

Page 69 — Impacts of Extracting Metals

Q1 Social factors include: new jobs available for locals, improved local services, influx of people might put strain on local services.
Economic factors include: more money in local economy, more goods made from the extracted metal are available.
Environmental factors include: pollution such as dust, noise and emissions from vehicles, habitat destruction, scarring of the landscape, after extraction the area may be turned into a conservation area.

Section 5 — Chemicals and Rocks

Q2 Aluminium is recycled because it takes a lot of energy to extract it from its ore, so even though it is very common extracting new aluminium is very expensive. Gold is recycled because it is rare and so it's too valuable to throw away.

Page 70 — Nanotechnology

Q1 a) 1-100 nanometres
b) E.g. seaspray
c) Any two of e.g. makes them stronger / makes them more durable / does not add weight to the racket.
Q2 a) silver
b) Silver nanoparticles have antibacterial properties.
Q3 B and C
Q4 Nanoparticles are being used in products today but the long term health impacts of many nanoparticles has not been worked out. Some people think that products containing nanoparticles should not be available until the effects on human health have been investigated properly.

Pages 71-72 — Mixed Questions — Section 4

Q1

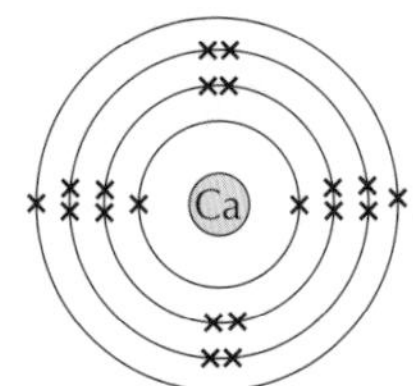

Q2 a)

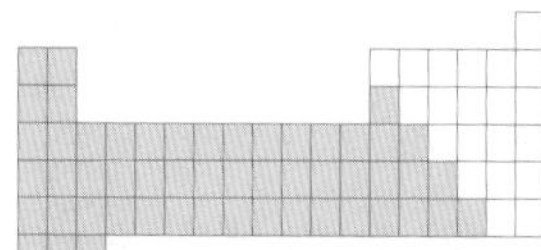

b) The following should be ticked:
Metals are generally strong but also malleable.
Metals conduct electricity well.
Properties of a metal can be altered by mixing it with another metal to form an alloy.
c) R. The material needs to be as light and as strong as possible with a high melting point and a reasonable price. S has a low melting point. T is expensive and fairly dense. U is not very strong and has a high density.
Q3 a) A finite resource is a resource of which there's a limited amount, which cannot be replenished.
b) i) In general, the more reactive the metal, the later it was discovered.
ii) Less reactive metals are easier to extract from their ores, for example by reduction with carbon. The least reactive metals are sometimes found uncombined in nature. The more reactive metals couldn't be extracted until electricity was discovered to do electrolysis.
c) i) iron(III) oxide + **carbon** → iron + **carbon dioxide**
ii) $2Fe_2O_3 + 3C \rightarrow 4Fe + 3CO_2$
d) i) Electrolysis produces very pure copper which conducts electricity better.
ii) Any two from: easily bent, easily drawn into wires, good conductor of electricity.
e) Aluminium is more reactive than carbon, and so cannot be extracted by reduction with carbon.

Section 5 — Chemicals and Rocks

Pages 73-74 — The Earth's Structure

Q1 a) 1.6 × 10 000 = 16 000 cm = **0.16 km**
b) 1.6 × 20 000 = 32 000 cm = 0.32 km
0.32 km + 325 km = **325.32 km**
Q2 The main earthquake zones are along the plate boundaries.
Q3 A sphere showing 3 layers.
Labels: Crust (outer layer) — very thin, it varies between 5 km and 50 km thickness.
Mantle (next layer down) — properties of a solid but flows very slowly like a liquid. Radioactive decay takes place here.
Core (centre) — mostly iron and nickel.
Q4 Crust — Thinnest of the Earth's layers
Mantle — Slowly flowing semi-solid layer that plates float on
Convection current — Caused by heat from radioactive decay in the mantle
Tectonic plates — Large pieces of crust and upper mantle
Earthquakes — Caused by sudden movements of plates
Volcanoes — Hot spots that often sit on plate boundaries.
Q5 Earthquake: Evidence — Strain in underground rocks.
How reliable is it? — Can only suggest the possibility of an earthquake. Low reliability.
Volcanic eruption: Evidence — Rising molten rock causing the ground to bulge slightly, leading to mini-earthquakes.
How reliable is it? — Molten rock can cool instead of erupting, so not a definite sign. Low/medium reliability.

Page 75 — Plate Tectonics

Q1 a) False
b) True
c) False
d) True
e) True
f) True
Q2 million, Pangaea, continents, tectonics
Q3 E.g. any three from:
Scientists studying the mid-Atlantic ridge discovered that the sea floor was spreading.
The magnetic orientations of rock bands on either side of the mid-Atlantic ridge are symmetrical.
The formation of new mountains suggests that the continents are moving and colliding with each other.
The coastlines of South America and Africa seem to match.
Fossils of identical plants and animals were found on different continents.
Rocks with matching layers have been found on different continents.

Page 76 — The Three Different Types of Rock

Q1 a) igneous rocks — formed when magma cools
sedimentary rocks — formed from layers of sediment
metamorphic rocks — formed under intense heat and pressure
b) i) e.g. granite
ii) e.g. limestone
iii) e.g. marble
Q2 a) Pressure forces out water. Fluids flowing through the pores deposit minerals that cement the sediment together.
b) granite
c) They are both the same chemical — calcium carbonate.
d) E.g. limestone is mostly made of layers of sediment cemented together. Marble is made up of small crystals. This gives it a more even texture than limestone and makes it much harder.

Section 5 — Chemicals and Rocks

Pages 77-78 — Using Limestone

Q1 calcium carbonate

Q2 a) calcium oxide, carbon dioxide

b) magnesium oxide

c) $CuCO_3 \rightarrow CuO + CO_2$

d) A Bunsen burner would not reach a high enough temperature for the reaction to happen.

Q3 The missing words are: limestone, mortar, concrete.

Q4 a) calcium carbonate → calcium oxide + carbon dioxide

b) To neutralise soils that are acidic.

Q5 Granite, paint and bricks should be circled.

Q6 a) neutralisation

b) The powdered limestone removes sulfur dioxide from the waste gases.

Q7 a) Any two from, e.g. it makes huge holes which permanently damage the landscape / noise / dust / destruction of habitats for plants and animals / transport is usually by lorry causing more noise and pollution / waste material causes unsightly tips.

b) Quarries provide employment for local people which can provide a boost to the local economy. There may also be improvements to infrastructure such as roads, recreational and health facilities.

Q8 a) Wood rots, is damaged by insects and is flammable. Concrete is not affected by any of these problems.

b) Metals corrode but concrete doesn't.

c) Bricks are made to a set size and shape but concrete can be poured into moulds of any size and shape.

Page 79 — Salt

Q1 a) False

b) True

c) True

d) True

Q2 Chlorine and sodium hydroxide.

Q3 a) A — brine
B — Cl_2
C — H_2
D — NaOH

b) Anode: $2Cl^- \rightarrow Cl_2 + 2e^-$
Cathode: $2H^+ + 2e^- \rightarrow H_2$

c) i) anode

ii) cathode

d) So they don't react with either the electrolyte or the products of the electrolysis.

Page 80 — Chlorination

Q1 chlorine, water supply, chlorination, chlorine, kills, microorganisms, water supply

Q2 a) oxidation of hydrogen chloride

b) The properties of compounds are different from the properties of elements from which they're made. So although chlorine will kill microorganisms, compounds that contain chlorine, such as sodium chloride, may not.

Q3 a)

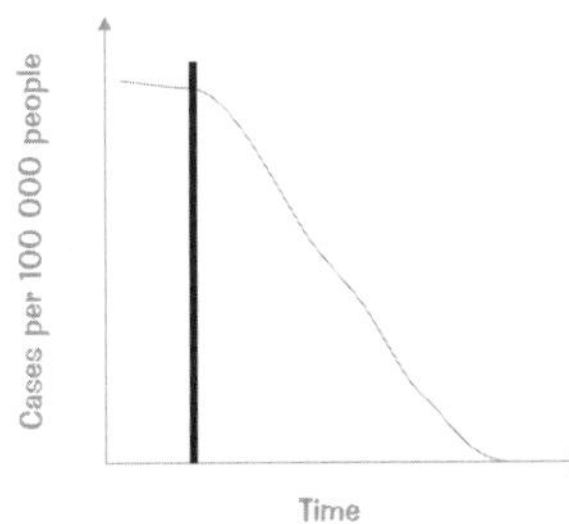

b) E.g. chlorination is a water treatment that kills disease-causing microorganisms. It is likely that it was introduced at the start of the decline in cases of typhoid.

c) E.g. chlorine can react with organic compounds in the water to make chlorinated hydrocarbons that can cause cancer.

Page 81 — Impacts of Chemical Production

Q1 a) polymer

b) carbon, hydrogen, chlorine

c) The plasticisers may leach out of the PVC into the environment, where they may have harmful effects.

Q2 a) The kestrels.

b) The organisms can't break down and excrete this type of substance, so it gets more concentrated as you move up the food chain (as each organism eats many of the organisms at the level below it). This means that animals at the top get the biggest dose of poison.

Q3 No. Some of the chemicals used to make the monitors may not have been tested thoroughly to see if they cause any long term problems to the environment or human health.

Page 82 — Hazard Symbols, Acids and Bases

Q1 a) — corrosive — attacks and destroys living tissue.

b) — irritant — causes reddening or blistering of the skin.

c) — toxic — can cause death if swallowed, inhaled or absorbed through the skin.

d) — oxidising — provides oxygen which allows other materials to burn more fiercely.

e) — harmful — like toxic but not quite as dangerous.

f) — highly flammable — catches fire easily.

Q2 a) i) purple — 14 — strong alkali

ii) yellow — 5/6 — weak acid

iii) dark green/blue — 8/9 — weak alkali

iv) red — 1 — strong acid

v) green — 7 — neutral

b) E.g. the colour can be difficult to judge exactly.

Page 83 — Reactions of Acids

Q1 a) hydrochloric acid + lead oxide → **lead** chloride + water.

b) nitric acid + copper hydroxide → copper **nitrate** + water.

c) sulfuric acid + zinc oxide → zinc sulfate + **water**

d) hydrochloric acid + **nickel** oxide → nickel **chloride** + water

e) **nitric** acid + copper carbonate → **copper** nitrate + **water** + **carbon dioxide**

f) phosphoric acid + **sodium** hydroxide → sodium **phosphate** + **water**

Q2 a) **ii)** and **iv)** should be ticked.

b) The two equations should be:
$H_2SO_4 + CuO \rightarrow CuSO_4 + H_2O$ and
$HCl + NaOH \rightarrow NaCl + H_2O$

Q3 a) NH_3

b) $NH_3 + HNO_3 \rightarrow NH_4NO_3$

c) No water is produced.

Section 6 — Chemicals from Oil

Pages 84-85 — The Evolution of the Atmosphere

Q1 True statements: When the Earth was formed, its surface was molten.
The early atmosphere was mostly made up of gases that had escaped from inside the Earth during volcanic eruptions.

Q2 The percentage of carbon dioxide has decreased by a large amount. This is because it dissolved into the oceans and green plants used it for photosynthesis. In both cases some of this carbon was incorporated into rocks, etc.

Q3 The statements should be in this order (from the top of the timeline):

1. The atmosphere is about four-fifths nitrogen and one fifth oxygen.
2. More complex organisms evolved.
3. Oxygen builds up in the air as plants photosynthesise.
4. Plant life appeared.
5. Water vapour condensed to form oceans.
6. The Earth cooled down slightly. A thin crust formed.
7. The Earth formed. There was lots of volcanic activity.

Q4 a) Largest sector is 'Nitrogen', second largest is 'Oxygen', smallest is 'Carbon dioxide and other gases'.

b) Nitrogen: 78%
Oxygen: 21%
Carbon dioxide: 0.035%

c) There is much more nitrogen and oxygen in today's atmosphere. There is far less carbon dioxide, water vapour and ammonia now. Oxygen is now a significant proportion of the atmosphere.

d) As the planet cooled, the water vapour condensed and formed the oceans.

e) Plants photosynthesised and produced it.

f) Any two from: e.g. killed off early organisms. / Allowed more complex organisms to evolve. / Created the ozone layer which blocked harmful rays from the Sun.

g) Nitrogen gas (N_2) was put into the atmosphere by denitrifying bacteria and by ammonia reacting with oxygen. N_2 gas isn't very reactive, so wasn't broken down, and its levels gradually increased.

Page 86 — Life and the Atmosphere Today

Q1 a) 1. Air is filtered to remove dust.
2. Air is cooled to -200 °C.
3. Carbon dioxide freezes and is removed. Water vapour condenses and is removed.
4. Liquefied air enters the fractionating column and is heated slowly.

b) mixture, boiling points

c) E.g. oxygen, nitrogen.

Q2 a) Billions of years ago, the earth's atmosphere was mainly nitrogen, hydrogen, ammonia and methane.
Lightning struck causing a chemical reaction between these gases and as a result amino acids were formed.
The amino acids collected in a 'primordial soup' — a body of water out of which life gradually crawled.

b) Miller and Urey sealed the gases, nitrogen, hydrogen, ammonia and methane in some apparatus, heated them and applied an electrical charge for a week.

c) Amino acids were created, but not as many as there are on Earth. This suggests that the theory is along the right lines but perhaps not quite right.

Pages 87-88 — Mixed Questions — Section 5

Q1 a) i)

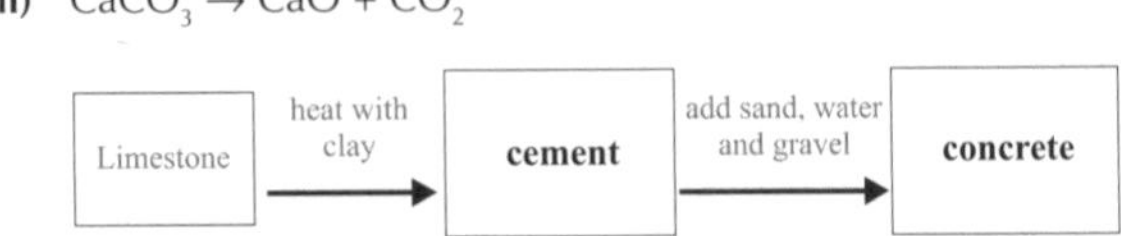

ii) $CaCO_3 \rightarrow CaO + CO_2$

b) Limestone —(heat with clay)→ **cement** —(add sand, water and gravel)→ **concrete**

c) Any two of: e.g. it doesn't rot when it gets wet / it's cheaper / it's fire resistant / it can't be gnawed away by insects or rodents.

d) cement, sand and water

e) calcium carbonate + hydrochloric acid → **calcium chloride** + **carbon dioxide** + **water**

Q2 a) Convection currents in the mantle.

b) Earthquakes and volcanoes

Q3 a) No. It would not support animal life because there is no oxygen. It could support plant life because there is plenty of carbon dioxide for photosynthesis.

b) i) Green plants and algae.

ii) The oceans absorbed CO_2.

c) i) True

ii) True

iii) False, scientists can't predict volcanoes and earthquakes with any accuracy.

Q4 The oceans are a natural store of CO_2 — they absorb it from the atmosphere. The increasing level of CO_2 means the oceans are becoming acidic because they are absorbing more. This could damage some sealife, e.g. coral and shellfish.

Section 6 — Chemicals from Oil

Page 89 — Fractional Distillation of Crude Oil

Q1 a) Crude oil is a **mixture** of different molecules.

b) Most of the compounds in crude oil are **hydrocarbon** molecules.

c) The molecules in crude oil **aren't** chemically bonded to each other.

d) Physical methods **can** be used to separate out the molecules in crude oil.

Q2

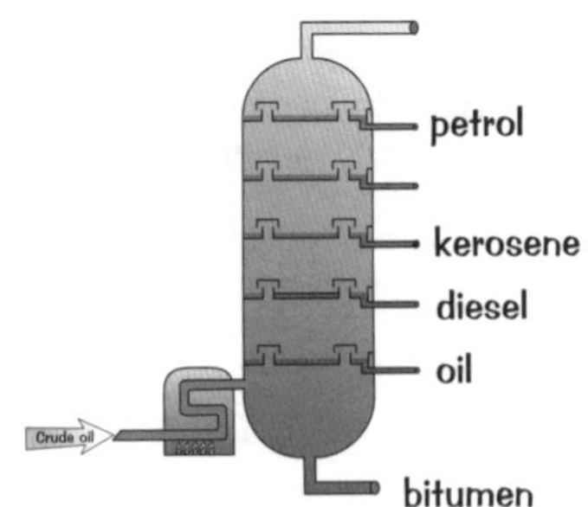

Q3 The larger the molecule the higher the boiling/condensing point.

Q4 The hydrocarbons all have different boiling points. During distillation the oil is heated and the different hydrocarbons boil off at different temperatures. The hydrocarbons can then be condensed individually and the crude oil is successfully separated.

Section 6 — Chemicals from Oil

Page 90 — Properties and Uses of Crude Oil

Q1 a)

```
   H          H H            H H H
H-C-H      H-C-C-H      H-C-C-C-H
   H          H H            H H H
methane     ethane       propane
```

b) propane

Q2 a) The longer the alkane molecule the **more** viscous (gloopy) it is

b) The shorter the alkane molecule the **lower** its boiling point.

c) The shorter the alkane molecule the **more** flammable it is.

Q3 a) C_nH_{2n+2}

b) $C_{20}H_{42}$ (n = 20 so 2n + 2 = (2 x 20) + 2 = 42)

Q4 a) Oils with long carbon chains are very viscous (gloopy) and so they cling to the moving parts of an engine, preventing damage.

b) Using a hydrocarbon with fewer carbon atoms would be problematic because it would vaporise when the engine got hot / could catch fire easily.

Page 91 — Cracking Crude Oil

Q1 shorter, petrol, diesel, long, high, catalyst, molecules, cracking

Q2 a) E.g. petrol, paraffin, ethene

b) thermal decomposition

Q3 a) ethene

b) 1. The long-chain molecules are heated.
2. They are vaporised (turned into a gas).
3. The vapour is passed over a catalyst at a high temperature.
4. The molecules are cracked on the surface of the catalyst.

Q4 a) kerosene → octane + ethene

b) $C_{10}H_{22} \rightarrow C_8H_{18} + C_2H_4$

Pages 92-93 — Alkenes and Ethanol

Q1 a) C_2H_4

b)

```
H     H
 \   /
  C=C
 /   \
H     H
```

c) Propene

d)

```
       H  H
H      |  |
 \C=C-C-H
 /       |
H        H
```

Q2 a) C_5H_{10}

b) C_6H_{12}

c) C_8H_{16}

d) $C_{12}H_{24}$

Q3 a) False

b) True

c) False

d) True

Q4 bromine water, decolourise, bromine water, orange, colourless

Q5 a) A

b) Method A — Uses yeast.
Method B — Uses a catalyst.

c) Any two of:
Needs lower temperatures so is cheaper. Can use simpler equipment. Uses sugar which is often grown as a major crop. Sugar is a renewable resource.

d) The ethanol produced is not very concentrated/needs to be purified.

Q6 Ethene is a product of crude oil and crude oil is a non-renewable resource. When crude oil starts running out, using ethene to make ethanol will become very expensive.

Page 94 — Burning Fuels

Q1 a) hydrocarbon + oxygen → carbon dioxide + water

b) oxidised, gives out

Q2 Any three from: e.g. how easily it burns / its energy value / how much ash or smoke it produces / how easy it is to store or transport.

Q3 a) CO_2 and H_2O

b) If there is not enough oxygen.

Q4 a) hydrocarbon + oxygen → **carbon** + **carbon monoxide** + **carbon dioxide** + **water**

b) Carbon monoxide is produced which is a very toxic (poisonous) gas.

Page 95 — Using Crude Oil as a Fuel

Q1 a) The sun would not always be bright enough to work well. / It wouldn't be possible to use solar power at night.

b) The wind wouldn't always be blowing when someone wanted to use the oven.

c) Nuclear substances would be very dangerous if they leaked. / It would be very expensive to develop a way of storing the fuel in a safe way.

Q2 New reserves of oil have been discovered since the 1960s. Also, new methods of extraction mean that oil that was once too expensive or difficult to extract can now be used.

Q3 a) When oil is transported by ship there is the possibility of spills into the sea. Crude oil is poisonous to birds and sea creatures.

b) Burning oil products releases carbon dioxide, which causes global warming, and carbon particles (soot) which cause global dimming. The sulfur in oil will make sulfur dioxide which causes acid rain.

Q4 Most technology around today is set up to use crude oil fractions as fuel and converting to alternatives would be time-consuming and costly. We need more energy than can currently be created using alternatives alone. Crude oil fractions are often more reliable than some alternatives, e.g. solar and wind power won't work without the right weather conditions.

Page 96 — Environmental Problems

Q1 a) true

b) true

c) false

d) false

Q2 The main cause of acid rain is... sulfur dioxide.
Acid rain kills trees and... acidifies lakes.
Sulfur dioxide is produced by burning fuels which contain... sulfur.
Limestone buildings and statues are affected by... acid rain.
In clouds sulfur dioxide reacts with water to make... sulfuric acid.

Q3 Ways of reducing acid rain include:
Removing the sulfur from the fuel before it is burnt (using low-sulfur fuels).
Using scrubbers in power station chimneys to remove sulfur dioxide from emissions.

Q4 Global dimming is the reduction in the amount of sunlight reaching the earth's surface. It's thought to be caused by particles of soot and ash produced when fossil fuels are burnt.

Section 6 — Chemicals from Oil

Page 97 — Carbon Dioxide in the Atmosphere

Q1 True statements:
Greenhouse gases act like an insulating layer around the Earth.
Greenhouse gases include carbon dioxide and methane.
Increasing amounts of greenhouse gases are causing global warming.

Q2 a) combustion (burning)
b) photosynthesis
c) respiration / combustion (burning)
d) coal

Q3 a) Global temperature has generally increased, although it has fluctuated.
b) Any two from: e.g. carbon dioxide is released when trees are burnt to clear land. / Microorganisms that feed on dead wood release CO_2 as a waste product of respiration. / Living trees use CO_2 for photosynthesis, so removing them means less CO_2 is removed from the atmosphere.
c) E.g. burning fossil fuels

Page 98 — Reducing Carbon Dioxide in the Atmosphere

Q1 a) seeding, injecting, phytoplankton, photosynthesis, hydrocarbons, high
b) Any one from:
E.g. there is no way of controlling what plankton grows — some is toxic.
When the plankton dies it is decomposed by microorganisms that use up oxygen, creating 'dead zones' in the ocean.
If carbon dioxide isn't converted into hydrocarbons using 'green' energy then this process just increases CO_2 levels.

Q2 a) water
b) When hydrogen is used as a fuel no carbon dioxide is produced so it doesn't contribute to global warming. It doesn't produce particulates either. Also it doesn't produce sulfur dioxide so it doesn't cause acid rain.
c) Hydrogen-powered vehicles are very expensive because the engines they use are expensive. Hydrogen is difficult to store, which makes it awkward to use as a fuel. Fuelling stations would need to be adapted / converted.

Q3 $0.9 \times 37\,000\,000 =$ **33 300 000 J** or **33.3 MJ**

Pages 99-100 — Using Alkenes to Make Polymers

Q1 The monomer of poly(ethene) is ethene.

Q2 Any three from: e.g. plastic bags / waterproof coatings for fabrics / tooth fillings / hydrogel wound dressings / memory foam.

Q3 a) Waste remains in landfill. Landfill sites are getting full and more are needed, which takes up useful land.
b) Recycle and reuse.
c) Plastic is currently made from crude oil. As this runs low, its price will rise.

Q4
$$n\left(\begin{array}{ccc} CH_3 & & H \\ | & & | \\ C & = & C \\ | & & | \\ H & & H \end{array}\right) \rightarrow \left(\begin{array}{ccc} CH_3 & & H \\ | & & | \\ -C & - & C- \\ | & & | \\ H & & H \end{array}\right)_n$$

Q5 Polymers and cornstarch.

Q6 Cracking is the breakdown of large molecules into smaller ones, whereas polymerisation is small molecules joining to form bigger molecules.
Cracking makes small alkenes and alkanes, polymerisation often uses alkenes to make alkanes.
Cracking usually involves breaking single bonds between carbon atoms. In polymerisation, the double bonds between carbon atoms are broken.

Page 101 — Structure and Properties of Polymers

Q1 together, can, flexible, low, more, higher

Q2 a) increasing the chain length, adding cross-linking agents, adding plasticisers, making the polymer more crystalline
b) shorten the length of the molecular chain
c) The polymer would become stiffer and have a higher melting point.
d) Cross-linking agents bond the polymer chains together chemically, making the polymer stiffer, stronger and more heat-resistant.

Q3 a) plasticisers
b) The molecules of the plasticiser get in between the polymer chains and reduce the forces between the chains.

Pages 102-103 — Plant Oils

Q1 a) Fruits: e.g. avocados and olives
Seeds: e.g. brazil nuts and sesame seeds
b) e.g. food or fuel
c) It squeezes the oil out of the plant material.

Q2 Vegetable oils provide loads of energy, and also contain nutrients.

Q3 a) False
b) True
c) False
d) True
e) False

Q4 a) They provide lots of energy.
b) e.g. biodiesel

Q5 Martin has produced the better method. It is a fair test. He gives accurate quantities. He labels his equipment so there is less opportunity for mistakes.

Q6 a) Reaction with hydrogen with a nickel catalyst at about 60 °C. The double bonds open up and bond to the hydrogen atoms.
b) It increases the melting points of vegetable oils.
c) Some vegetable oils are only partially hydrogenated as turning all the double bonds into single bonds would make the oil too hard. Margarine is an example of this. It is partially hydrogenated so that it is spreadable.

Q7 a) saturated
b) They increase the amount of cholesterol in the blood, which can block arteries and lead to heart disease.

Page 104 — Emulsions

Q1 a) E.g. emulsions can be formed from oil suspended in water or water suspended in oil.
b) E.g. the thicker an emulsion, the more oil it contains.
c) E.g. emulsions can be combined with air and it makes them fluffier.
d) E.g. emulsions are found in foods as well as in non-food items such as moisturisers and paints.

Q2 a)

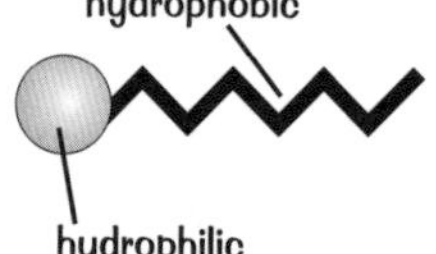

b) Lecithin molecules surround the droplets of oil, with their hydrophilic heads facing out into the water and their hydrophobic tails in the oil droplet. This layer keeps the oil droplets from joining together to separate out from the water.

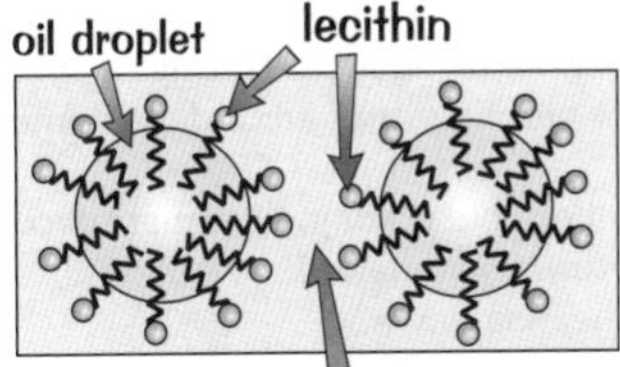

Q3 a) Emulsifiers increase the shelf-life of food by stopping emulsions from separating out.

b) Some people are allergic to certain emulsifiers, e.g. egg yolk, so they would need to check the ingredients very carefully.

Pages 105-106 — Mixed Questions — Section 6

Q1 a) There are twice as many hydrogen atoms as there are carbon atoms in each molecule (and no other atoms).

b)

```
  H H   H
  | |  /
H-C-C=C
  |    \
  H     H
```

c) Alkanes only have single bonds, alkenes have a double bond between some carbon atoms. (The general formula of an alkane is C_nH_{2n+2}.)

Q2 a) cracking

b) Ethene can be hydrated with steam to produce ethanol. This requires a high temperature, high pressure and a catalyst.

c) Ethanol can be made by fermentation of sugar. Sugar is obtained from plants which are renewable.

Q3 a) Lots of small molecules (monomers) join up to make long chain molecules (polymers).

b) Name: polystyrene / poly(styrene)

```
  H   H   H   H   H   H   H   H
  |   |   |   |   |   |   |   |
--C - C - C - C - C - C - C - C--
  |   |   |   |   |   |   |   |
  H  C6H5 H  C6H5 H  C6H5 H  C6H5
```

Q4 a) The following can be in any order:
Petrol has a lower melting and boiling point than diesel.
Petrol is more flammable (ignites more easily) than diesel.
Petrol is less viscous (flows more easily / is runnier) than diesel.

b) When it's burnt, there are fewer pollutants than from petrol or diesel. / It's carbon neutral because it's made from plants.

Q5 a) Ace oil

b) The viscosity becomes much less.

c) Do the experiment at the average temperature of a car engine.

d) Duncan XYZ oil

Section 7 — Heat and Energy

Page 107 — Heat, Temperature and Kinetic Theory

Q1 Heat is a measure of **energy**
Temperature is a measure of **hotness**.
Heat travels from a **hot** place to a **cold** place.
When a substance is heated its particles vibrate **more** quickly.

Q2

Solid | Liquid | Gas

Gas — There are almost no forces of attraction between the particles.
Liquid — There are weak forces of attraction between the particles.
Solid — There are strong forces of attraction holding the particles close together.

Q3 a) False

b) True

c) True

d) True

e) False

Q4 As you heat a solid, its particles will gain more kinetic energy. They will vibrate more and move faster and eventually overcome the strong forces of attraction that hold the particles in a solid together. Eventually the particles will move fast enough and far enough apart that the substance will become a liquid.

Page 108 — Conduction and Convection

Q1 a) True

b) False

c) True

d) False

Q2 The metal spoon feels colder because metal is a better conductor, so it conducts heat energy away from his hand more quickly.

Q3 The very bottom of a hot water tank stays cold... because water isn't a good heat conductor.
Warm air rises... because it is not so dense.
A small heater can send heat all over a room... because heat flows from warm places to cooler ones.

Q4 The experiment shows that convection works very well in water — the ice melts at the top because convection currents carry warm water upwards. It also shows that water is a poor conductor of heat — convection currents do not warm the water below the flame, and the water below the heater stays cold because conduction only occurs very slowly.

Q5 A blanket with holes in traps more air than a blanket without holes. This reduces conduction as air is a better insulator than the blanket material.

Page 109 — Heat Radiation

Q1 a) False

b) True

c) True

d) False

e) False

Q2 a) Dark, matt surfaces are **good** absorbers and **good** emitters of heat radiation.

b) The best surfaces for radiating heat are **good** absorbers and **good** emitters.

Section 7 — Heat and Energy

c) The best materials for making survival blankets are **poor** absorbers and **poor** emitters.
d) The best surfaces for solar hot water panels are **good** absorbers and **good** emitters.

Q3 a) As it cools down, the tea is emitting more heat than it is absorbing.
b) It must be absorbing the same amount of heat that it is emitting.
c) A system that's at a constant temperature — radiates the same average power that it absorbs.
A system that's warming up — radiates less power than it absorbs.
A system that's cooling down — radiates more power than it absorbs.

Page 110 — Condensation and Evaporation

Q1 liquid, cools, kinetic energy, attractive.
Q2 a) i) True
ii) False
iii) False
b) ii) Particles can evaporate from a liquid at temperatures much lower than the liquid's boiling point.
iii) E.g. The speed of a particle, the direction it's travelling in and how near the surface it is all affect whether it can escape a liquid.
Q3 When the sweat on your skin evaporates it causes a cooling effect. This is because the fastest particles (the ones with most kinetic energy) are most likely to evaporate from a liquid (the sweat). When they do, the average speed and kinetic energy of the remaining particles decreases. This decrease in average particle energy means the temperature of the remaining liquid falls. Sweating more will increase this cooling effect, as more particles will evaporate from skin.
Q4 a) Any two from: e.g. if the liquid has: a high temperature / low density / large surface area. / If there is a low concentration of the liquid in the air it's evaporating into. / If there's greater airflow.
b) Any two from: e.g. if the temperature of the surface the gas touches is lower. / If the surface area of the surface the gas touches is larger. / If the temperature of the gas is low. / If the gas is dense. / If there's lower airflow.

Page 111 — Rate of Heat Transfer

Q1 a) To maximise the amount of heat transfer.
b) Metal is a good conductor so it will conduct heat away from the radiator much faster than air, as air is an insulator.
Q2 Any four from:
Shiny mirrored surfaces — reduce radiation.
Sponge supports — reduce conduction.
Vacuum gap between walls of bottle — reduce conduction and convection.
Plastic cap filled with cork — reduces conduction.
Air space between bottle and outer case — reduces conduction.
Plastic case — reduces conduction.
Q3 E.g.

Type of Transfer	Suggested Improvements to reduce heat loss
Radiation	Make the outside surface shiny / white / silvery.
Conduction	Cover the tank with 'lagging' material that conducts poorly, e.g. fibreglass.
Convection	Have the tank in a cupboard so warm air can't 'escape', or put a loose cover over it.

Pages 112-113 — Energy Efficiency in the Home

Q1 sources, radiators, sinks, windows, insulate, efficient.
Q2 a) Through the roof — e.g. loft insulation.
Through the walls — e.g. cavity wall insulation.
Through the doors — e.g. double glazing of any glass panels / draught-proofing strips around the frames and letter box.
b) She could install double glazing, fit draught-proofing strips around the windows, and have thick curtains. (Or she could turn her heating down.)
Q3 a) Payback time = 200 ÷ 100 = **2 years**.
b) Yes, because although the hot water tank jacket is cheaper, it has a longer payback time so the loft insulation will save him money sooner.
Q4 a) Cavity wall insulation — reduces heat transfer by convection, because pockets of air are trapped in the foam, and can't move between the two walls.
b) Loft insulation — layers of insulation reduce heat transfer by conduction from the ceiling to the roof space. (Heat transfer by radiation from the loft floor is also reduced, because the loft floor is not so warm.)
c) Double glazing — a layer of air between two panes of glass reduces heat transfer by conduction because the air acts as an insulator.
Q5 a) U-values measure how effective a material is as an insulator / how fast heat can transfer through a material.
b) Gary should choose brand A because it has a lower U-value — the lower the U-value, the better the material is as an insulator, so heat transfer will be less.

Page 114 — Specific Heat Capacity

Q1 a) Specific heat capacity is the amount of energy needed to raise the temperature of 1 kg of a substance by 1 °C.
b) Substance A
Q2 a) Concrete
b) Water is used because it has a really high specific heat capacity so it can store large amounts of heat, and can be easily pumped around pipes.
Q3 $E = m \times c \times \theta$.
The temperature change for both is 50 °C.
Energy from mercury = 27.2 × 139 × 50 = 189 040 J.
Energy from water = 2 × 4200 × 50 = 420 000 J.
Difference = 420 000 – 189 040 = **230 960 J** (≈ 231 kJ).
Q4 Rearrange the energy equation:
$m = E \div (c \times \theta)$.
Mass = 3040 ÷ (380 × 40) = 3040 ÷ 15 200
= **0.2 kg** of copper (or **200 g**).

Page 115 — Energy Transfer

Q1 conservation, transferred, dissipated, created.
Q2 a) **chemical energy** → heat and light energy.
b) electrical energy → **sound and heat energy**.
c) **electrical energy** → **light and heat energy**.
Q3 a) i) chemical energy
ii) heat/thermal energy (and kinetic energy)
b) Any two from:
Chemical energy → heat energy (as the coal burns).
Heat energy → kinetic energy (as the steam drives the engine).
Chemical energy → light energy (in the lamp).
Other answers are possible.
Q4 a) Gravitational potential energy.
b) Chemical energy from the porridge is transferred to kinetic energy in Bruce's muscles and the moving bar. This kinetic energy is then transferred to gravitational potential energy.
c) The gravitational potential energy is transferred into kinetic energy as it falls downwards.

Section 7 — Heat and Energy

Page 116 — Efficiency of Machines

Q1 a) True
b) True
c) False
d) False
Q2 a) 100 J
b) 5 J
c) 100 – 5 = 95 J
d) 5 ÷ 100 = 0.05
Q3

Total Energy Input (J)	Useful Energy Output (J)	Efficiency
2000	1500	**0.75**
4000	2000	0.50
4000	**1000**	0.25
600	200	**0.33**

Q4 The winch, like all other devices, is not 100% efficient — some of the input energy will be 'wasted'. Much of this waste is likely to be heat energy, generated by friction in the motor and between the moving parts of the winch.

Page 117 — Energy Transformation Diagrams

Q1 See diagram below — where the scale is 1 small square = 2 J. Different scales are possible.

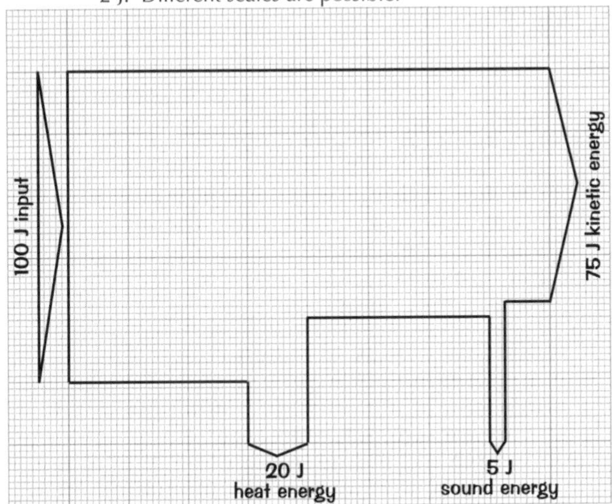

Q2 a) 100 J heat + 40 J GPE = 140 J
b) 60 J
c) Efficiency = 60 ÷ 200 = **0.3**.

Page 118 — Power Stations and Nuclear Energy

Q1 Most power stations use **non-renewable** sources of energy, such as coal, oil or gas. These **fossil** fuels are initially burnt in a boiler. This converts the **chemical** energy in the fuel to **heat** energy. A turbine then converts this energy into **kinetic** energy, which, in turn is converted to **electrical** energy by a generator.
Q2 a) False
b) True
c) False
Q3 Both coal and nuclear power stations produce steam which is used to drive a generator. The method of steam production is different, but the method of electricity production is identical.
Q4 a) Irradiation does not involve contact with the source. Contamination involves some of the source becoming attached to you (so you continue to be irradiated).
b) Contamination is worse because you are exposed to the ionising radiation for a longer time, so it does more damage.

Page 119 — Wind and Solar Energy

Q1 a) E.g. they make a lot of noise. They spoil the view/ landscape. A lot of turbines are needed to replace one power station.
b) Any three from: e.g. there's no permanent damage to the landscape. / They use a renewable/free source of energy. / Running costs are low. / They don't emit greenhouse gases.
Q2 a) So he could compare the amount of energy that had been stored each night.
b) Any sensible answer, e.g. there hadn't been much wind the night before. / The generator wasn't working properly.
Q3 Disadvantages — the initial costs are high, most solar cells are not very efficient, they don't work well when it's cloudy, it's not very practical to connect them to the National Grid. Advantages — they use a renewable and free source of energy (there are no fuel costs), they are a good way to provide energy in remote places, there is no pollution when they are in use.

Page 120 — Wave and Tidal Energy

Q1 1. A wave forces air through a turbine.
2. The air makes the turbine spin.
3. The spinning turbine drives a generator.
4. Electricity is produced by the generator.
Q2 a) Both
b) Wave
c) Tidal
d) Wave
e) Tidal
Q3 Any two from: e.g. initial costs are fairly high. / Barrages can look unattractive. / Barrages can prevent access for boats. / Barrages can damage habitats. / No energy is available at the turn of the tides.
Q4 a) Any two from: e.g. no pollution. / No fuel costs. / Minimal running costs. / Good for small-scale use.
b) Any two from: e.g. high initial costs. / Spoiling the view. / Can be unreliable because it depends on winds. / It is currently only suitable for small-scale use. / Can be a hazard to boats.

Pages 121-122 — Biofuels, Geothermal and Hydroelectricity

Q1 Biofuels are used to generate electricity in a similar way to **fossil fuels**. Biofuels are burnt to heat **water** and make **steam**, which is used to drive **turbines** to power generators and make electricity.
Biofuels can be solids (e.g. **woodchips**), liquids (e.g. **ethanol**) or gases (e.g. **methane**).
Q2 a) False
b) False
c) False
d) True
Q3 E.g. in some areas where hot rocks lie near to the surface of the Earth, water is pumped in pipes down to hot rocks and returns as steam to drive a turbine. / In some areas where hot rocks lie near to the surface of the Earth (e.g. volcanic areas), hot water and steam rise to the surface. This steam can be used to drive turbines to generate electricity.

Section 7 — Heat and Energy

Q4 E.g. it's expensive to drill down several kilometres to the hot rocks. / There are very few places where it's suitable to drill.

Q5 Answer will depend on student's opinion:

a) E.g. the student could say that no pollution is produced when electricity is being generated, or that building the dams and manufacturing the turbines, generators etc. does cause pollution.

b) E.g. the student could say that there are no fuel costs, or that building dams and purchasing turbines etc. is expensive.

c) E.g. the student might argue that dams are unsightly, they disturb the natural environment and disrupt wildlife etc., or they could argue that an impressive engineering structure has a positive visual impact, and/or that not all hydroelectric projects involve building dams.

d) E.g. the student could say that it is rare for reservoirs to be empty even in dry weather, and water can be released to power the generators when it's needed most, or they could say that power supplies are less reliable during droughts, and this may be a more serious problem in the future.

e) Any two from: e.g. it is a renewable source of energy. / It does not contribute to global warming (once running). / The output can be varied more quickly than that of most other power stations. / There are minimal running costs.

f) Any two from: e.g. people may be required to move from their homes in the valley. / Rotting vegetation releases greenhouse gases (methane and CO_2) when the valley is flooded. / Set-up costs are high. / Set-up times are long. / Reservoirs look unsightly when they dry up.

Page 123 — Energy Sources and the Environment

Q1 Acid rain... sulfur dioxide formed by burning oil and coal.
Global warming... releasing CO_2 by burning fossil fuels.
Dangerous radioactive waste... using nuclear power.
Spoiling of natural landscapes... coal mining OR sulfur dioxide formed by burning oil and coal.

Q2 Answer will depend on student's opinion but should include an explanation of their reasoning, e.g. Lisa because nuclear power produces long-lasting, dangerous, radioactive waste.
Or Ben because nuclear power is carefully controlled to reduce any dangers. Also, nuclear power doesn't produce any carbon dioxide, whereas using fossil fuels adds to the carbon dioxide in the atmosphere, leading to climate change / an increased greenhouse effect / global warming.

Q3 Plants that are used to produce biofuels (or to feed animals that produce biofuels) absorb carbon dioxide from the atmosphere. Burning the biofuel puts the carbon back into the atmosphere as carbon dioxide, so overall there is a neutral effect on the atmosphere.

Q4 a) This is the process of collecting carbon dioxide from power stations before it is released into the atmosphere.

b) E.g. in empty gas fields, oil fields, dissolved in seawater at the bottom of the ocean, capturing with algae.

Pages 124-125 — Comparison of Energy Resources

Q1 Gas

Q2 a) Any one of: gas supplies often need to be imported and there may be steep price rises, gas will run out eventually, burning gas causes atmospheric pollution and contributes to the global warming.
Other answers are possible.

b) Any one of: high set-up costs, high maintenance and/or decommissioning costs, long set-up times, dangerous radioactive waste, risk of catastrophic accidents, threat from terrorism, nuclear fuels need to be imported.
Other answers are possible.

c) Any one of: it's dependent on the weather / only works when the wind is blowing, unreliable, visual pollution / spoils the view, noise pollution. Other answers are possible.

d) E.g. high set-up costs. Other answers are possible.

Q3 a) Most (about 75%) of the UK's electricity generation depends on supplies of coal, oil and gas. These fuels are all non-renewable and will run out eventually.

b) 1. We don't know how to dispose of the radioactive waste safely.
2. Nuclear power stations and radioactive waste are targets for terrorists.

c) Shutting down / removing from active status.

d) Answer will depend on student's opinion. 'I agree' could be backed up by mentioning that sea levels change in a predictable and reliable way, twice every day, and/or that the UK has a long coastline and plenty of opportunities to use the resource. 'I disagree' could be backed up by saying that there are only a few suitable estuaries, or that at neap tides, the difference in sea level between low and high tides is small, so there is not much energy available.

e) E.g. the running costs are low / it doesn't release greenhouse gases.

Pages 126-128 — Mixed Questions — Section 7

Q1 a) i) The heat is used to turn water into steam, which drives turbines. Generators then convert the kinetic energy of the turbine blades into electrical energy.

ii) Find the total energy input and subtract the 1000 J of useful output.
Efficiency = Useful energy output ÷ Total energy input,
so Total energy input = Useful energy output ÷ efficiency.
= 1000 J ÷ 0.38 = 2632 J.
So wasted energy = 2632 – 1000 = **1632 J**.

b) nuclear energy, biomass

Q2 a) i) E.g. solar cells require little maintenance and no fuel, making them suitable for remote locations (where transporting fuel and arranging repairs would be difficult and expensive). / Solar power is a renewable source of energy and won't pollute the island.

ii) E.g. the island is likely to be quite windy. / Wind turbines are fairly cheap to install. / As with solar power, wind power is renewable, doesn't cause pollution and doesn't require fuel.

b) Wave power / biofuels / hydroelectric power / tidal / geothermal energy.

c) Both solar and wind power are unreliable/dependent on the weather. / On days which weren't sunny or windy, there would be little or no electricity.

Q3 a) The freezer compartment cools the warmer air at the top of the fridge, which then falls, forcing warmer air to rise.

b) In the ice, the particles are close together in a fixed, regular arrangement. The particles in the ice have less energy than in the liquid water. In liquid water the particles are close together, but can move past each other, and form irregular arrangements.

Section 8 — Electricity and Waves

Q4 a) Chemical energy.
b) E.g. below, using a scale of 1 small square = 25 joules. Other scales are possible.

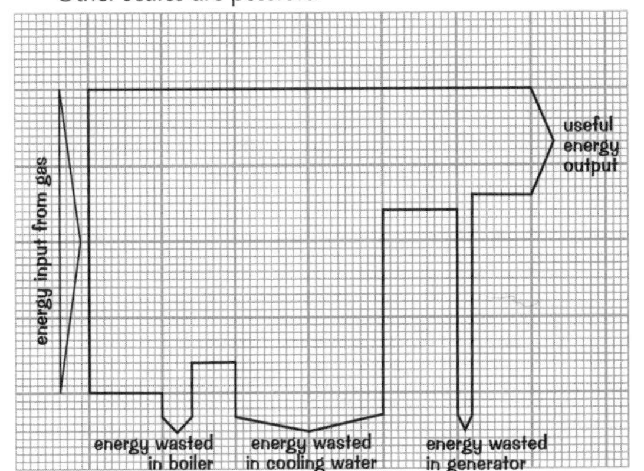

c) Useful output energy = 1000 J – 100 J – 500 J – 50 J = 350 J. So efficiency = 350 ÷ 1000 = **0.35** (or 35%).
Q5 a) Hot water tank jacket.
b) Over 5 years, the savings would be:
Hot water tank jacket: (5 × £15) – £15 = £60
Draught-proofing: (5 × £65) – £70 = £255
Cavity wall insulation: (5 × £70) – £560 = –£210
Thermostatic controls: (5 × £25) – £120 = £5.
So **draught-proofing** would save the most money.
c) The temperature change required is 36 – 14 = 22 °C.
$E = m \times c \times \theta$
= 90 × 4200 × 22 = **8 316 000 J** (= 8316 kJ = 8.316 MJ).
Q6 a) Any three of: e.g. set-up costs / set-up and decommissioning time / reliability / running costs / environmental issues (waste and pollution) / suitable locations.
b) Carbon capture and storage technology is used to collect CO_2 from fossil-fuel power stations before it is released into the atmosphere. This reduces the amount of CO_2 building up in the atmosphere and reduces the strength of the greenhouse effect.

Section 8 — Electricity and Waves

Page 129 — Generating Electricity

Q1 voltage, moving, electromagnetic induction, magnet, coil, alternating, complete, magnetic, reverses.
Q2 a) E.g.

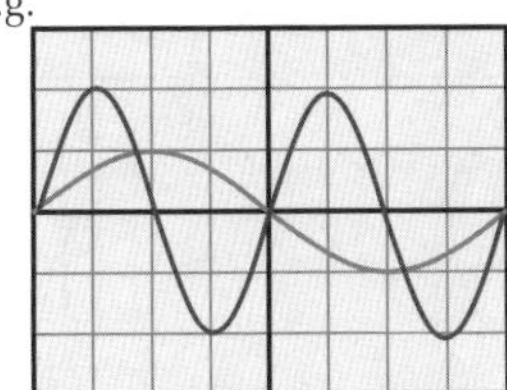

The trace should have a higher frequency and a higher amplitude.
b) E.g. use a stronger magnet / use a coil with a larger number of turns / use a coil with a larger area.
Q3 As the wheels on the bike go round, they turn the magnet inside the dynamo. As Sebastian slows down, the magnet turns less quickly, which means less electric current is induced to power the lights.

Pages 130-131 — Electricity and the National Grid

Q1
1. Electrical energy is generated in power stations.
2. The voltage of the supply is raised.
3. An electrical current flows through power cables across the country.
4. The voltage of the supply is reduced.
5. Mrs Miggins boils the kettle for tea.

Q2 a) Underground cables
b) Overhead cables
c) Overhead cables
d) Overhead cables
e) Underground cables
f) Overhead cables
g) Underground cables
Q3 a) Step-up transformer, pylons, step-down transformer.
b) At higher voltages, less energy is wasted as heat. This saves more money than the cost of the equipment.
Q4 a) The National Grid transmits energy at high voltage and **low current**.
b) A step-up transformer is used to **increase** the voltage of the supply (OR reduce the **current**) before electricity is transmitted.
c) Using a **low current** (OR high **voltage**) makes sure there is not much energy wasted.
Q5 a) Supply is the amount of electricity generated and delivered to consumers. Demand is the amount of electricity needed by the consumers.
b) Consumer demand for energy is increasing, so the National Grid has to increase the supply to meet this demand.
c) E.g. more plants can be built, power output of power plants can be increased.
d) E.g. use energy efficient appliances, being more careful not to waste energy in the home (e.g. by turning off lights).

Pages 132-133 — Power and the Cost of Electricity

Q1

Appliance	Power (W)	Current (A)
Kettle	2600	11.3
Radio	13	0.057
Laptop computer	736	3.2
Lamp	39.1	0.17

Q2 a) Energy supplied = power × time = 2 kW × 3 h = **6 kWh**.
b) Cost = 6 kWh × 7p/kWh = **42p**.
c) Lamp: Energy used = 0.06 kW × 9 h = 0.54 kWh.
Shower: Energy used = 8 kW × 0.25 h = 2 kWh.
So Boris is **right** — the shower uses more energy.
Q3 a) 34783 – 34259 = **524 Units**.
b) Total cost = 524 × 9.7 = **5082.8p** (or **£50.83** to the nearest penny).
Q4 a) E.g. night storage heating. (Also accept, e.g. washing machine or dishwasher run on a timer switch.)
b) i) It's cheaper.
ii) It's cost-effective because power stations can't be switched off at night, so it's better for power companies to sell electricity generated at night than to waste it.
Q5 a) Number of kWh used = 7 × 275 × 1000
= 1 925 000 kWh so cost = kWh × night time cost per kWh
= 1 925 000 × 3.7 = 7 122 500p or **£71 225**.
b) kWh generated = 5 × 288 × 1000 = 1 440 000 kWh so cost = kWh × daytime cost per kWh
= 1 440 000 × 7.2 = 10 368 000 or **£103 680**.

Section 8 — Electricity and Waves

Q6 a) Power = Voltage × Current
= 230 × 10 = 2300 = 2.30 kW.

b) Units used = 2.30 × 2 = 4.6.
Cost on peak = 4.6 × 11.3 = 51.98p.
Cost off peak = 4.6 × 6.0 = 27.60p
Saving = 51.98 – 27.60 = **24.38p**
Or 4.6 × (11.3 – 6.0) = **24.38p**

Page 134 — Choosing Electrical Appliances

Q1 E.g. it can be used in locations where there is no access to mains electricity. / It's easier to use as there is no power cord to get in the way/restrict movement.

Q2 a) Battery powered lamp: Energy used to fully charge (enough for 8 hours use) = 0.4 kW × 6 hours = 2.4 kWh
Mains powered lamp: Energy used in 8 hours = 1.6 kW × 8 = 12.8 kWh
So, difference in energy used = 12.8 – 2.4 = **10.4 kWh**

b) Difference in cost = 10.4 × 12 = **124.8p**

c) E.g. there might not be an electricity supply where they are camping, so they will not be able to use a mains powered lamp or recharge the battery powered lamp when it runs out. The wind up lamp does not require any electricity to recharge.

Q3 Any two from: e.g. can be used to power X-ray machines / refrigeration of medicines/vaccines / can power lighting/ equipment for operations / refrigeration of food.

Pages 135-136 — Wave Basics

Q1 energy, matter

Q2 a) Transverse — 2, Longitudinal — 1.

b) E.g. vibrations in a transverse wave are perpendicular to the direction of energy transfer, whereas in longitudinal waves they are parallel to the direction of energy transfer. / Transverse waves can travel in a vacuum but longitudinal waves cannot.

Q3 a) A and C

b) A and B

c) A and C

Q4 Transverse:
vibrations are at 90° to the direction of energy transfer
produced by a slinky spring whose end is wiggled at 90° to the spring itself
ripples on water
electromagnetic radiation
Longitudinal:
vibrations are along the same direction as the energy transfer
sound waves
produced by a slinky spring whose end is pushed and pulled towards and away from the rest of the spring

Q5 a) metres (m)

b) There are 25 waves per second.

c) A

Q6 ~~Frequency = Speed × Wavelength~~ ~~Frequency = Wavelength / Speed~~ Wavelength = Speed / Frequency
~~Speed = Frequency / Wavelength~~ Speed = Frequency × Wavelength Frequency = Speed / Wavelength

Q7 You need to work out the frequency.
Using v = fλ and rearranging gives
frequency = speed ÷ wavelength.
So frequency = $(3 \times 10^8) \div (5 \times 10^{-7})$ = $\mathbf{6 \times 10^{14}}$ **Hz**.

Q8 a) He has drawn a wave with a wavelength of 4 m rather than 2 m.

b)

Q9 You need to work out the wavelength.
Using v = fλ and rearranging gives:
wavelength = speed ÷ frequency.
So wavelength = $(3 \times 10^8) \div (4.6 \times 10^{15})$ = $\mathbf{6.5 \times 10^{-8}}$ **m**

Page 137 — Wave Properties

Q1 a) The normal is an imaginary line that's at right angles to the surface at the point of incidence (where the light hits the surface).

b)

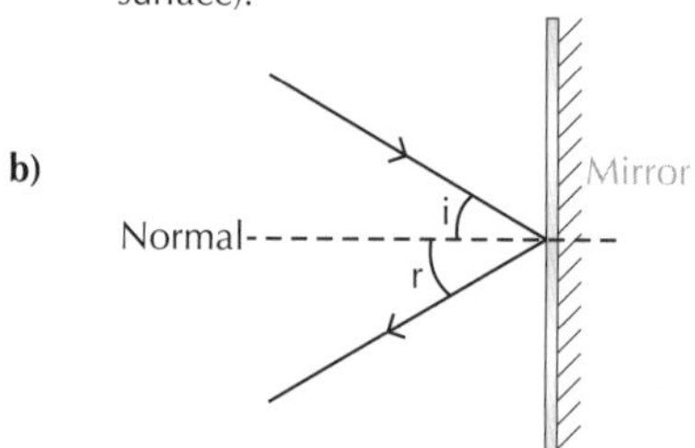

Q2 a)

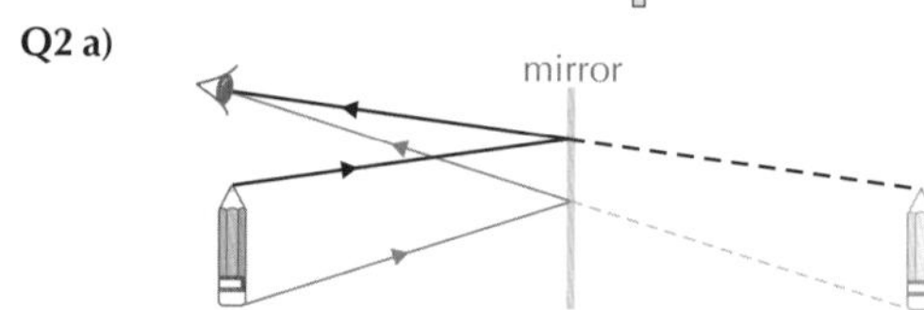

b) virtual

c) upright

d) The left and right hand side of the object are swapped round in the image. E.g. the right hand side of the actual pencil appears to be the left hand side of the pencil on the image.

Page 138 — Diffraction and Refraction

Q1 a) Diffraction is the spreading out of waves when they pass through a gap or past an obstacle.

b)

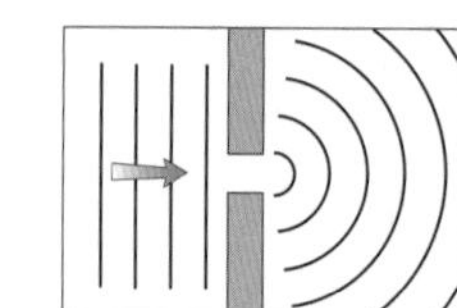

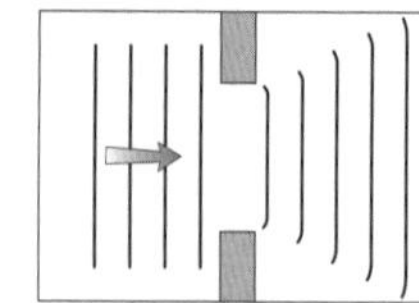

Q2 a) B

b) Because the wave met the boundary face on. / Because the wave is travelling along the normal. / The angle of incidence is zero.

c) The wavelength gets shorter.

d) The frequency remains the same.

e) The wave slows down.

f) The wave would speed up again, the wavelength would increase and the frequency would stay the same.

Section 8 — Electricity and Waves

Page 139 — Sound Waves

Q1 C, A, D, B.
Q2 vibrate, high, low.
Q3 The bigger the **amplitude** of a sound wave, the **louder** the sound.
Q4 2000 (2 kHz = 2000 Hz)
Q5 a) 30 Hz
b) 5 Hz, 630 Hz, 8 kHz, 21 kHz, 400 kHz, 3 MHz
c) i) ultrasound
ii) infrasound

Page 140 — Analogue and Digital Signals

Q1 weaken, amplified, interference, noise, analogue.
Q2 E.g.

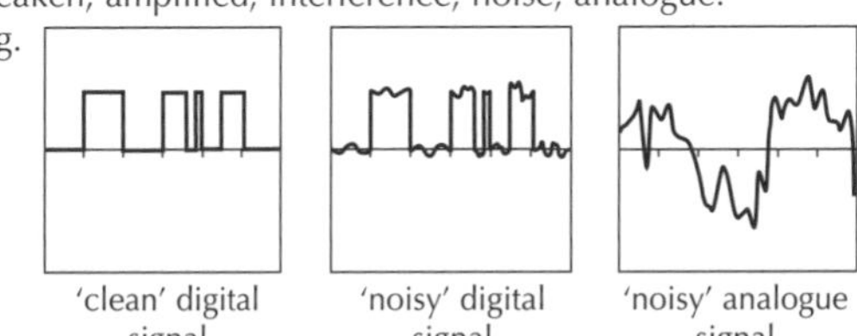

'clean' digital signal — 'noisy' digital signal — 'noisy' analogue signal

Q3 a) Computers process digital information only. Analogue signals would first have to be converted to digital ones.
b) The 'on' and 'off' phases of a digital signal can usually be recognised as 'on' and 'off' even when the signal is noisy, and noise can be removed when the signal is amplified.
c) E.g. more information can be sent at one time / digital signals are easier to encrypt.
Q4 E.g.

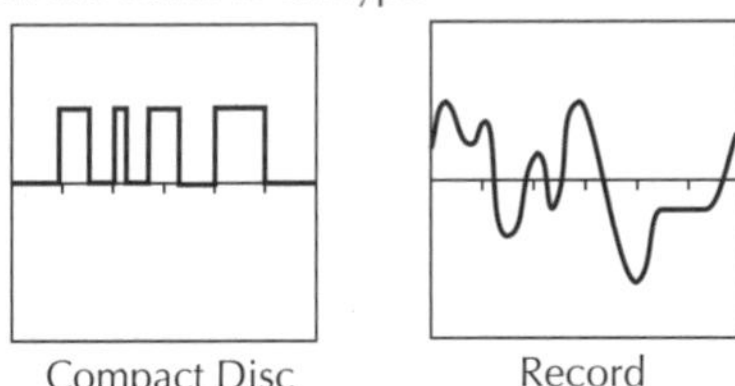

Compact Disc — Record

Pages 141-142 — EM Waves and Communication

Q1 a)

Radio waves	Micro-waves	Infrared		Ultraviolet	X-rays	Gamma rays
1m-10^4m	10^{-2}m (1 cm)	10^{-5}m (0.01mm)	10^{-7}m	10^{-8}m	10^{-10}m	10^{-15}m

b) The energy of the waves **increases** from **left to right** across the table.
Q2 a) i) False
ii) False
iii) False
iv) True
b) i) Visible light travels **at the same speed** in a vacuum **as** both X-rays and radio waves.
ii) **Gamma rays** have the highest energy of all EM waves.
iii) Radio waves have the **longest** wavelength of all EM waves. / **Gamma rays** have the shortest wavelength of all EM waves.
Q3 A, B and D should be circled.
Q4 EM waves with higher frequencies have **shorter** wavelengths.
The **higher** the frequency of an EM wave, the greater the energy of the wave.
Q5 The house can receive **long-wave** signals because they can diffract around the mountain. It also receives **short-wave** signals because they are reflected by the **ionosphere**. However **FM** signals are not received at the house as the transmitter is not in direct line of sight of the house.
Q6 Things they have in common — any two from, e.g. they can both travel in a vacuum. / They both travel at the speed of light. / They both transfer energy.
Ways in which they differ — any two from, e.g. they have different wavelengths. / They have different frequencies. / They have different energies.

Page 143 — Microwaves

Q1 a) This allows the satellite to send signals to (and receive signals from) a large area of the Earth.
b) Microwaves can pass through the Earth's watery atmosphere for use in satellite communications.
c) E.g. to cook food.
Q2 a) Microwaves heat up the water inside cells (and this could kill/damage them).
b) Mobile phones use microwaves of a different wavelength that are not absorbed as much as the microwaves used by microwave ovens.
c) There could be a risk we haven't discovered yet that may have serious consequences.
d) People who live near the mobile phone transmitters/masts.

Page 144 — Infrared and Visible Light

Q1 a) True
b) False
c) True
d) False
e) True
Q2 E.g. sensors in security equipment such as burglar alarms which detect heat from an intruder. / Sensors that detect heat loss from houses in order to see where insulation is needed. / Night vision equipment that detects heat and displays it as an image to show where living things might be hiding.
Q3 a) Visible light or infrared waves.
b) They are reflected down the core of the fibre.
Q4 E.g. the lens focuses the light onto a light sensitive film or electronic sensor. The film or sensor then records the image.

Page 145 — X-Rays and Gamma Rays

Q1 a) True
b) True
c) False
Q2 a) True
b) ultraviolet, X-rays, gamma rays.
c) Ionising radiation is radiation that transfers enough energy to knock electrons off atoms.
Q3 kill, cells, cancer, focused, normal, ill, dose.
Q4 1. Passengers' baggage can be X-rayed to check that no dangerous or illegal items are being taken on planes.
2. Passengers can be X-rayed to see if they are concealing any dangerous or illegal items on or in their body.

Page 146 — UV Radiation and Ozone

Q1 a) Ultraviolet radiation.
b) The DNA in human cells can be damaged or destroyed. / Cells can become cancerous.
Q2 a) The pigment in dark skin absorbs UV, preventing it from reaching the more sensitive cells deeper down.
b) Any two from: e.g. stay in the sun for as short a time as possible. / Wear clothing and hats to reduce the amount of UV absorbed. / Use a protective sun cream.
c) Marie can stay in the sun 25 times as long before burning as she could without any cream on.

Section 8 — Electricity and Waves

Q3 a) The ozone layer is high up in the atmosphere.
b) It absorbs some of the UV rays from the Sun.
c) E.g. CFCs.
Q4 a) E.g. by repeating studies in different locations and using different equipment to measure the same things.
b) E.g. they banned/restricted the use of CFCs.

Page 147 — The Greenhouse Effect

Q1

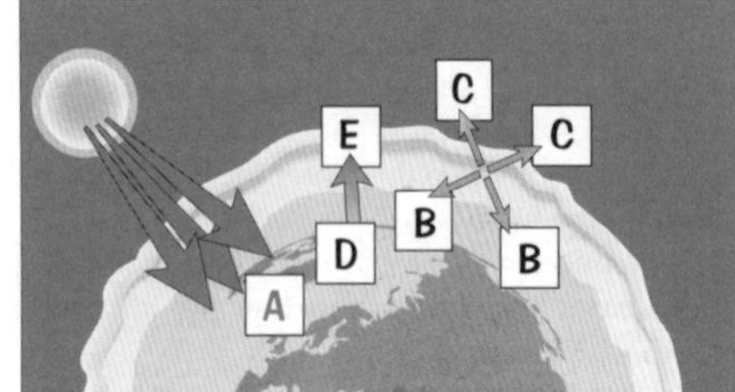

Q2 water vapour, carbon dioxide, methane
Q3 B
Q4 a) i) E.g. respiration in plants and animals / volcanic eruptions.
ii) Any two from: e.g. burning fossil fuels for energy. / Burning fossil fuels for transport. / Chopping down trees for more land.
b) E.g. man-made sources of methane include cattle digestion from cattle farming and decaying waste in landfill sites. Methane is released naturally from volcanoes, wetlands and digestion of wild animals.

Page 148 — Global Warming and Climate Change

Q1 temperatures, increased, greenhouse, carbon.
Q2 a) Description of Data
b) Description of Data
c) Explanation of Data
d) Description of Data
e) Explanation of Data
Q3 a) They might have to grow different crops — traditional crops might not grow well in drier conditions.
b) i) E.g. hurricanes, floods, droughts.
ii) E.g. if droughts became more common/the seasonal rains became unreliable, crops might fail more regularly and animals would die, leading to food shortages. / Rain might become heavier/more frequent, farmers could benefit from higher yields.

Page 149 — Seismic Waves

Q1 Disturbances in the Earth produce **seismic** waves which can travel **through** the Earth. These waves can be recorded on a seismograph, which draws a **seismogram**.
Q2 a) P-waves
b) P-waves
c) S-waves
Q3 **B** and **C** are true.
Q4 a) They change speed (and hence direction) as the nature of the material of the Earth changes. This is refraction.
b) This happens to P-waves e.g. as they enter the outer core, which is a liquid. The change from solid to liquid causes refraction to take place more suddenly.
c) i) S-waves don't reach the other side.
ii) This tells us that part of the Earth's interior must be liquid.

Pages 150-151 — Mixed Questions — Section 8

Q1 a) A
b) B
c) E.g. use of products (such as hairsprays and fridge coolants) which release CFCs into the atmosphere has caused a thinning of the ozone layer (which absorbs UV radiation from the Sun). / People spend more time sunbathing.
Q2 a) $P = V \times I$ so, rearranging, $= P \div V = 360 \div 230 =$ **1.57 A**.
b) Energy = Power × Time = 0.36 kW × 0.75 h = 0.27 kWh. Cost = 0.27 × 15.2 = **4p**.
Q3 a) 0.02 m
b) 10 Hz
c) Speed = Wavelength × Frequency = 0.02 × 10 = **0.2 m/s**
Q4 a) Visible light or infrared.
b) E.g.

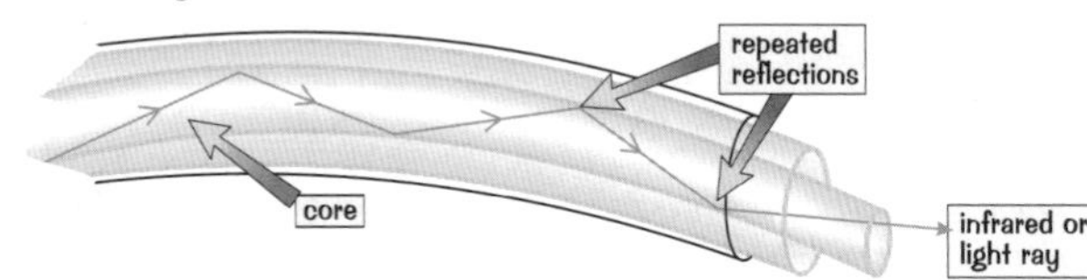

Q5 a) reflection
b)

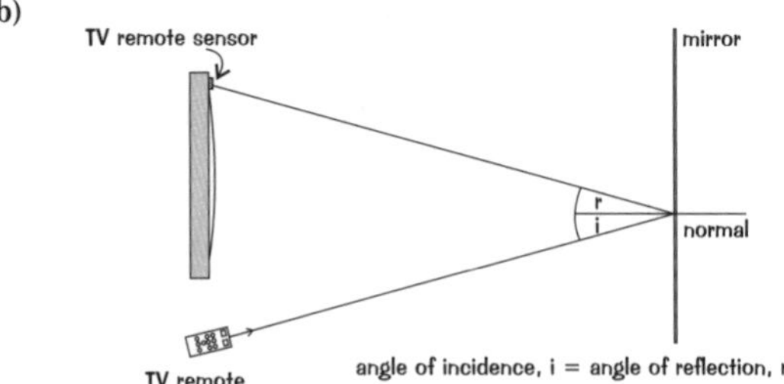

Q6 a) Frequency = Speed ÷ Wavelength $= 3 \times 10^8$ m/s ÷ 1500 m = **200 000 Hz** (= 200 kHz).
b) Longer waves diffract more around large objects than shorter waves. So the long-wave radio signal diffracts around the mountains and can be received in Mr Potts' holiday cottage. The short-wave radio and TV signals (which also use short waves) don't diffract much and so they can't be received in his cottage.
c) When Radio Roary's analogue signal is amplified, any noise affecting the signal will be amplified too, because it's difficult to remove. It's much easier to remove noise from a digital signal, so Radio Piracy will sound clearer than Radio Roary because any noise can be removed.

Section 9 — The Universe

Section 9 — The Universe

Page 152 — Galileo and Copernicus

Q1 a) geocentric
b) Copernicus
c) Sun
d) circles
e) Universe
f) elliptical
Q2 a) The telescope.
b) E.g. Galileo looked at Jupiter on different nights and saw some 'stars' in a line near the planet. When he looked again he saw that these stars seemed to be carried along with the planet. He suggested they couldn't be stars and were actually moons of Jupiter.
He also observed that Venus has phases (like the Moon).
c) E.g. the moons of Jupiter proved that not everything orbited the Earth. Changes in the phases of Venus were only possible if Venus orbited the Sun.
d) The church believed Galileo's ideas went against the Bible (which said that the Earth was at the centre of the Universe). / The Ptolemaic model had been around for a long time.

Page 153 — The Solar System

Q1
1. Mercury
2. Venus
3. Earth
4. Mars
5. Asteroids
6. Jupiter
7. Saturn
8. Uranus
9. Neptune

Q2
1. The planets do not give out their own light *OR* the planets only reflect light.
2. The planets are much smaller than the stars.
3. The planets are much closer than the stars.

Q3 a) Because when the Solar System was forming, the gravitational attraction of Jupiter kept interfering, which left millions of asteroids orbiting the Sun between the orbits of Mars and Jupiter.
b) i) Rock, dust and ice.
ii) The ice in the comet melts as it approaches the Sun and gets hotter.

Page 154 — Beyond the Solar System

Q1 a) thousands, millions, galaxy, halfway, arms.
b) galaxies, stars
Q2 Its actual brightness. How far away it is. (It will also be affected if there is dust between the star and the Earth that will absorb some of the star's light.)
Q3 a) There are $365 \times 24 \times 60 \times 60 = 31\ 536\ 000$ seconds in a year. Speed = distance ÷ time. Rearranging,
distance = speed × time
$= 3.0 \times 10^8 \times 31\ 536\ 000$
$= 9\ 460\ 800\ 000\ 000\ 000 \approx \mathbf{9.5 \times 10^{15}\ m}$
b) $13 \times 10^9 \times 9.5 \times 10^{15} = \mathbf{1.2 \times 10^{26}\ m}$ (to 2 s.f.)
Q4 a) Stars A and B are closer to us than the other stars. The angle at which we see them, relative to the distant stars, has changed as the Earth has moved around the Sun.
b) Star A — it appears to have moved further than B.

Page 155 — Looking into Space

Q1 Light pollution is light thrown upwards from street lamps and other forms of artificial lighting. This can make it hard to see dim objects.
Q2 a) e.g. X-rays / radio waves
b) e.g. exploding stars
Q3 a) Improved magnification means we can look further into space and discover more and more galaxies.
b) E.g. this has helped improve our understanding of the Universe as it allows us to collect more information about the Universe. It also means that it is quicker and easier to increase our knowledge of the Universe.
Q4 a) It takes time for their light to reach us.
b) Radio waves would take 200 years to reach them and we weren't transmitting radio waves 200 years ago.

Page 156 — The Life Cycle of Stars

Q1 a) heat (from thermonuclear fusion)
b) gravity
c) The force pulling the star inwards and the force pushing it outwards are equal, so they balance and cancel out.
d) A main sequence star.
Q2 a) Gravitational attraction pulls the material together.
b) Energy is released when hydrogen nuclei fuse together to form helium nuclei/from thermonuclear fusion.
Q3 a) It runs out of hydrogen.
b) Its surface is cooler than a main sequence star's surface.
Q4 planetary nebula, white dwarf, supernova, neutron star, black hole.

Pages 157-158 — The Life of the Universe

Q1 a) It will sound lower pitched.
b) Doppler effect
c) The wavelength seems to increase.
d) The frequency would seem to have increased.
Q2 As the train leaves, it moves away from Brian's microphone. So the frequency appears to get slightly **lower**. E.g.

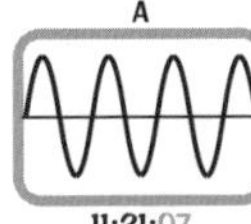

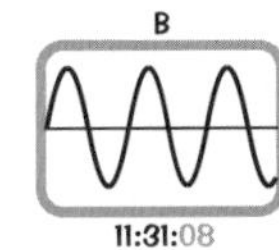

Q3 Light from other galaxies is red-shifted — all the frequencies are lower in the spectrum than is the case for stationary objects. This tells us that the galaxies are moving away from us. Also, the further away the galaxy, the greater the red-shift. This tells us that more distant galaxies are moving away from us at a faster rate than nearer galaxies.
Q4 a) The Universe started as a single point that exploded in the Big Bang and has been expanding ever since.
b) Space itself is expanding.
Q5 a) Low frequency electromagnetic radiation coming from all parts of the Universe.
b) Very shortly after the beginning of the Universe, the Universe was very hot and emitted very high energy, high frequency radiation. As the Universe expanded it cooled, and this radiation dropped in frequency and is now detected as the CMBR.
Q6 Any one from: e.g. it can't explain observed acceleration and expansion of the Universe. / It doesn't tell you anything about the Universe before the Big Bang.

Section 9 — The Universe

Page 159 — Mixed Questions — Section 9

Q1 a) Hydrogen nuclei combine (by fusion) to form helium. Over time more and more of the hydrogen is used up, producing more and more helium.

b) Using: distance = speed × time
= 300 000 × 500 = 150 000 000 km = **1.5×10^8 km**.

Q2 a) Astronomers take pictures of the sky six months apart and measure how far a star appears to have moved. The further it's moved the closer it is to the Earth.

b) E.g.

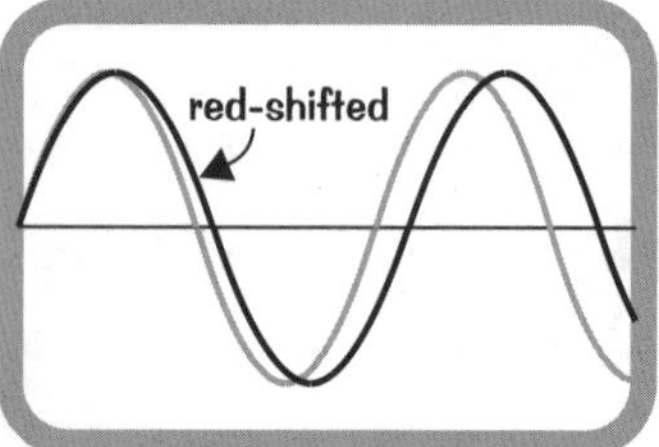

c) More distant galaxies have greater red-shifts than nearer ones, showing that more distant galaxies are moving away from us faster. This is evidence that the Universe is expanding and started in a very dense state.

Q3 E.g. the planets orbit the Sun in elliptical orbits. There are eight planets which go in the order (from nearest to the Sun): Mercury, Venus, Earth, Mars, Jupiter, Saturn, Uranus, Neptune. Some planets have moons orbiting them. A belt of asteroids orbits the Sun between Mars and Jupiter.
E.g.

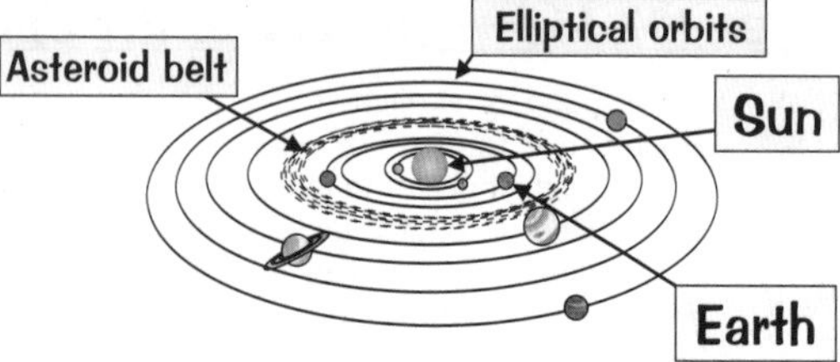